T0281812

Grace & Grit

Grace & Grit

A HISTORY OF BALLET IN MINNESOTA

Georgia Finnegan

AFTON PRESS

The publication of *Grace & Grit:*
A History of Ballet in Minnesota
has been made possible by
our generous donors:

Mary Anne Anderson

Thomas J. Arneson

Karen Bachman

Tim Bechtold

Beth E. Bergman

Priscilla Brewster

Susan Brewster

Eleanor Crosby

Sheldon Damberg

Lauren Dwyer

Ruthena and Doug Fink

John and Donna Finnegan Jr.

Bruce Goodman

Shirley and Barry Hannine

Sonja and Johan Hinderlie

Kathryn Keefer

Thomas Klas and Lisa Swan

Laurie Koltes and Bob Tranmer

Sarah-Jane McCarthy

In Memoriam, Malcolm W. McDonald

Pamela Neal

Richard and Nancy Nicholson

Jina Penn-Tracy

Sarah and Joel Quie

William White

Archie D. & Bertha H. Walker Foundation

Hubbard Broadcasting Foundation

Minnesota Arts and
Cultural Heritage Fund

Front Cover: Sally Rousse, Co-founder of James Sewell Ballet, 1993. Courtesy of Erik Saulitis, photographer.
Back Cover: Abdo Sayegh Rodríguez, Dance Artist with Minnesota Dance Theatre, ca. 2004. Courtesy of Erik Saulitis, photographer.
Opposite Half Title Page: *Les Sylphides*, Col. W. de Basil Original Ballet Russe de Monte Carlo. Anna Adrianova, pictured on the left, second up from the bottom of the page. Courtesy of Marius J. Andaházy, Artistic Director. © 2000 Andaházy Souvenir Book.
Frontispiece: Hitomi Yamada, Dance Artist with James Sewell Ballet, ca. 1996. Courtesy of Erik Saulitis, photographer.
p. 7: John J. Finnegan, ca. 1940. Courtesy of the Finnegan family.
p. 8: *Falling off pointe*, Sally Rousse with James Sewell Ballet, ca. 1993. Courtesy of Erik Saulitis, photographer.
p. 11: Cathy Young and her company, Young Dance, ca. 1995. Courtesy of Erik Saulitis, photographer.

Copyright © 2024 by Georgia Finnegan. All rights reserved. No part of this book may be used or reproduced by any means, graphic, electronic, or mechanical, including photocopying, recording, video, taping or by any information storage retrieval system, without the written permission of the publisher except in the case of brief quotations used in critical articles and reviews.

Afton Press
Ian Graham Leask, Publisher
6800 France Avenue South, Suite 370
Edina, MN 55435
www.aftonpress.com

ISBN: 978-1-7361021-3-8

Book design by Mayfly Design
Cover design by Gary Lindberg
LC record available at https://lccn.loc.gov/2022033635

Printed in the United States of America
Distributed by the University of Minnesota Press
111 Third Avenue South, Suite 290
Minneapolis, MN 55401-2520
www.upress.umn.edu

CLEAN
WATER
LAND &
LEGACY
AMENDMENT

This project was made possible in part by the people of Minnesota through a grant funded by an appropriation to the Minnesota Historical Society from the Minnesota Arts and Cultural Heritage Fund. Any views, findings, opinions, conclusions, or recommendations expressed in this publication are those of the author and do not necessarily represent those of the State of Minnesota, the Minnesota Historical Society, or the Minnesota Historic Resources Advisory Committee.

Dedication

In Memory of John J. Finnegan
My beloved father, writer, and musician

Table of Contents

En Pointe, Saint Paul City Ballet School. Elizabeth Kappes, ca. 2006.
Artist, Charles Gilbert Kapsner. Oil on panel, 12 x 24 inches.
Courtesy of the Private Collection of Charles Gilbert Kapsner.

Foreword and Author's Note

Rochelle Zide-Booth, Ballet Russe de Monte Carlo, "Bluebird Pas de Deux" from *The Sleeping Beauty, Act III, Dance Magazine,* ca. 1954. Courtesy of Rochelle Zide-Booth.

Foreword

Those of us, even the dance professionals, when dealing with the history of ballet in America, have tended to write about the two coasts: San Francisco and Los Angeles; and New York, Boston, Philadelphia, and Washington, D.C. Before this, there simply wasn't enough material about the great middle of America's ballet history for us to quote from. Thanks to Georgia Finnegan, that's no longer going to be a problem.

Her new book, *Grace & Grit: A History of Ballet in Minnesota*, opens the rest of American dance to our eyes, our brains, and our hearts. The form she has chosen makes her work interesting and accessible even to people whose "first language" may not be "the language of ballet." She starts with a brief history of ballet, from its European beginnings, before zeroing in on the history of ballet in the Midwest, specifically in Minnesota. Georgia finishes her book acknowledging modern and contemporary dance that emanated out of ballet.

Having worked in the ballet and dance world quite a bit myself, I recognized several names and learned several new ones in both the ballet and modern dance fields. The book reads like a charming work of fiction, which it definitely is not. It is a history and a really good one—an important one for dance students, for dance professionals, for anyone who is interested in American dance, or for someone who is just looking for a good book to read.

—Rochelle Zide-Booth, former dancer with Sergei Denham's Ballet Russe de Monte Carlo.

Dancers of the Ballet Russe de Monte Carlo, Washington, DC, ca. 1954-1956.
Rochelle Zide-Booth, bottom, second from the right; and Jo Savino, top first from the left.
Photography by Cameramen, Inc.
Courtesy of Joseph Savino.

Aspen River, Colorado, 2015. Courtesy of Erik Saulitis, Photographer.

Ouverture d'Esprit

As a child, I danced, not as a ballet student at a local ballet school, but as a child smitten by the dance muse. I walked on my toes; I moved my arms and body into various shapes; I fearlessly leaped from branch to branch of a neighbor's tree; I balanced on the playground's teeter-totter. I vividly recall my first visit to a dance studio. I went with my friend and stood outside the large studio window, intensely watching her take ballet class, yearning to be dancing with her. Once home, I told my parents that I wanted to take ballet lessons. "No, Georgia Ann. Not possible right now." *Right now* became a ten-year wait.

I decided to keep moving and dancing on my own accord, with my own made-up choreography. I often danced and moved in our home as my father played on his favorite instrument—a 1939 Gibson lap steel guitar. I grew up hearing him in his study practicing a wide range of music, from the "Flight of the Bumblebee" by Nikolai Rimsky-Korsakov to "Sweet Leilani," a classic Hawaiian song. One childhood summer, I asked my father to be the musician in my backyard dance production. He was seated behind a large blanket that served as the makeshift curtain. The sidewalk and grass in front became the stage. My siblings and neighborhood friends danced to my imaginative choreography. The show opened with my father's Hawaiian music wafting from behind the curtain. Pop music of the mid-1960s, blaring from a vinyl 45 RPM on a small record player, opened the second act with my choreography entertaining a friendly audience.

In eighth grade, a music class assignment was to take a piece of music we had studied and create a group presentation. I took charge of my group, chose a section from Igor Stravinsky's music to the ballet *Petrouchka*, and set movement on my fellow students, completely naïve to the foolhardiness of my choreographic efforts. To this day, I am amazed that I designed dance steps to a story about a traditional Russian puppet show held during a pre-Lenten carnival. I owe a tremendous debt to the music teacher at my West St. Paul junior high school, who taught me that music and dance have a symbiotic relationship. Michel Fokine choreographed *Petrouchka* in 1911 and said, "I wanted all the dancers strolling at the fair to dance gaily, freely, as if the dances were not staged but arose spontaneously from an overabundance of emotion and gaiety. . . . "[1] Dance, notably ballet, drew me in "with an overabundance of emotion," and my fervor for it has never diminished.

This fervor piqued my desire to train in classical ballet, to perform, and to eventually produce ballets, collaborating with dancers, musicians, and theater artists. A close friend once said to me, "Ah, you are a Diaghilev!" I shook my head and replied, "No." I then slowly nodded my head in humble memory

I believe in all that has never yet been spoken.
I want to free what waits within me
so that what no one has dared to wish for
without my contriving . . .
May what I do flow from me like a river,
no forcing and no holding back,
the way it is with children . . .[2]

Vaslav Nijinsky as Petrouchka, 1933. Photo credit: Lebrecht Music Arts / Bridgeman Images.

My early childhood dance efforts foreshadowed my own future ballet story, similar to the overture of a ballet giving the audience a musical browse with hints, tunes, and glimpses of the story to come. This book on Minnesota's ballet history asks readers to engage in *ouverture d'esprit*, French for open-mindedness, as they browse this book. Like the headwaters of the Mississippi, ballet's headwaters began far away in Renaissance Italy. The first chapter reveals this long, meandering history and how it flows into Minnesota. One of my favorite quotations from Renaissance genius Leonardo da Vinci states, "In rivers, the water that you touch is the last of what has passed and the first of that which comes; so with present time." So with ballet's history.

As I researched, I found the "present slipping away . . . overpowered by the hypnotic strength of the past."[3] My writing space at Afton Press resembled an old bookstore, its shelves filled with "Rare and Used Books," giving barely any room for my computer and monitor. Hours slipped away as the fascinating and intriguing stories from ballet's past enticed me to read more and more. We are heirs to a tradition extending back centuries, and it is comforting to know

of this tireless ballet producer of the early twentieth century. One musical collaboration with Minnesotan jazz musician George Maurer opened me to one of his favorite poets, a Bohemian-Austrian poet, Rainer Maria Rilke. Written in 1899, the following excerpt from the poem, "I believe in all that has never yet been spoken," speaks to the energy and fervency I bring to writing this history of Minnesota ballet.

that the ballet performed now will become the history of tomorrow.

Ballet is one of many varying dance disciplines in Minnesota because dance defies an absolute definition. Dance such as contemporary, modern, post-modern, lyrical, hip-hop, jazz, tap, ballroom, social, and ethnic dances have all found a valued place in Minnesota's dance scene. My historical binocular will focus on ballet schools that maintain a close working relationship with either a professional ballet company and/or professional dance artists who adhere to the gravitas of a technically strong ballet foundation in their training and performing. Classical ballet's turnout of the legs marks the salient difference from other theatrical dances. Turnout technique and training "offers maximum base and support for any ensuing movement; it is the bedrock of ballet style and practice."[4] A bedrock for the well-trained and versatile dancer. In addition to turnout, the five classic positions of the feet allow the dancer the possibility to control dance movements while moving and stepping in any direction.

Despite this defined focus and scope, my research displayed here is not exhaustive; so much more could have been written. My bibliography presents the major sources of my erudition, including several interviews with dance artists and enthusiasts. The historical literature, as well as the artists' stories, inspired me to dig deeper and to "look beyond the barre."

I drew elements from one of the gems of classical ballet, *The Sleeping Beauty*, *Op. 66*, for this book's structure. Imagine

Nic Lincoln, Dance Artist with James Sewell Ballet, ca. 2000. Courtesy of Erik Saulitis, photographer.

attending a concert stage performance of *The Sleeping Beauty*. The Ouverture d' Esprit is my author's note; Prologue, a short ballet history divided into seven sections; Acts I, II, Entr'Acte, and Act III chapters; Coda, artists' stories; Apotheosis, sacred dance; and Coda Générale, ballet collaborators. The history of ballet in Minnesota concludes with an Encore. I explain how ballet, primarily a euro-russe-centric dance, established deep Minnesota roots while vibrancy and a fierce independence also took the stage. Minnesota ballet stretched beyond its classical structure and emerged with an exuberant embrace of contemporary ballet, dance, and diversity.

Creative individuals with grace and grit ushered ballet into Minnesota's contemporary dance age. As Michel Fokine, one of the great early-twentieth-century ballet choreographers, wrote at the beginning of his memoirs:

If you are looking for an easy and simple choice, the most peaceful, the most practical way of navigating in the sea of art is to float with the tide—be it in the calm of a carefree day when the waters are quiet and clear to the point of boredom, or in the nightmarish turbulence of a night of raging waves surrounded by darkness and impenetrable turmoil. But if such a course offers you little challenge, and you wish to choose your own course in the direction of your own goal—if you are ready to challenge the struggle and sufferings confronting you, the elements do not frighten you, you do not require favorable weather, you do not have to inquire about favorable trade winds—you can boldly set your course against the tide.[5]

Like any art form, ballet is inseparable from prevailing cultural, social, political, and economic trends. The dawning of artistic visionaries and bravura technique pushed ballet beyond the barre, studio walls, and proscenium stages. A myriad of performance venues and dancers of various ethnicities, socioeconomic levels, abilities, and ages also took center stage. Ballet no longer remained exclusively the realm of professional ballet dancers. An intriguing story of Minnesota ballet history unfolds by sharing dance artists'

Da'Rius Malone, resident choreographer with James Sewell Ballet, Minneapolis, Minnesota, September 2021. Courtesy of Erik Saulitis, photographer.

riveting experiences and reminiscences. Their voices will be the words that write themselves, and this book will become the stage on which their dance stories perform.

The Foundations of Ballet

A Nod to Antiquity: Dance Artists with James Sewell Ballet, ca. 1995.
Courtesy of Erik Saulitis, photographer.

At the Beginning

It is the movement of people and things which consoles us.
If the leaves on the trees didn't move, how sad the trees would be—and so should we.
—Edgar Degas (A French artist known for painting dancers)[6]

Ballet is dance, and dance is movement. Human beings move from their first borning cry to their final breath, a moving rhythm that vibrates from the beginning of the human continuum. Prehistoric rock paintings of human figures found in India, Africa, and Brazil have been interpreted as musicians and dancers. A sense of performance, or perhaps a rite of passage for youth, is found in the Tuc d'Audoubert cave in the Pyrénées of southwestern France. Imprints of youths walking on their heels and fingertips pressed into the clay floor richly decorate this cave.

In ancient Egypt, tomb paintings with many stylized images of dance portray the importance Egyptian culture had for an afterlife journey to a resting place. More than three thousand years ago, exquisite Egyptian tomb paintings of Nefertari, the first and favorite queen of the Pharaoh Rameses the Great, adorn the walls in various poses and *port de bras* (arm movements). Decorations on ancient Greek and Roman pottery portray people dancing and pagan dances with nymphs, fauns, and satyrs.

Early recorded history also contains references to dance in Plato and Aristotle's writings. Plato wrote, "All well-bred [people] should have mastered the art of singing and dancing."[7] In Greek mythology, the muse of dance and choral song is Terpsichore, whose name has entered the English language, terpsichorean, defined as "pertaining to dancing." In the fifteenth century, the choristers of Seville Cathedral danced *Los Seises* during the six days following the feast of Corpus Christi (about sixty days following Easter).

Before fur traders, missionaries, soldiers, and the influx of settlers set foot on Minnesota soil, indigenous tribes, primarily the Dakota/Sioux and the Ojibwe/ Chippewa, lived here and danced. Dancing held a crucially significant role in indigenous rituals, ceremonies, and life celebrations and continues to be vital today. A sacred ritual in preparing to dance involves putting on various dance regalia, such as moccasins, beadwork, feathers, headdresses, bells, breastplates, shawls, or ribbons. Movements portray the purpose of a dance, augmented by drums, bells, and song. The powwow dance (from the Algonquian Pau-wau or pauau) originally meant a healing ceremony. Today powwows honor tribal people's rich heritage of spiritual and social dances, quintessential to their belief that "To dance is to share both the joy and the pain. . . . To dance is to be able to go beyond one's injuries, to reclaim your right to exist . . . your right to flourish . . . the right of all to flourish. To dance is to know the freedom of living fully. . . ."[8]

Minnesota's indigenous tribes lost their foothold on the land of their ancestors in the mid-1800s. An inpouring of settlers from the eastern states and emigrants from northern and western Europe, including Great Britain, Ireland, and Scandinavia, made the long journey westward to the Minnesota Territory. Enticed by the promise of open land and seemingly limitless opportunities, these newcomers carried with them precious commodities: books, clothing, some furniture, music, and dances. The first newspaper of the territory, *The Minnesota Pioneer*, documented the popularity of social dancing in large halls or at private parties. Mazourka Hall, the second story of a small frame building that housed Elfelt's dry goods store at Third and Cedar Streets in Saint Paul, was one such place. Rebecca Marshall Cathcart, who was twenty years old when her family moved to Saint Paul in 1849, later remembered, "Almost all our public dancing parties were held there." and "Mr. and Mrs. Elfelt were most hospitable, and many dancing parties were given in their beautifully appointed home in Irvine Park."[9]

Minnesota Territory became a state in 1858, and like the rest of the country, the temperance movement had its strong tethers in the state. Alcohol's frequent presence at these dances fueled the efforts by "dry" promoters to limit social dancing events. One such person wrote, hearkening back to the Greek muse of dance, " . . . 'no harm in *dancing*' but isn't it strange . . . how a few dozen cannot gather together in the name of Terpsichore, without one at least getting his head broken mysteriously, and a bevy of his first cousins groping their oblivious ways home about sunrise. . . ."[10]

In the Spirit of Terpsichore. Guest dance artist with James Sewell Ballet, ca. 2012. Courtesy of Erik Saulitis, photographer.

Movements, be they primeval, ritual, social, or choreographic, are intrinsic to dance, intrinsic to ballet. Many consider ballet a fine art and the pinnacle of dance training, while many others not familiar with ballet may have no idea of its origins and development. In the United States, the proliferation of Nutcracker productions during the winter holidays may cause some to believe ballet's roots are in America: "What would December be without *The Nutcracker*? It is as loved and leaned upon as Handel's *Messiah* and Dickens's *A Christmas Carol*."[11]

Some Minnesotans, if they saw *Black Swan*, directed in Hollywood by Darren Aronofsky, may pinpoint the eastern United States. This psychological-horror motion picture follows two rivaling ballerinas in a New York City ballet company rehearsing the classic ballet, *Swan Lake*. Those that recognize the name Mikhail Baryshnikov because of his 1977 film debut in *The Turning Point* may consider Russia as ballet's origin. Some of us living in *L'Étoile du Nord* and who took ballet lessons when we were young may herald France because ballet terms are all French. Others might say that Britain holds this honor if they watched *Billy Elliot*, the motion picture screenplay by Lee Hall set in a coal mining town in northern England. Young Billy discovers his passion for ballet, hangs up his boxing gloves, and against all odds, pursues his dream.

Actually, the unsown seeds of ballet in Minnesota began in the early twentieth century by the progenitors of Les Ballets Russes, a company that received both euphoric accolades and absolute disdain. In 1909 the company's performance of *Les Sylphides* received brilliant accolades. The choreographer, Michel Fokine, was inspired by the ballerinas of the Romantic ballet period, dressed in long, white tutus, giving them an ethereal appearance, with the ballet veering between reality and dream. The male role, first danced by Nijinsky, was, according to Fokine, "the personification of poetic vision."[12] Fokine had reworked his 1907 ballet, called *Chopiniana*, but with the 1909 Ballets Russes in Paris, Diaghilev renamed the work *Les Sylphides*. This name and version remain the one performed today in the West.

With a different Ballets Russes performance, *Le Sacre du Printemps* (*The Rite of Spring*), in 1913 at Le Théâtre de Champs-Élysées in Paris, pandemonium broke out as the audience reacted viscerally to the performance with shouting, booing, and stamping feet. The producer of the ballet stood up in his box and shouted to the crowd: "I beg you, permit us to finish the performance!"[13] Change in ballet style and technique can bring dissent and division only to be embraced by the next generation of ballet dancers and choreographers. A museum masterpiece, ballet is not. An ever-new work of art it is.

Louis XIV as Apollo from *Ballet de la Nuit*, seventeenth century, artist unknown.
Photo credit: © rmn-Grand Palais / Art Resource, NY.

SCENE 2
When Kings and Nobility Danced

A king may be judged by the standard of dancing during his reign.
—A Chinese saying[14]

Ballet's impressive history traces its watershed era not to the twentieth century, but to the courts of the Italian Renaissance, where kings, princes, and courtiers danced. Amid a flourishing Renaissance, the nobility became patrons of artists, philosophers, poets, and scientists. In these regal spaces, the first intimations of ballet technique began. Dance developed from a pastime into an art possessing a definite technique called a *balletto*, the root word for *ballet*. The earliest ballets, staged to carry political messages glorifying rulers, became an established aspect of Italian court life. In 1533, Catherine de' Medici of Florence married the future King Henri II of France, both just fourteen. Catherine came to France with her love of the arts, court dance, Italian pageantry, and spectacular and opulent court entertainments.

With Henri II's death only six years later, Catherine dominated the French court for many years, and her sons, King Charles IX and King Henri III, carried her Italian artistic tastes forward. Both monarchs shared their mother's interest in ceremonial and theatrical events and were known to stroll through the streets dressed *en travesti* and adorned with gold and silver veils and Venetian masks.[15] Shrewd, determined, and unscrupulous, Catherine wielded the power behind her sons' thrones. A veritable political and cultural force in France, she brought Italian fashion into France, such as cosmetics and face powder. Catherine made wall mirrors popular by decorating her Paris mansion with 119 mirrors; she upgraded the manner of eating and introduced the fork—when even the nobles ate with their fingers or a knife.

In October 1581, during the monarchy of King Henri III and his wife, Queen Louise, nobles of all ranks gathered as the royal family's honored guests at the Salle Bourbon near the Louvre Palace in Paris. A grand and lavish spectacle to celebrate the marriage of Marguerite de Lorraine, the sister of Queen Louise, entertained guests for nearly six hours. Catherine commissioned Balthasar de Beaujoyeulx, an Italian virtuoso violinist and ballet master, to create *Ballet Comique de la Reine* as part of the festivities for the marriage. Members of the court, nobility, and royalty danced accompanied by a mixture of music, song, verse, and spectacle—

27

such as the entrance of Queen Louise in a golden carriage, designed like a fountain, with sirens and tritons singing and playing musical instruments. The *Ballet Comique de la Reine* began at the late hour of 10:00 p.m. Nevertheless, it attracted crowds in the thousands intent on seeing the event, which cost France several million francs. The performance took place on the floor of the hall, where the royal family watched from the end of the room, and the crowds of people watched from above in the galleries.

The *Ballet Comique de la Reine* had political undertones. Its narrative told of the suppression of conflicts by the king and queen that brought a triumphant peace to France. Beaujoyeulx named this mixture of music, song, dance, and spectacle a *ballet comique* to show that dance and drama (*comédie* in French) together made a unified whole. The *Ballet Comique de la Reine* only vaguely resembles today's ballets, although it does reign as the first true ballet with choreography and a libretto. These *ballets de cour* (court ballets) thrived for the next century as court entertainment. Beaujoyeulx wrote in the preface to the ballet, "And now, after so many unsettling events . . . the ballet will stand as a mark of the strength and solidity of your Kingdom . . . The blush of color has returned to your France."[16] One hundred years later, and firmly established on French soil, ballet would emerge with Louis XIV holding sovereignty over ballet with his crown and scepter. Dancing for both pleasure and power, ballet was codified, cultivated, and advanced during his reign.

A ballet celebrated Louis XIV's birth in 1638 with a spectacle called the *Ballet de la Félicité*. He was christened *Louis-Dieudonné* (Gift of God). As a boy, he studied dance, and his tutor, Cardinal Mazarin, was accused of emphasizing dance over grammar lessons. Louis inherited the throne at almost five years old, but his mother served as sole regent for her son until his coronation at age fifteen in 1653. At this young age, Louis XIV danced the role of Apollo, the Roman sun god, in a thirteen-hour ballet called *Ballet de la Nuit* (Ballet of the Night). Performed at night with themes of darkness and chaos, Louis XIV entered dressed in gold, rubies, pearls, and diamonds with a headpiece of costly ostrich plumes, taking center stage as the rising sun god, Apollo, and dispelling the night evils.[17]

Ballet de la Nuit, performed eight times in the ensuing months, cleverly achieved theatrical success while solidifying Louis XIV's absolute power as a monarch. Impassioned about dance, Louis trained assiduously, and every morning he practiced vaulting, fencing, and dancing. His personal ballet master, Pierre Beauchamps, worked with him daily for twenty-two years.[18] As the *Roi-Soleil* (Sun King), he chose the sun as his emblem and surrounded himself with some of the greatest artists and intellectuals of that time—the playwright Molière, the painter Charles Le Brun, and the composer Jean-Baptiste Lully—while making France the dominant power in Europe with a flourishing colonial presence. Under his scepter, Louis XIV raised ballet to a brilliant level. As a "magnificent monarch, ruler of a rich nation insatiate for pleasure, dazzling spectacles were produced with glamour and opulence."[19]

Louis XIV made an indelible mark on the destiny of ballet. He is attributed with taking French peasant dances, bringing them into his court, and elevating dance from its plebian roots to a cultivated, refined art form. Under Louis XIV's absolute auspices, the principles governing classical ballet were born, and men were the masters of the art—the era of the *danseur*, later to be upstaged by the ballerina. To this day, French is the language of ballet technique, steps, and poses. His ballet master, Beauchamps, defined the five basic foot positions—one of the first lessons for every ballet dancer to this day. As an avid dancer and acutely proud of his legs, the famous portrait of Louis XIV by Hyacinthe Rigaud highlights Louis XIV's legs. He stands in ballet's fourth position of the feet, wearing high heels and a tall wig, all for the sake of appearing taller, regal, and refined. By 1681, Louis XIV had appeared on stage more than one hundred times. This date marks his retirement from performing. He had noticeably gained weight, but his love for ballet persisted.

Louis had already established the Académie Royale de la Musique in 1669, and dancers performed in its productions. Ballet became more structured and grew beyond court entertainment to performances with paying audiences in theaters. The Académie

Louis XIV of France in his Coronation Robe, 1701. Hyacinthe Rigaud, Musée du Louvre.

eventually became the Paris Opéra. Today the Paris Opéra Ballet holds the title of being the world's oldest ballet company. At his death in 1715, his seventy-two-year reign ended, a reign longer than any other known European monarch, and his ballet legacy continued to the modern day. Louis XIV's long reign brought stability to France, and his ballet legacy continued to wax strong during the eighteenth century. Choreographers achieved a rank of their own, and *les danseurs* (male dancers) dominated the stage.

Pavel Homko, Dance Artist with Minnesota Dance Theatre, ca. 2004.
Courtesy of Erik Saulitis, photographer.

SCENE 3
Les Danseurs

According to Aristotle, ballet expresses the actions of [people],
their customs and their passions.
—Claude-François Ménestrier[20]

Gaétan Vestris (1729–1808), famous for his technical acuity and outstanding dramatic ability, was the first danseur to take off his mask, preferring instead his facial expressions and mime. Often referred to as *Le Dieu de la Danse* (The God of Dance), but equally known to be quite conceited, he is said to have proclaimed, "Europe had only three great men, Frederick the Great of Prussia, Voltaire, and himself."[21] His son Auguste, another brilliant dancer, assumed his father's title as *The God of Dance* and stunningly pioneered and performed many virtuoso steps. After he retired from the stage, he influenced the new generation of dancers by passing along the principles of the French style. Marie Taglioni, Fanny Elssler, Jules Perrot, August Bournonville, and Marius Petipa were some of his star pupils who developed into great dancers and choreographers. At the same time, the emergence of social dancing, not associated with the court, spread throughout the middle classes. English dancing master, John Weather, typified this rise in social dancing.

Ballet reached far beyond the court of Louis XIV and spread throughout Europe and eastward into the realm of the Russian Empire into a different court. Under the monarchy of Peter I, also known as Peter the Great (1682–1725), ballet was not for entertainment but for creating a new Russian people. During his reign, Russian society opened up to the West; French and Italian ballet masters came; Saint Petersburg, a port city on the Baltic, was built like a European city; and magnificent palaces and courts were established. After his death, Empress Anna continued to Westernize Russia, and during her short reign (1730–1740), the Imperial Russian Academy of Dancing was founded to rival both Europe and Moscow. Other acclaimed centers for ballet in Copenhagen, Stuttgart, Vienna, and Milan made their debut during the eighteenth century, while France remained the "source-mother and father-home" of ballet.

A wellspring of interest, study, and reform in ballet technique ensued. The famous French choreographer and the most outspoken advocate for ballet reform, Jean-Georges Noverre (1727–1810), was one of the first to recognize ballet as an artistic medium.

His *Lettres sur la Danse et sur les Ballets*, published in 1760, set forth many of his ideas and ideals for ballet reform. Noverre believed ballets had to tell a story, not just a comic, lighthearted, or entertaining story but a story with a narrative of substance, including life's dark side, such as love, betrayal, murder, and tragedy. He said, "A ballet is a picture, or rather a series of pictures connected one with the other by the plot."[22] In other words, a *ballet d'action* moves a plot forward and is not simply a *divertissement* (entertainment).

In addition to espousing change in ballet's structure, he took aim at ballet's dress and costuming. He wrote, "Children of Terpsichore . . . abandon these cold masks . . . they denature your expressions, they eclipse, to put it bluntly, your soul. . . . get rid of these huge wigs and gigantic coifs . . . do without these tight and fashionable underskirts, which deprive movement of its charms, which disfigure elegant positions and efface the beauty of the upper body in its different poses."[23] Noverre's *Lettres* also set forth guiding principles for ballet composers—that is, music in ballet exists in connection

Abdo Sayegh Rodríguez, Dance Artist with Minnesota Dance Theatre, ca. 2004.
Courtesy of Erik Saulitis, photographer.

with the action and helps the action develop on the stage. Similar to Noverre's efforts at ballet reform, his close friend, German composer Christoph Gluck, experimented with music and opera reform.

The ideas in his *Lettres* resonated throughout France, England, and Europe for decades, embracing inevitable reform. By the 1780s, ballet and opera were no longer in lockstep with each other. "For the first time, ballet was recognized . . . as a self-sufficient art that could explain itself without words—*better* than words."[24] Noverre believed he was a champion of reform—not to change the elegant steps and poses of the noble style but to mix pantomime, dance, drama, and music into an aesthetically integrated narrative.

The reign of Louis XVI (1754–1793) poignantly revealed an undermining of Noverre's belief in the noble style of ballet while an increased interest in ballets with populist themes and lighter fare gained acceptance—and box office superiority. Louis XVI half-heartedly, and only when required, acquiesced to the pomp and ritual of royal power. He disdained public appearances and, for example, preferred to observe the majestic Versailles gardens through a telescope from on high in a private alcove. He preferred simple and relaxed dress and manners. In the late eighteenth century, aristocrats began emulating the more relaxed dress—off with the silk stockings, fancy breeches, powdered wigs, and hoopskirts. Louis XVI's queen, Marie Antoinette, only exacerbated the decline of the noble ideals of royal authority. Vicious gossip, scandal,

Pastel of Marie Antoinette, ca. 1775. Probably after Jean-Baptiste Gautier Dagoty. Le Musée des Beaux-Arts Antoine Lécuyer.

and scrutiny by the court because she did not produce an heir to the throne, and her sartorial excesses with ostentatious gowns and hairstyle poufs further diminished the absolute authority of the monarchy.

In 1789, the monarchy faced escalating financial and political crises. It would take the French Revolution to force balletic change. On July 1, 1789, *La Fille Mal Gardée* premiered at the Grand Théâtre de Bordeaux. In the picnic scene of the ballet, the dancers rushed downstage, closer to the audience, and sang a song in support of a revolution.[25] By July 14, with the famous charging of the Bastille prison, rioting had taken to the

Parisian streets, and the palace guards called out to squelch rioters flipped loyalties and joined the people. The Paris Opéra and other royal institutions drew angry crowds. One afternoon, some three thousand men and women gathered outside the Opéra, hurling insults and threatening to torch the theater. Revolution erupted throughout France during the last weeks of July. Angry peasants ransacked châteaux and abbeys, destroying documents of serfdom and symbols of the nobility and clergy. The French Revolution's deepest *raison dêtre* was a disdain for nobility and the aristocracy. People sang and danced in the streets, reveling in their victorious overthrow of the aristocracy. *Ici On Danse!* "Here We Dance!" the people asserted, while many dancers from Parisian theaters fled to the French provinces or abroad.[26] This artistic diaspora benefited ballet; it spread beyond the doors of the Paris Opéra.

Despite the Revolution's turmoil, gruesome executions, and reigning terror, ballet performances continued at the Paris Opéra under the direction of Pierre Gardel. Even when the monarchy fell in 1790, Gardel retained his post as *maître de ballet* at the Opéra.

Venziana mask from Verona, Italy.

He possessed incredible tenacity for survival and survival of the art he loved. In fact, "A list existed of some twenty-two singers and dancers who were destined to be executed, but its author, the murderous Jacques Hébert, admitted he did not act on the list because he liked being entertained."[27] Saved by the art! The Opéra continued, barely, at the *fin de siècle* (end of the eighteenth century). Often on the verge of bankruptcy, the Opéra reorganized to survive. Creative vitality languished, with only its former repertoire on stage—reruns of the *ancient régime*. Public balls and *bals masqués* had become the rage, and hundreds of Parisian dance halls filled days and nights with dancing. A new favorite social dance, the waltz, swept through Europe and became wildly popular since dancers now gazed at each other—not the king—their bodies entwined in a sensuous embrace and often scantily dressed. The waltz made its stage appearance at the Paris Opéra in 1800 with the ballet *La Dansomanie* by Pierre Gardel.

The Paris Opéra held extravagant masked balls that were open to crowds of every social distinction. Instead of scantily dressed patrons, outlandish dress made its appearance at the Opéra. With an air of total insouciance, some men and women came to the Opéra in bizarre dress—or undress—bordering on the uncouth. Men were seen sporting skintight pants and bold-colored short coats. Josephine de Beauharnais (Napoleon's wife) appeared in a gown made of rose petals and nothing underneath. Another woman came wrapped loosely in a tiger skin pulled around her naked body. Gardel's forty-two-year ten-

Liberty Leading the People, 1830, Artist Eugène Delacroix. Oil on canvas. Musée du Louvre.

ure at the Opéra endured some of the most volatile periods in French history, languishing as the esteemed seat of Noverre's noble style. His tenacious character served him well, and the Opéra survived. The era that began with Louis XIV and the noble style ended with the Revolution. French courts and ballet no longer carried the cachet as ballet's citadel. The beginning of the nineteenth century saw ballet shift back to its original roots—Italy.

At La Scala in Milan, Italy, its classical ballet company's influence and prestige spread throughout Europe. The French novelist Stendhal wrote, "See you at La Scala, they say."[28] The Italian school of ballet rightfully attributes its founding to Carlo Blasis (1797–1878). He directed the Ballet School of La Scala for more than a decade and produced a generation of exceedingly exceptional dancers.

Born in Naples, Blasis's family moved to Marseille. The story is told that his father, while traveling to London, had been kidnapped by pirates and ended up in southern France. His family joined his father in Marseille. Blasis trained in the French style and went on to Bordeaux, where he performed works by Noverre and Gardel. In 1817, Blasis made his debut at the Paris Opéra with the kindly patronage of Gardel. At the Opéra, he met Auguste Vestris and was deeply impressed by his virtuosity and innovative dancing. Dissatisfied with the contract that the Opéra offered him, Blasis moved back to Italy, his artistic-soul base.

In 1820, he published an analysis of ballet technique in his *Traité Élémentaire, Théorique et Pratique de l'Art de la Danse* (*Elementary Treatise Upon the Theory and Practice of the Art of Dancing*) and *The Code of Terpsichore* (1830), the first comprehensive ballet textbook. By codifying ballet's poses, Blasis believed that dancers could achieve an ease of motion and elegance with every gesture and movement layered with seductive grace. His belief in bold, virtuosic dancing found a home in Italy. Blasis and his pupils enhanced pointe work and pirouettes with new technical feats of bravura. Legend has it that it was he who originated ballet's attitude pose. Readers may be surprised to learn that he did not. Blasis wrote in his Treatise: "The position that dancers specifically refer to as the attitude is the loveliest and most difficult of execution in dancing. In my opinion, it is an adaptation of the much-admired pose of the celebrated Mercury of Bologna."[29] So perhaps he did claim it in later years because he was the first dancer to pirouette in attitude.

Blasis, considered by his contemporaries as a universal genius, could have easily won accolades as a writer, painter, and musician, but Blasis chose dancing. In his lifetime, his sphere of influence rippled throughout Europe and to the far-reaching cities of Warsaw and Moscow. His *Treatise* and *Code* influenced the development of Enrico Cecchetti (1850–1928), Blasis's direct artistic descendant. Cecchetti toured Europe as a premier danseur and became an instructor at the Imperial Ballet School, Russia, in 1892. A superb ballet teacher, many Russian dancers made brilliant technical progress under him and later became well-known dancers and choreographers. Cecchetti significantly improved classical ballet pedagogy throughout Europe—a key contribution to modern classical ballet training.

Attitude, a classical ballet term. Emily Tyra, Guest dance artist with James Sewell Ballet, 2017. An *attitude* pose shown with a *renversé*, a bending of the head and body from the waist while turning with a knee in *attitude*. Courtesy of Erik Saulitis, photographer.

SCENE 4
Danseuse to Ballerina

And then you have the classical ballerinas—
they're like sopranos. Applied to the dance.
—Ninette de Valois[30]

The Industrial Revolution in commerce, manufacturing, water, and steam power swept through Europe in the nineteenth century. It marked a major change in human lifestyle and caused a yearning for an idealized memory of the past as well as an awakening of interest in spirituality and the supernatural. "In literature, painting, and music, the Romantic period was a progressive development; in ballet, it was little short of a revolution."[31] The romanticists embraced themes of human struggle between the actual and the ideal, between the flesh and the spirit. Noverre's belief that music and stage action together created *ballets d'action* became a reality.

The rise in prominence of the *danseuse* in the mid-nineteenth century forever changed ballet's choreography and look. The *ballerina*, Italian for female dancer, took artistic precedence. Male dancers lost their sovereignty in the ballet world and became delegated to simply a *porteur* (carrier) role; female dancers now ruled center stage. Enter the ballerina, moving on her toes—*en pointe*—giving her an appearance of lightness

and a longer line of the body. Softly rounded arms and a forward tilt of the upper body gave the ballerina a willowy look. A new costume enhanced this appearance of lightness and line. Ballerinas dared to wear a tight-fitting bodice presenting their bare necks and shoulders. Pale pink tights and satin pointe shoes gave glimpses of their legs through long, white, gossamer tutus. The *ballet blanc*, a ballet or scene in a ballet where ballerinas wore white tutus or costumes accompanied by otherworldly spirits, established its place in the "mystique of the mysterious."[32]

Marie Taglioni (1804–1884), born with rounded back and shoulders, seemed destined to never become a ballet dancer. Her father, Filippo Taglioni, was an Italian dancer, ballet master, and choreographer, and her mother was a Swedish dancer. Despite Marie's physical challenges, she began ballet at a young age while living in Paris with her mother. One of her teachers had asked rhetorically, "Will that little hunchback ever learn to dance?"[33] Absolutely. Her perseverance, charm, and unique artistry overcame those challenges.

In her mid-teens, Marie Taglioni joined her father in Vienna, where he was ballet master at the Court Opera. She trained under his guidance for two years, achieving a brilliance of technique and an ethereal quality that would make her soundless landings a Paris sensation.[34] At eighteen years old, Marie Taglioni made her ballet debut in Vienna dancing in *La Réception d'une Jeune Nymphe à la Cour de Terpsichore*, staged by her father for this occasion. Another dancer, Fanny Elssler, a Spanish-looking Viennese *danseuse*, also made her debut with this ballet. These two debutantes and future lifelong rivals would not meet up again until eleven years later while dancing at the Paris Opéra.

Marie Taglioni in *La Sylphide*, 1845.
Artist Richard James Lane after Alfred Edward Chalon. "Souvenir D'Adieu. La Sylphide mourns James's betrothal." Color lithograph with watercolor. Bibliothèque de l'Opéra Garnier, Paris, France. Photo © Leonard de Selva/ Bridgeman Images.

Filippo Taglioni's stellar masterpiece *La Sylphide* premiered in 1832 at the Paris Opéra. It was inspired by Charles Nodier's novel *Tribly, ou le Lutin d'Argile* (*The Elf of Argyll*), published in 1822. The novel's story told of an elf in the Scottish Highlands who lures the wife of a fisherman away from her husband. However, *La Sylphide's* storyline takes a romantic era departure from the novel. Instead of an elf, the ballet has an otherworldly spirit, a diaphanous woodland sylph. The sylph succeeds in luring a betrothed man to a forest glade on his wedding day, stating she loves him and has watched over him for years. He follows her to where the sylph and her sisters dance for him. He attempts to catch her with a scarf given to him by an old sorceress, but when he wraps the scarf around her shoulders, her wings fall off, and she dies. Sister sylphs carry her aloft to an otherworld. Alone at the end, he views his fiancée in a wedding procession going to church to marry another man; he collapses lifeless.

Like a clarion bell, success echoed throughout Europe, including London and Saint Petersburg, and inspired the Romantic era of ballet. One observer noted, "Taglioni's style was 'Romanticism applied to dance.'"[35] *La Sylphide* featured Marie Taglioni, dancing with superb technique and ethereal beauty. Taglioni performed *sur les pointes* (on the pointes dancing, not simply posing) supported only by darning the toes of the satin shoes. It was the first ballet where pointe work enhanced the ballet's choreography. Her white silk tutu, shortened to highlight her pointe work, became the iconic classical ballerina tutu. With her light and graceful style, she seemed to float over the stage, a winged wonder and otherworldly sylph—a defining contrast to the virtuosic earthbound movements popular at the time.

La Sylphide benefited from the advanced theatrical techniques of the nineteenth century such as flying harnesses accenting lightness of being and modern gaslight producing a moonlight glow shimmering through Taglioni's white tutu. Her debut in *La Sylphide* redefined ballet and Marie Taglioni became the archetypal ballerina, a *prima ballerina assoluta*. She reigned supreme in the ballet world. Her name became a new Franch verb, *taglioniser*, as others imitated her style. Her hairstyle became the height of fashion; her name branded products; Queen Victoria named a racehorse after her. Taglioni ascended the throne as Queen of Dance.

Fate pursued Fanny Elssler and Marie Taglioni when they met at the doors of the Paris Opéra. No longer ballet debutantes, both had triumphantly captured audience acclaim, admiration, and devotion, but differently. Taglioni danced discreetly and otherworldly; Elssler danced sensuously with earthy intensity. Théophile Gautier, the nineteenth-century French poet, writer, leader in the Romantic movement, and prominent dance critic, famously compared the two, "Mlle. Taglioni is a Christian dancer . . . she flies like a spirit in the midst of transparent clouds of white muslin. Fanny is quite a pagan dancer; she reminds one of the muse Terpsichore, tambourine in hand,

her tunic exposing her thigh, caught up with a golden clasp."[36] She danced with her entire body, not only her feet and brought the high energy of Hungarian, Polish, Spanish, and Russian ethnic dances to ballet, called *danse caractère*—traditional folk dances or dance with acting. Audiences raved about Elssler's *cachucha*, a fiery solo dance from Andalusia (southern Spain) performed *sur les pointes* with castanets.

Elssler's debut at the Opéra in 1834 thrilled the audience with her dancing the lead role in *La Tempête*, and an ardent rivalry began. Elssler was as brilliant a dancer as Taglioni, but where "Taglioni glowed, Elssler glittered."[37] Paris audiences called

Fanny Essler in "The Cracovienne Dance" from *La Gypsy*. Photo credit: Lebrecht Music Arts / Bridgeman Images.

themselves either Elsslerites or Taglionists. The rivalry never ceased until 1838, when Taglioni accepted a Russian invitation to perform with the Imperial Ballet at the Mariinsky Theatre in Saint Petersburg. In Russia, Taglioni's career reached its zenith, and her appearances rekindled an interest in ballet. After her last performance at the Mariinsky in 1842, fans allegedly purchased a pair of her pointe shoes, cooked them, and served them in a sauce. Another canard from Taglioni's time states that on a trip, Taglioni's party was accosted by bandits who simply wanted to see her dance.[38]

Marie Taglioni formally retired from the stage in 1847. She spent time in Italy and eventually returned to Paris and became the *Inspectrice de la danse* at the Paris Opéra. She choreographed her only ballet, *Le Papillon* (1860, *The Butterfly*), for her most promising protégée, Emma Livry. The hope was that this ballet would forever link Emma Livry as a Romantic icon, similar to Taglioni with *La Sylphide*. Her brief, brilliant career was brought to its terrible close when her costume caught fire from the gas winglight alongside her. Dance critic Théophile Gautier wrote, "Emma Livry was barely twenty-one. . . . She belonged to that chaste school of Taglioni, which makes the dance an almost spiritual art. . . . She could imitate the charming, whimsical flight of a butterfly settling on a flower without bending its stem."[39] Years later, Emma Livry achieved distinction by being chosen, along with the luster of former stars Marie Taglioni and Carlotta Grisi, as one of the three *danseuses* to have their portrait busts commissioned to be placed in the Paris Opéra, where they honorably remain to this day.[40]

After Taglioni left the Paris Opéra for the Imperial Ballet, the absence of Elssler's archrival gained Elssler luminosity as the sole *étoile* at the Opéra. Then an invitation to America in 1840 caught her fancy. She wrote in *The Letters and Journal of Fanny Elssler*, "I am about to cross the Atlantic and proceed to America! . . . I cannot look upon this strange intention as other than a mad freak that has seized my fancy in a thoughtless moment . . . My sober judgment could never have brought me to such a resolution…" One event onboard the ship displayed Elssler's utmost aplomb and strength. She retired to her cabin to find a sailor with a knife in the process of robbing her jewelry. She stepped back and to defend herself, took a preparation, made a pirouette, kicked him so forcefully with an extended leg, she knocked him to the floor. The sailor was seriously injured and died a few days later.[41]

Fanny Elssler arrived in America with a tour contract of three months. She stayed for almost two years. Fanny dazzled the American public with her voluptuous charm, bravura, and free spirit. Performances were sold out, and enthusiastic ovations occurred wherever and whatever she danced. Elsslermania swept the country with her luscious intensity and sensuous beauty. On the day she performed in Washington, D.C., Congress adjourned for lack of quorum. At a formal gathering at the Capitol, a toast was raised to her health and drunk from a dance shoe. Richmond, Virginia, greeted her with tolling bells and cannon salutes. Pen and ink artists sketched copious portraits of her, and to the buying public's delight, thousands of lithographs were made. She performed in almost every principal city in America and also accepted an invitation to Havana, Cuba. On her return to Europe, Elssler danced in London, Vienna, and Berlin and in the eastern realm of Russia. In both Moscow and Saint Petersburg, her dramatic intensity in the mad scene of the ballet, *Giselle*, brought the houses down in both cities and made her personal mark on *Giselle*.

In the shadows of Taglioni and Elssler, a new *étoile* was rising at the Paris Opéra: Carlotta Grisi. At sixteen years old, she danced with a ballet company in Naples when she met Jules Perrot, one of the few male dancers acclaimed during the Romantic era, also known as a choreographer. Gautier wrote this bravo to Perrot in 1840, "quiet agility, perfect rhythm, and easy grace . . . Perrot the aerial, Perrot the sylph, Perrot the male Taglioni."[42] Grisi's sublime talent and beauty enchanted Perrot, and a few years later, when she arrived in Paris, Perrot trained Grisi himself, instilling "elegance and clarity of pose into her movement style."[43] As lovers and dancers, they toured together to Munich, Vienna, Lyon, and London—a couple on stage and off. A daughter was born in 1837, and they never married, but as artists of the Romantic era, they remained cordial and continued to work together when their paths crossed.

Enamored with the ideals of the Romantic movement, Gautier and Perrot discussed a ballet collaboration with Grisi in

Carlotta Grisi in *Giselle*. Photo credit: Lebrecht Music Arts/Bridgeman Images.

mind as the heroine. After reading Heinrich Heine's poem *De L'Allemagne*, the genesis of *Giselle* took shape in Gautier's mind. In Heine's poem, the spirits of brides who died before their wedding day lured men into the forest and forced them to dance until their deaths. This cluster of romanticist stars—Perrot, Gautier, and Grisi—together created a triumphant success. Carlotta Grisi danced the lead role in the original title of the ballet, *Giselle ou Les Wilis*, a ballet in two acts, for its 1841 premiere at the Paris Opéra. This ghostly ballet of love, betrayal, suicidal grief, and sylphide-like wilis became a sensational hit and catapulted Grisi to fame. During the 1840s, she also performed at Her Majesty's Theatre, which from the early 1830s until the late 1840s, was the home of London's Romantic ballet.

Giselle, the archetypal ballet blanc and icon of the Romantic period, continues to be danced today. Its legacy that choreography establishes the narrative of a ballet story endures. Perrot's intense choreographic fusion of dance and storyline was his symbolic nod to Noverre's revered ideals. Gautier saw in Grisi a unique blend of the earthiness of Fanny Elssler and the ethereal quality of Marie Taglioni. She was his muse as well as his lifelong love. Gautier's talent and collaboration with the writer Jules-Henri Vernoy de Saint-Georges, composer Adolphe Adam, choreographers Jean Coralli and Jules Perrot (who choreographed all of Grisi's solos), dancers, musicians, and the production staff produced a classic ballet of artistic strength and sensibility. Gautier brought out the finest in all his collaborators, similar to what the dance world would see with Serge Diaghilev and the Ballets Russes in the early 1900s.

Under the radar of the overwhelming glow of *Giselle* at the Paris Opéra, another extraordinary Romantic ballerina *étoile* had already made her mark in Italy and beyond. Fanny Cerrito (1817–1909), born and trained in Naples, adhered and profited from Carlo Blasis's pedagogy. With an amazing *ballon* (ability to jump), captivating charm, and a radiant stage presence, she captured the hearts of dance audiences in many Italian cities and then accrued equal success beyond Italy. At the young age of only twenty-one, Cerrito obtained prima ballerina status at La Scala, an indication of what would become a spectacular career. In 1840 London, Cerrito made her debut at Her Majesty's Theatre and was fortunate to be the leading dancer when Perrot became its principal ballet master. The British public adored Cerrito, and the press even changed the accent in her surname and adoringly called her Miss "Cherry Toes."[44] She remained the darling of London until 1847.

After a successful production of *Giselle* in London, Jules Perrot created numerous short ballets as principal ballet master at Her Majesty's Theatre. Benjamin Lumley, director of the theatre, envisioned four of the most celebrated ballerinas dancing together in honor of Queen Victoria's birthday celebrations. In 1845, at Her Majesty's Theatre in London, a stirring murmur moved

Fanny Cerrito in *Ondine*.

Lucile Grahn in *Eoline ou La Dryade*. Photo credit: Lebrecht Music Arts/Bridgeman Images.

throughout the audience. Both the public and critics waited in heightened anticipation for the curtain to rise and to see on stage, together for the first time, the four greatest *étoiles* of the Romantic ballet world: Marie Taglioni, Carlotta Grisi, Fanny Cerrito, and Lucile Grahn. Fanny Elssler, the fifth *étoile* at that time, was invited to dance, but she declined, and young Lucile Grahn, without a second thought, gladly accepted the invitation. Grahn was a Danish-born ballerina known as the "Taglioni of the North."[45]

Together, the ballerinas danced the Opening and the Finale of *Pas de Quatre* choreographed by Perrot with music by Cesare Pugni. In between these bookends of the ballet, Perrot choreographed a unique variation for each ballerina, capturing the shimmering essence of her romantic style. Dissension broke out between the dancers during a rehearsal concerning who would perform immediately before Taglioni. A diplomatic decision was made to have the solos performed in age order: Lucile Grahn, the youngest, followed by Carlotta Grisi, then Fanny Cerrito, then Taglioni the oldest and a *grande dame* dancing the most sought-after last solo. Gautier, dance critic extraordinaire, wrote, "At the curtain call, Cerrito crowned Taglioni with a wreath of white roses while the public deluged the stage with bouquets."[46] *Pas de Quatre* with Jules Perrot's composition, illuminating the brilliance of each artist, blended with an excellent choreographic design, demonstrated that ballet at its best does not need a storyline to survive. It seems almost impossible that Perrot could convince four of the most celebrated Romantic era ballerinas to perform together; they did, but only four times with the original four. However, *Pas de Quatre* retains its allure and continues to draw ballerinas to perform the ballet and entices audiences to attend.

Romantic ballet began to languish during the last half of the nineteenth century. Ballet lost its poetic status and dreamy idealism to literary men and women who espoused realism, not romanticism. Even though the Paris Opéra continued operating with support from the state, it lacked artistic distinction. The danseuses became the main attraction to many people, "in particular for members of the select Jockey Club . . . " They had the right of entry to the Foyer de la Danse, a

Pas de Quatre, Stroia Ballet Company, Little Falls, Minnesota. Janine Ersfeld (en pointe in back), Megan Magwire (penché on the right), Katie Dehler (kneeling on the left), and Ann Marie Ethen (kneeling on the right). Dropps Photography, Saint Cloud, MN, 1995. Courtesy of Ann Marie Ethen.

room behind the stage where the ballerinas visited them before the ballet.[47]

Vestiges of the Romantic ballet did linger, not on the Opéra's stage but on the canvases, drawings, and sculptures of Edgar Degas. "He paid homage to dancers and the dance, and he did so in part by invoking the Romantic ballet. Indeed, the future of *La Sylphide* and *Giselle*—and ballet—lay elsewhere. *Giselle* was mounted in Russia in 1842 by a little-known French ballet master and later staged by Jules Perrot himself, assisted by the young French danseur, Marius

Petipa."[48] When Petipa became ballet master of the Imperial Ballet, he kept the ballet in the repertoire and restaged scenes as he saw necessary. ". . . Petipa replaced the softness of Romantic style with a gemlike sharpness; his ballets were conceived as treats for the eyes." [49] Petipa's restaged *Giselle* came back home to Paris in 1910, sixty-nine years after its premiere at the Paris Opéra, by Serge Diaghilev and Les Ballets Russes. *Giselle*, an ever-popular ballet, continues to be performed around the globe.

SCENE 5

Marius Petipa, Father of Classical Ballet

Dancing means Music made visible.
—Théophile Gautier[50]

With a seismic shift, the center of ballet moved from France to the Russian Empire. Saint Petersburg and its state-controlled Mariinsky Theatre became its epicenter and Marius Petipa its focus. Petipa (1819–1910), an accomplished French danseur and choreographer, partnered Fanny Elssler for his debut at the Paris Opéra in 1841. He then left Paris for a more profitable position in Bordeaux, where he danced lead roles and choreographed many works before accepting a principal danseur role at the King's Theater in Madrid. Enamored with Spain and its national dances, he once said, "I danced and played the castanets no worse than the best dancers of Andalusia."[51] Petipa had a love affair with the wife of a marquis, which forced him to flee Spain. In 1847, he arrived in Saint Petersburg. A lingering love of Spanish dance made its appearance in many of his major ballets he later developed. Still in the prime of his dancing career, Petipa accepted a one-year contract as principal danseur for the Imperial Ballet. A contract for one year that lasted his entire lifetime.

After only a few months at the Imperial Ballet, young Petipa and a fellow danseur, Pierre-Frédéric Malevergne, staged to high acclaim a Russian production of Joseph Mazilier's *Paquita*. When Jules Perrot arrived in Saint Petersburg in 1848 as chief choreographer of the Imperial Ballet, Petipa assisted Perrot with the staging of Perrot's ballet *La Esmeralda*. Petipa continued to teach, dance, and choreograph, acquiring more esteem in the Russian ballet system. His

Marius Petipa. Photo credit: Bridgeman Images.

45

rise to the top of the Russian ballet hierarchy had not yet come. Petipa's breakthrough happened after 1858 when Perrot left Russia and went back to France. The director of the Imperial Ballet needed a new full-length ballet for a guest ballerina. Petipa was chosen, with only six weeks to opening night.

Petipa always kept his eye on the news of the day to intuit a possible connection between news and a possible ballet. The building of the Suez Canal began in 1859, fostering the public's interest in Egyptian antiquities. An Egyptian-themed romance, *The Mummy's Tale* by Gautier became the basis for Petipa's *The Pharaoh's Daughter*. The ballet premiered in 1862 to tremendous success and remained in the repertoire until the 1920s. Petipa danced the role of Ta-Hor. It was his last dance, but also his apogee. *The Pharaoh's Daughter* honored Petipa's choreographic skills by naming him chief choreographer of the Imperial Ballet.

As chief choreographer, Petipa refined the theatrical elements of ballet and developed the rules, or rather the tradition, of the classical ballet. He became known as the "master of the grand spectacle." His ballets had a plot with fully developed scenes, vibrant *danses caractères* (ethnic dances), and pantomime. Petipa believed that choreography took precedence over the other artistic expressions in the ballet, such as music, decor, and libretto; he gave detailed and precise instructions to all the artists involved with his ballets. Under his tenure, the Imperial Ballet achieved recognition as second to none. Its school absorbed the

The Egyptian Couple, 1975.
Artist L. "Gretch" Holl-Blaustein.
Egyptian silk screen, 24 x 16 inches.
Courtesy of L. "Gretch" Holl-Blaustein.

best characteristics of the French and Italian styles, and by the *fin de siècle* its pupils were in demand internationally, similar to the Italian ballerinas in the two previous decades.

Petipa embraced the wave of Italian *étoiles* to Russia with their fresh technical and dramatic skills. Pierina Legnani, considered by many the greatest ballerina from La Scala, joined the Imperial Ballet from 1893 to 1901. She debuted in *Cinderella* with an astonishing performance in the final act: thirty-two *fouettés en tournant*—a feat of tremendous difficulty never before seen in Russia. She caused a sensation in the audience, and they cried, "Encore, encore!" Not to be outdone by an Italian ballerina, when Mathilde Kschessinska mastered the same feat, rejoicing erupted in

Pierina Legnani. In an 1893 interview for London's *The Sketch*, Legnani said, "I have breakfast, quite a heavy breakfast—café au lait, with yolks of egg in it, and fillet of beef."

Mathilde Kschessinska symbolized Imperial Russia. After the 1917 Bolshevik Revolution, she fled Russia with her husband, the Grand Duke André of the Romanov family and their son. They settled in Paris and sold her jewels. With that money, she opened her ballet school.

the Russian audience. Legnani became Petipa's muse. He created several roles for her to highlight her talents, and she was given the title of *prima ballerina assoluta* obtained by only one other ballerina, Mathilde Kschessinska. Legnani, Kschessinska, and Preobrajenska held the distinction of being the three greatest ballerinas in Russia in the late nineteenth century, and the three greatest rivals. Kschessinska allegedly ushered live chickens on stage during a solo of Preobrajenska.[52]

From the 1860s to his retirement from the Imperial Ballet in 1903, Petipa collaborated with many composers, but only

according to a musical plan he had already laid out for a ballet. During Petipa's tenure as principal ballet master, he and Pyotr Ilyich Tchaikovsky (1840–1893) formed a celebrated collaboration. Tchaikovsky passionately admired ballet and understood that music is an aural art form and ballet a visual one. Tchaikovsky's scores bridged the human ear and eye for Petipa's choreography in *The Sleeping Beauty*, which premiered in 1890. The ballet was hugely successful and the Imperial Ballet commissioned Tchaikovsky to compose music for *The Nutcracker* (1892). When Petipa fell ill, Lev Ivanov, the second

Pyotr Ilyich Tchaikovsky in 1888 with nephew Georgy Kartsev (right), Vladimir Zhedrinsky (far left), and lifelong friend and poet Alexei Apukhtin (left).

ballet master, took over the choreography and followed Petipa's detailed notes for the plot. Ivanov also choreographed Acts 2 and 4 of *Swan Lake* (1895). These ballets transported Mariinsky Theatre's audiences to faraway times and places, and they remain to this day the image of classical ballet.

In nearly fifty years as a choreographer, Petipa created more than sixty full-evening ballets and an immeasurable number of short ballets and dance numbers. Many of his ballets have stood the test of time, performed either in their entirety or with brilliant selections showcasing the dancers' agility and technical skills. Some of these ballets include *The Sleeping Beauty, Don Quixote, La Bayadère,* and *Raymonda.* Among those that he restaged—*Paquita, Giselle, Le Corsaire, Coppélia, La Sylphide, Swan Lake (Acts 1 and 3)*—have also had staying power. Petipa retired from the Imperial Ballet and remained in Russia until his death. Reminiscing about his years there as chief choreographer, he once said, "I created a ballet company of which everyone said: 'Saint Petersburg has the greatest ballet in Europe.'"[53] He established the style and structure of the classical ballet as it is known today. Petipa can be regarded as the "father of classical ballet" and Tchaikovsky as its "godfather." Together they left an indelible mark on ballet, as did Louis XIV two hundred years earlier.

SCENE 6
A Creative Force

Classical ballet is to the dance, what poetry is to literature.
—Serge Diaghilev[54]

Another ballet legend takes center stage: Serge Pavlovich Diaghilev. He was not a dancer, a choreographer, or a composer, but "He displayed characteristics of the enlightened despot, of the natural leader who knows how to drive the most unyielding elements, at times using persuasion, at others, charm."[55] His far-reaching legacy forever changed ballet, resonating across the twentieth century with the global impact of innovative showstoppers.

Diaghilev (1872–1929) was born into a family of Russian nobility that encouraged the arts, and he grew up surrounded by musical evenings with chamber music, songs, and an occasional opera. He was raised by his stepmother, who instilled in him a will to succeed. From his father, he inherited some of his physically unattractive genes—a large head proportionally bigger than his thick-set body, deeply set sad eyes, a protruding jaw, and a plump, fleshy underlip. He smiled only with his mouth while the rest of his face remained serious.

Diaghilev's family traits of enthusiasm and stubbornness also formed his character. He moved from the family's country mansion

Portrait of Serge Diaghilev with his Nurse, 1906. Artist Léon Bakst. Oil on canvas, 63.39 x 45.67 inches. Credit: State Russian Museum, Saint Petersburg, Russia/Bridgeman Images.

in Perm and entered Saint Petersburg University in 1890 to study law. He stayed with his cousin, who introduced him to a small band of creative art enthusiast friends, such as Léon Bakst and Alexandre Benois. His cousin's friends thought Diaghilev was provincial and boorish. Diaghilev diligently immersed himself in becoming socially prudent, adamant about not compromising his social status. Along with his law studies, Diaghilev also studied music at the Conservatoire. After being criticized for his musical efforts by Rimsky-Korsakov and his friends, Diaghilev began to take an interest in painting. About five years later, ballet sparked his interest.

In 1899, Diaghilev became an assistant to the director of the Imperial Theatres as the "Official for Special Missions." He marvelously carried out his first assignment to edit the annual report of the Imperial Theatres. Diaghilev converted a useful, yet utterly dull publication, into a finessed work of art with excellent reviews. Despite overrunning his budget, he approached the director with bold conditions that the director would not grant. A faux pas for being young and newly hired. Further criticism ensued, and his overbearing attitude and snobbish belief in his rightness on any issue made working with him difficult. At that time, Diaghilev denied being homosexual, even though spiteful rumors circulated, and he had received a powder puff as an anonymous gift. The Imperial director warned him to be discreet; he was not.[56] Tensions increased, and in 1901 Diaghilev was "dismissed." This dismissal meant exclusion from any Imperial employment in the future, including the use of Imperial Theatres or entering a theatre to watch a ballet or hear a concert.

The words of Benois, Diaghilev's close friend and artist collaborator, speak to Diaghilev's resiliency and how dismissal from the Imperial Theatres did not deter his artistic ambitions. Benois wrote, "It was he who had contrived to knit us young Russian painters into a homogenous group . . . he who founded the influential art magazine; it was he again who organized the splendid exhibit of Russian portraiture that entirely filled the immense Tavrida Palace. But all this activity took place in Russia, and was aimed at raising the artistic understanding of Diaghilev's compatriots. . . . all our activity was aimed at glorifying Russian art—indeed, everything around us in Russia that held beauty and spiritual meaning."[57]

Alexandre Benois, 1935. Plate XXII Peter Lieven. *The Birth of Ballets-Russes.*

Diaghilev's nationally acclaimed *Exhibition of Russian Historical Portraits* in 1905 received accolades from friends, artists, critics, and even Czar Nicholas II who had opened the display. His exhibition exemplified an appreciation of Russian art and identity. Even his enemies acknowledged the extraordinary success of this exhibition during growing opposition to Imperial rule, political tensions, and the escalating violence in 1904 and 1905. At the Metropole Hotel in Moscow, near the spot where the czar's uncle and brother-in-law had been assassinated, a gala banquet honoring Diaghilev took place. Tall, heavy-set, and elegantly dressed, Diaghilev took the floor and spoke these words, "We are witnessing the greatest historic hour of reckoning, of things coming to an end in the name of a new, unknown culture—one which we will create but which will also sweep us away . . . I raise my glass . . . to the new commandment of a new aesthetic."[58] Perhaps as he spoke, Diaghilev sensed a harbinger of his own future.

With growing revolutionary fervor and opposition to Imperial control, Diaghilev knew that instability would reduce Imperial subsidies and new cultural events. Diaghilev's source for many of his artistic endeavors over the past six years had been the czar. Ever resilient and resourceful and aware that Russia had become more dependent on French loans and needed to maintain good Franco-Russian relations, he decided to approach the government, asking for support for cultural initiatives to Paris. Diaghilev's export campaign of Russian art had begun.

"He no longer found in his own country enough scope and freedom for his nature, temperament, and ambitions to function."[59]

Early in 1906, Diaghilev conceived the idea of staging a major art exhibition of painting and sculpture in the new Salon d'Automne (August art salon) in Paris. As a Russian cultural initiative, and with Russia slowly recovering from the recent political turbulence, he had time to make contacts and establish his reputation with Parisian cultural officials. He did not travel straight to Paris; he took a tour of the Mediterranean with his boyfriend and arrived in Paris in May 1906. By June, he had the list of artists and began the work of organizing the loan and transportation of seven hundred and fifty works in preparation for the October opening. The exhibition, a tremendous success with an appreciative French audience, affirmed Diaghilev's decision to promote Russian art abroad. His circle of close artist friends "could not help but love our country or fail to respond to the strange charm of her soul . . ."[60]

He followed the exportation of Russian art and culture with music concerts in 1907 and the production of the opera *Boris Godunov* in 1908. In 1909, the czar withdrew all financial support for his export campaign to Paris. What appeared to be an insurmountable obstacle, but with flinty and determined ambition, he decided to drop opera because of its greater expense and present an entire ballet season. He wrote to his promoters in Paris, "No opera this year. Bringing brilliant ballet company, eighty strong, best soloists, fifteen performances . . . Start big publicity."[61] A fiduciary decision that would give birth to Les Ballets Russes and dramatically make ballet the center of his life. Nevertheless, sensing his power to influence people and experiencing the rapture of talking and convincing others of his ideas, he defined his mission in life in a letter to his stepmother: "First of all, I am a great charlatan . . . second, I'm a great charmer; third, I've great nerve; fourth, I'm a man with a great deal of logic and few principles; and fifth, I think I lack talent; but . . . I think I've found my real calling—patron of the arts."[62]

Serge Diaghilev. Overleaf, V&A Publishing, 2010. p.6. Photograph by Jan de Strelecki. Jerome Robbins Dance Division, New York Public Library for the Performing Arts.

Diaghilev's Les Ballets Russes

Diaghilev was the greatest impresario ballet ever had.
—Serge Lifar[63]

Diaghilev collaborated with composers, choreographers, designers, and dancers with one goal in mind, as he said to a young artist and writer, Jean Cocteau: *Étonne-moi.* (Astonish me.)[64] Those two words speak volumes about Diaghilev's character and how twentieth-century ballet would change. Diaghilev's company, Les Ballets Russes, flourished from 1909 to 1929. He allowed the creative artists he worked with to explore the limits of their artistic yearnings. His company danced to new music by composers Stravinsky, Debussy, Prokofiev, Ravel, Sati, and several others. He commissioned visual artists for decor from Picasso, Matisse, Bakst, Benois, Rouault, and a great many others. In addition, he encouraged innovative creativity from five significant choreographers of the twentieth century—Michel Fokine, Vaslav Nijinsky, Léonide Massine, Bronislava Nijinska, and George Balanchine.

For Diaghilev's export campaign to Paris, the Saison Russe 1909, everything was well underway when the Imperial Court withdrew its financial support. The Théâtre du Châtelet had been leased; dancer and

Théâtre du Châtelet Program of Anna Pavlova by Jean Cocteau, Les Ballets Russes in Paris, 1909.

technician contracts signed; sets were being painted by several artists, including Bakst and Benois; and substantial borrowed money from benefactors had been spent. Michel Fokine, an outstanding young choreographer with creative and inventive fervor, had accepted Diaghilev's invitation to join the company. Diaghilev's will of iron to surmount enormous obstacles continued to amaze the court, which believed he would give up. The court kept an eye on Diaghilev's activities, ready to stop any of his activities if he accessed the hallowed and forbidden Imperial Theatres, buildings, or halls.

The theatre chosen for all the rehearsals for Diaghilev's 1909 export campaign to Paris was the Hermitage Theatre, which adjoined the Winter Palace, the residence of the czar. Dancers had gathered under Michel Fokine's direction. Rehearsal had just begun when a messenger from the court arrived and stated that access to the hall for Diaghilev and his dancers was strictly forbidden. Nothing could be done. Diaghilev had made the unforgivable *faux pas* to the Imperial Court. Fokine was enraged, and the company was completely confused and distraught. Everyone lost their heads except for Serge Diaghilev, who promptly set to work finding a new rehearsal space. In less than an hour, Diaghilev's secretary arrived and announced that arrangements had been made and carriages were waiting to escort everyone to a recently renovated theatre. Once at the theatre, a buffet of light meal selections awaited them. Serge, as his company called him, had taken care of his "family."

Michel Fokine. *Mikhail Fokine*, Mariinsky Theatre Souvenir Booklet, 2008. The Museum of the Mariinsky Theatre, Saint Petersburg.

Les Ballets Russes, Diaghilev's new ballet company of young artists and dancers from the Mariinsky Theatre in Saint Petersburg and the Grand Theatre in Moscow, descended on Paris, full of zeal and excitement. Paris offered them an infinitely freer and more colorful life than back home in Russia. They had never seen anything but the streets of their cities, the walls and floorboards of their ballet schools, and the stages of the Grand and Mariinsky Theatres. Fokine, the choreographer and régisseur (stage manager), worked the dancers assiduously. They responded with more enthusiasm and discipline than they usually showed in Saint Petersburg and Moscow. Fokine had seen Isadora Duncan when she came to Saint Petersburg in 1907, exhibiting her rebellion against classical ballet. Her ideas aligned

Léon Bakst's costume design for *The Red Sultana*, choreography by Michel Fokine, 1910. *Mikhail Fokine, Mariinsky Theatre Souvenir Booklet*, 2008. The Museum of the Mariinsky Theatre, Saint Petersburg.

with Fokine's own personal struggles with the old forms of ballet, and Diaghilev gave him *carte blanche* with his choreographic creations.

Diaghilev did everything to make opening night memorable for his dancers. The theatre was in poor condition, so he completely refurbished and redecorated it according to his fine taste. For publicity, he sent free tickets to the most beautiful actresses in Paris. The opening night at the Théâtre du Châtelet on May 19, 1909, of Les Ballets Russes went off exceptionally well. The dancers performed with completeness,

Vaslav Nijinsky. Photo credit: Private Collection, Prismatic Pictures/Bridgeman Images.

unity, and artistic originality. Fokine's inventiveness charmed and amazed the French. Another artist, Vaslav Nijinsky, stood out—a new "god of the dance." Once on stage, the audience remained keenly and ardently focused on him, with roaring ovations for his impeccable technique, for seemingly defying gravity, and for floating on air like a weightless spirit. As the curtain closed on a stage full of fierce warriors leaping in the *Polovtsian Dances* from Borodin's *Prince Igor*, Parisians did more than applaud. "An ecstatic audience ran down the aisles and tore off the orchestra rail in an attempt to embrace the dancers."[65] That night, Diaghilev and Benois took a night walk, "Our sense of well-deserved success filled us with happiness . . . wandering through the streets and squares of Paris lasted until dawn, drunk as we were on extraordinary amounts of champagne and the emotions we had just experienced."[66]

In Paris, at the Théâtre National de l'Opéra in 1910, Diaghilev premiered *Schéhérazade*, the first true ballet created for Les Ballets Russes—except for the *Polovtsian Dances* from the opera *Prince Igor* that Fokine had choreographed in 1909.[67] *Schéhérazade* with an exotic Oriental theme based upon *The Arabian Nights*, music by Nikolai Rimsky-Korsakov, erotic choreography by Michel Fokine, an orgy in a harem, and Léon Bakst's avant-garde setting and costumes transformed the stage into an Arabian palace and "tapped into the French obsession with a perceived sensual Orient . . . "[68] *Schéhérazade* had a far-reaching effect even on the Parisian fashion. People began to dress differently; turbans and harem pants found their way to the runway. With *Schéhérazade*, the audience saw the ballet's focus turn from the grace and beauty of the ballerina to the strength and sensuality of the male dancer. The brilliant male dancer Vaslav Nijinsky, with stunning power and theatrics, performed the role of the Golden Slave. His dancing and physicality returned the male importance to the ballet stage. Les Ballets Russes caused a shift in classical ballet and the beginnings of modern ballet. If Fokine could be called the *father of modern ballet*, then Diaghilev could be called the man who made it possible.

With the Saison Russe 1911, the ballets *Petrouchka* and *Le Spectre de la Rose* were added to the repertoire, with Nijinsky in the title roles. Parisians effusively embraced both the impresario Serge Diaghilev and the Russian-Polish dancer Vaslav Nijinsky.

Vaslav Nijinsky as the Golden (Favorite) Slave 1910. *Mikhail Fokine*, Mariinsky Theatre Souvenir Booklet, 2008. The Museum of the Mariinsky Theatre, Saint Petersburg.

Poster advertising Les Ballets Russes at the Théâtre de Monte Carlo, April 19, 1911. Artist Jean Cocteau. Color lithograph. This is an image of Nijinsky originally created for Les Ballets Russes de Serge Diaghilev's premiere of *Le Spectre de la Rose* at Monte Carlo, 1911. Photo © Christie's Images / Bridgeman Images and © ARS / Comité Cocteau, Paris / ADAGP, Paris 2022.

Le Spectre de la Rose. Tamara Karsavina as the Girl and Vaslav Nijinsky as the Spectre. *Mikhail Fokine*, Mariinsky Theatre Souvenir Booklet, 2008. The Museum of the Mariinsky Theatre, Saint Petersburg.

Parisians adored Nijinsky's classical style and his virtuosic elevation that reached and maintained pinnacle heights. His sister, Bronislava Nijinska, wrote, "He did not come down completely on the balls of his feet, but barely touched the floor with the tips of his toes . . . His toes were so strong . . . and his rebound so quick, that his push up from the ground was imperceptible, creating the impression that he remained at all times suspended in the air."[69] Nijinsky's "super potent projection," said the actress Elizaveta Timeh, "stirred the audience of both sexes equally."[70] Returning to Russia in 1911 to fulfill his contract obligations with the Imperial Ballet, Nijinsky decided to wear the fashionable Parisian male costume for his leading role in the romantic ballet *Giselle*—a short tunic and tights, but minus the Russian required trunks over his tights. He was asked by a dowager empress to cover up for Act Two. Nijinsky refused.

Nijinsky as Albrecht from *Giselle, (Act II)*, 1910. Costume after Alexandre Benois. Silk velvet with replica silk shirt. Photo credit: Private Collection, Prismatic Pictures/Bridgeman Images.

Nijinsky returned to Paris and Diaghilev's Les Ballet Russes in 1912 with his first choreographic work *L'Après-midi d'un Faune (The Afternoon of a Faun)*. In the final movement, Nijinsky extended himself, lying face-down on a Nymph's scarf, giving it one slow sensual movement. One half of the audience responded with frenzied applause, and the other half with frenzied protests. Some spectators denounced the final movement as bestial and dissolute. In his diary, Nijinsky wrote, "When I composed this ballet, I was not thinking of perversity."[71] With Nijinsky's *Le Sacre du Printemps (The Rite of Spring)* in 1913, the "riot at the Rite" goes down in history as the most scandalous event in the arts. The shocking choreography, a complete reversal of classical ballet technique, and Igor Stravinsky's discordant score caused a visceral reaction in the

L'Après-midi d'un Faune with Andrew Lester as the Faune, Claire Westby (lower left), Allison Doughty Marquesen (middle), Claire Laine (right) as the Nymphs, 2007. Choreography by Phillip Carman for Saint Paul City Ballet. Courtesy of Louis Wendling, photographer.

audience. Spectators began hissing, shouting, laughing, shrieking, and some actually fighting. An artistic riot ensued. Diaghilev's response after the complete debacle of the opening night: "Exactly what I wanted."[72]

Diaghilev's bold invitation to Paris began Russian ballet's diaspora to the West, influencing the ultimate change to ballet style for the first half of the twentieth century. Diaghilev's "passionate devotion to the cause he served and to the ideas he was then promulgating and his complete disinterestedness and lack of personal ambition in all his enterprises won the hearts of his coworkers. Working with him, they realized, meant working solely for the great cause of art."[73] In 1916, Diaghilev and Les Ballets Russes received an invitation to present a season of performances at New York City's Metropolitan Opera. However,

this engagement and the company's 1916–1917 tours in nearly sixty American cities, including Saint Paul and Minneapolis, Minnesota, aroused both disdain and delight.[74] The company's sensually charged repertoire of exotic scenes and erotic movements caused fury from American moralists, and censorships plague the company throughout the tour. It was not until 1933 that the Ballets Russes returned, but with a slightly different name and a different impresario.

Les Ballets Russes toured from 1914 until 1929. World War I stopped the touring only in

Le Tricorne (The Three Cornered-Hat, The Miller's Dance), 1920. Ballet by Martinez Sierra after Alarcon, music by Manuel de Falla, choreography by Léonide Massine. Set of pochoirs (stencils) made after the original sets and costumes designed by Picasso. Art Resource, NY. © 2023 Estate of Pablo Picasso /Artists Rights Society (ARS), New York.

Pablo Picasso (in the cap) and artists sitting on the curtain of the Ballet *Parade*, 1917. Credit: Private Collection/Bridgeman Images. © 2023 Estate of Pablo Picasso/Artists Rights Society (ARS), New York.

1915. A notable artistic shift occurred in 1917 when the Saison Russe unveiled a new work, *Le Parade*. The ballet had flawless modernist details with curtain, decor, and costumes by Pablo Picasso, music by Erik Satie, libretto by Jean Cocteau, and choreography by Léonide Massine ". . . historians have identified this work as the cradle of Les Ballets Russes modernism."[75] The doors of the world opened to the artists during their whirlwind tours of South America, England, France, Belgium, Italy, Monaco, Austria, Germany, Switzerland, and Hungary from 1918 to 1929. Anna Pavlova, prima ballerina of the Mariinsky Theatre and one of the most influential ballet dancers of her time, joined Les Ballets Russes but left the company in 1910 and traveled to America. Pavlova popularized Russian ballet, bringing it from coast to coast in America from 1910 to 1924, attracting young people to ballet.

The last performance of the Diaghilev Ballets Russes took place at Covent Garden in London on July 26, 1929. Following this London season, Diaghilev, who had chronic diabetes, went to Venice for a rest. On August 15, Boris Kochno, his private secretary and artistic adviser to Les Ballets Russes, received a telegraph message from Diaghilev saying, "Am sick. Come at once. Diaghilev."[76] Kochno arrived the next day and went to the Grand Hotel des Bains in Venice, where Diaghilev and Serge Lifar were staying. For the next two days, Diaghilev had some rally moments with smiles, chatting, and visiting with two close friends and advisers, Misia Sert and Coco Chanel.

Then came the fever, shivering, and breathing loud and hard. At dawn, "Diaghilev stopped breathing. The first rays of the sun came through the window and touched his forehead. His head sank toward his shoulder, and a tear rolled down his cheek. It was six o'clock in the morning of August 19, 1929."[77] Diaghilev's death closed the story of the man whose towering creative spirit devoted twenty years of life to ballet, music, and stage design. He is not forgotten. And, "to honour his memory only as the creator and soul of the Ballets Russes is to appreciate him in part only. He was the anthology of the epoch remarkable for the vitality and rapid maturing of its artists, he was the sum and substance of his time."[78]

Igor Stravinsky (left) and Serge Diaghilev meet at Croydon Airport, UK, in 1926.
Photo credit: Tully Potter/Bridgeman Images.

Anna Pavlova with her pet swan, Jack. *The Dying Swan* was Pavlova's signature solo dance.
Legend has it that her last words were asking to have her swan costume prepared.
Photo credit: Private Collection © Look and Learn/Bridgeman Images.

The Nascence of Ballet in Minnesota

Colonel Wassily de Basil.

SCENE 1

Early Ballet Schools in Minnesota

On the brink of the Great Depression, with the deaths of Diaghilev in 1929 and Pavlova in 1931, the Ballets Russes succumbed to division, intrigue, and dissension, leaving an emptiness in the cultural life of Europe and America. Like a phoenix rising from the ashes, new companies formed, drawing from the Diaghilev repertoire, dancers, and formula for presenting innovative works. The first company to form in 1932 was the Ballets Russes de Monte Carlo under the direction of a Russian businessman, Vassili Voskresensky, known historically as Colonel Wassily de Basil. His influence and direction of the Ballets Russes, with various changes and names, continued for twenty years. Other companies formed and flourished from the 1930s through the early years of the 1960s under the direction of either René Blum or Sergei Denham. The new Ballets Russes companies filled the artistic void by renewing the public's interest in nineteenth-century classical ballet while exploring avant-garde integration of dance and music.

Léonide Massine, dancer and choreographer with the Ballets Russes de Monte Carlo, choreographed *Choreartium* in 1933 set to Brahms's Fourth Symphony.[79] The backdrop evoked the coolness of a Grecian setting, and the women's costumes, modeled after classical tunics, made their mark in the early 1930s and became known as symphonic costumes. *Choreartium* aroused international attention and controversy never seen before in music and dance circles. Symphonies were thought of as a musical whole, and nothing should be added to them. In his autobiography, Massine wrote, "I decided to do the choreography of the ballet . . . according to the instrumentation of the score, using women dancers to accentuate the delicate phrases,

Sergei Denham. Courtesy of Rochelle Zide-Booth.

65

The Dying Swan, first performed by Anna Pavlova in 1907 by Michel Fokine, who said that *The Dying Swan* was his answer to criticism that he was generally opposed to pointe shoe dancing. *Mikhail Fokine*, Mariinsky Theatre Souvenir Booklet, 2008. The Museum of the Mariinsky Theatre, Saint Petersburg.

while the men interpreted the heavier, more robust passages."[80] Ernest Newman, a much-celebrated English music critic in the first half of the twentieth century, fervently championed Massine's work. He wrote, "If dancing is to be restricted to music that was specifically written for dancing, I am afraid that at least half of the present ballet repertory must henceforth be banished from our sight . . ."[81]

From 1935 to 1936, de Basil's Ballets Russes toured America, and at one of the stops, a young man happened to watch a *Choreartium* rehearsal. One of the soloists in the first scene of the ballet, a girl in blue, caught and held his attention. Besides inflaming international controversy, *Choreartium* also kindled an interest in a man's heart to begin serious ballet training. Years later, his friend, Stanley S. Hubbard, would say, "How many people do we know who would, as a young person, see someone dance and say, 'That's the person I want to marry.' Then change their whole life around to become a dancer in order to meet the one they love?"[82]

The impresario Sol Hurok had, in Agnes de Mille's words, "imported de Basil's Ballets Russes de Monte Carlo and the craze that was to endure seventeen years and sweep everything else to corners."[83] Hurok's exceptionally fine publicity, along with the cross-country tours totaling twenty-five thousand miles, Russian ballet had suddenly become a rage and the most popular form of entertainment besides radio and cinema.

The various Ballets Russes companies continued to tour extensively and globally until 1962, when it took its swan song—final bow—in the United States. Ballets Russes dancers, comprising many nationalities, had spread across the USA, like windswept wildflower seeds, taking root on fertile ground throughout the nation, prepared in part by Anna Pavlova's travels through several states, "It was a triumphal march," Pavlova exclaimed, "but an exceedingly fatiguing one."[84] Many superb Ballets Russes dancers, choreographers, and teachers remained in America following both Pavlova and the Ballets Russes tours.

In Minnesota, Ballets Russes dancers, Russian-trained dancers, and other ballet advocates proved their mettle and established ballet schools primarily in the metropolitan area of Minneapolis-Saint Paul. Victor Stengel founded his School of Ballet in Minneapolis circa 1948–1960s. His studios occupied spacious rooms in the Kugler Music and Dance Studios at 807 Hennepin Avenue. Eventually, Victor Stengel founded his own ballet studio on Hennepin Avenue, not far from the Kugler space. Before coming to Minnesota, he graduated from the Kiev and Moscow academies. His accolades included being a soloist, choreographer, and ballet master in several Russian and European cities. In January 1950, a Ballets Russes dancer, Lóránt Andaházy, taught ballet at the Kugler studios.[85] The Ballet Concertant of Minneapolis founded by three former Ballets Russes dancers—Sonia Orlova (de Basil Ballets Russes), William Glenn and George Verdak (both of the Ballet Russe de Monte Carlo)—traveled to Grand Marais from Minneapolis in 1956 and performed near the shore of Lake Superior.

Another Russian-trained ballet dancer, George H. Bonnarens (b. 1921 in Iowa), moved to Minnesota from Paris, where he trained in classical ballet under the tutelage of two famed Russian teachers, Olga Preobrajenska and Elvira Rone. A student of the world's leading flamenco artists in Spain, France, Mexico, and New York, Bonnarens also taught flamenco and led the area's first

Ballet Concertant brought eight dancers, costumes, makeup, and dances suitable for chamber music as part of Grand Marais's summer concert series, a program that began in 1947 and directed by Gerard Samuel, the associate conductor of Minneapolis Symphony Orchestra. Courtesy of Katherine Goertz.

performing group, Los Amigos. He became the Ballet Director at the Sivanich School in Hopkins from 1954 until it closed in 1985.

Marianne Gallinger Casoria (b. 1921, Dusseldorf, Germany) came to Minnesota, after having danced as an "International Danseuse." She founded the School of Ballet on 4317 Excelsior Boulevard in St. Louis Park in the late 1940s and directed the Minneapolis Civic Opera Ballet and the Northwest Ballet Troupe. Ms. Casoria died in 2018 and was preceded in death by her veteran husband of fifty-one years. The director of a Minneapolis Ballet Company in the 1970s, Hy Somers, formerly a choreographer and dancer for the Illinois Ballet, briefly resided in the Twin Cities. In May 1971, the Duluth Civic Ballet invited him and his company to perform at the Ordean Junior High Auditorium.[86]

These early windswept seeds that established ballet schools in Minnesota found abounding interest but lacked longevity. In 1945 two Ballets Russes dancers found their way to Minnesota, bringing their virtuosic dancing, elegance, beauty, and grace with them. They began their first ballet school, the Russian Ballet School, above a bicycle shop in downtown Saint Paul at 134 West 6th Street. This building was demolished to make room for I-94 and 35-E. With virtuosic energy, tenacity, and grit, they established their ballet school at various other sites: a second studio in Minneapolis taking up two street addresses, 4758 and 4860 Grand Avenue; one at 7000 Cahill Road in Edina; and one at 3208 Xenwood Avenue in St. Louis Park. A lease was signed for 1680 Grand Avenue in Saint Paul, above a grocery store—soon to turn hardware store—in June 1949. The newly named Andaházy Borealis Ballet School became the first classical ballet academy in Minnesota that established an enduring legacy. The two sites that garnered the most attendance and support were the St. Louis Park studio and the Grand Avenue studio in Saint Paul.

THE DULUTH CIVIC BALLET
GEORGE MONTAGUE, Director
presents

the MINNEAPOLIS BALLET COMPANY

HY SOMERS, Director

with special guest artists
ORRIN KAYAN
premier danseur
National Ballet of Washington
and
GEORGE MONTAGUE
☆

ONE PERFORMANCE ONLY
Sat., May 8 - 8 p.m.
Ordean Junior High Auditorium
Tickets on sale at Glass Block & Goldfines
Prices: $4.00 & $3.00. Students $1.50.

Hy Somers. Advertisement for the Duluth Civic Ballet, 1971. Courtesy of Marius Andaházy.

Coda: Artist Story

Annette Atwood-Piper: Dance Artist, Physical Therapist, Ballet and Anatomy Teacher (Interview 10/17/21)

In the 1940s, neighborhood ballet schools existed, but most of them taught a one-hour class divided into fifteen-minute segments of ballet, tap, jazz, and acrobatics. Annette Atwood-Piper of Minneapolis recalls attending a ballet school on Lyndale Avenue in a building "across from where the Walker Art Center now stands." Annette's recollection as a six-year-old in that class is the teacher forcing her leg into splits on the barre and the "blue and white tiles in the foyer," where she made a screaming and dramatic temper tantrum. Her mother embarrassingly picked her up, and Annette never went back to that ballet school.

Rambunctious, active, and constantly moving, Annette's family learned of Ruth Wagner's Ballet School on Lake Street East across from the art deco Avalon movie theater—only a five-block walk for Annette from her address on 2500 16th Avenue South. For fifty cents an hour, Ruth Wagner taught ballet, tap, jazz, and acrobatics. What endeared Annette to Miss Wagner was the Spanish *caractère* dance included in the ballet class. After a few years at Miss Wagner's school, Annette's mother enrolled her at MacPhail Music Center in Minneapolis, which also offered a potpourri of ballet, tap, jazz, and ballroom. Annette distinctly remembers her tap teacher, Lillian Vail, and her recital number to "Yes, We Have No Bananas."

After MacPhail, Annette heard of a Victor Stengel School of Ballet (ca. 1948) next to the State Theatre on Hennepin Avenue. Drawn to ballet, she wanted to be challenged with a "pure ballet school." She had heard of the Andaházys teaching ballet in Saint Paul, but she would need to take the streetcar. Her father did not want her to go to Saint Paul, "Too dangerous," he told her. Annette enrolled in the Stengel school and continued taking ballet classes throughout her high school years.

Her school, St. Margaret's Academy, was within walking distance of the Stengel studio on Hennepin Avenue. Annette described in fond detail her architecturally stunning high school, the former McNair residence built in the 1920s on Linden Avenue North. Every classroom had a fireplace. The study room was a ballroom, and two buildings were in the backyard. One building housed science and math classrooms; the other was the school's cafeteria and the sisters of St. Joseph of Carondelet's residence. "It was gorgeous," and sighing regretfully, "it was demolished for a freeway ramp."

Annette walked downtown to the State Theatre, entered the main doors on Hennepin

Avenue, walked through the box office area, and then took a right to a stairway that led to spacious dance and music studios where William and Ida Kugler also taught music. Annette remembered Stengel as a handsome, dark-haired, well-built, muscular man. He had a pianist for his ballet and *caractère* classes. Records and taped music were not available or considered not adequate for classical ballet training. He adroitly managed both the artistic and business sides of his ballet school. A master networker, he procured several contracts to perform at entertainment events. Annette remembers performing in the Ice Capades, but not on skates. However, Annette vividly recalls performing on ice, and in skates, for a winter-themed window at Donaldson's department store on Sixth Street and Nicollet Avenue. Stengel's dancers also performed for various conventions at the Minneapolis Auditorium and once across the Mississippi River at a nightclub in Mendota. After a few years, Stengel moved across the street to 824 Hennepin Avenue, where they had more studio space and windows on the avenue.

Annette graduated in 1951 from St. Margaret's Academy and worked at Dayton's department store on Seventh Street and Nicollet Avenue to earn money for college and ballet lessons. She decided to take ballet lessons at The Kugler Music and Dance Studios, which had moved to a space on Sixth Street between Nicollet and Hennepin Avenues, not far from Dayton's on Seventh Street. William and Ida Kugler traveled the world collecting antique musical instruments. They also had

Lyceum Theatre Advertisement for The One and Only Ballet Russe de Monte Carlo, March 1952. Courtesy of Judith Brin Inger.

connections with the Royal Ballet in London. They hired Alex Martin from England's Royal Ballet to teach ballet classes at their studios. Annette took classes every day for two years from Martin and became trained in the Royal Academy of Dance syllabus (RAD). During her tenure with the Kugler studios, the Royal Ballet came through Minneapolis, and at the Kugler studios, she met Margot Fonteyn. "It thrilled me to meet Margot Fonteyn," and "I greeted her, and we shook hands."

In 1952, Annette's aunt, Florence Roers, invited her to a performance of The One and Only Ballet Russe de Monte Carlo at the Lyceum Building in Minneapolis. The program rendered her completely captivated by ballet,

The Lyceum Theatre Building, originally built as the Minneapolis Auditorium Building, opened in 1905. From road shows to live theatre to movies, the Lyceum presented various programs until the late 1950s, when it closed due to a dramatic increase in rent. The building was razed in the early 1970s and a new building, Orchestra Hall, opened in 1974. Courtesy of the Minnesota Historical Society.

especially the production of *Schéhérazade*. Marius Andaházy recalls his father, Lóránt Andaházy, as a guest artist, danced the role of the Golden Slave in this performance. Going to the ballet *Schéhérazade* forever changed the trajectory of her life. At the University of Minnesota, Annette studied pre-physical therapy and theater education. She blended her theater interests with ballet in many of the university's Showboat performances. Annette decided to finish her physical therapy degree and went to San Francisco, where she received her degree at the University of California Medical Center while continuing ballet lessons and becoming RAD accredited to teach ballet.

Minnesota drew her back home as a physical therapist and a ballet teacher. Under Nadine Jette at the University of Minnesota, she took ballet classes two or three mornings each week. She admired Nadine's relentless pursuit to permanently establish dance as its own department at the university—not as part of the theater department. Annette became well-known for her ballet classes she taught from an anatomy perspective. As a registered physical therapist and a lifetime member of the Royal Academy of Dance, Annette continues to be a font of wisdom for physical therapists who need advice when working with dancers.

Gabriela Komleva as Nikiya in *La Bayadère*. People's Artist of the USSR (1983).
And They Danced On. Jack and Waltraud G. Karkar. Photography by Kirk Fleischauer.

Hungarian Roots

The story of two Ballets Russes dancers, one with American roots and the other of Hungarian ancestry, begins not in Minnesota but overseas with the two world wars of the twentieth century. How could these two wars contribute to the nascence of ballet in Minnesota? The answer begins with a Russian ballerina telling her story in what became an iconic ballet studio, above a hardware store, on Grand Avenue in Saint Paul.

On a hot summer day in July 2002, ballet dancers entered an 1890s red brick building located near Macalester College on Grand Avenue in Saint Paul. Originally built as Herman Marten's Grocery store, this building eventually became an Ace Hardware store in the 1950s. The second floor of the building became a ballet studio in 1949, an iconic landmark where neighbors would say, "You can find everything you need there, from tools to tulles." With an excited flurry, a bevy of young dancers hurried up a broad staircase with its chipped white walls and painted blue steps to the ballet studios above the hardware store. A once-in-a-lifetime personal visit with Gabriela Komleva, ballet mistress of the Mariinsky Theatre in Saint Petersburg, Russia, awaited them.

At the apex of her ballet career, Gabriela was known throughout Russia. She reigned supreme with her interpretation of the lead role in *La Bayadère* (The Temple Dancer). This ballet story of a doomed love between the young warrior, Solor, and the beautiful temple dancer, Nikiya, premiered in 1877 at the Mariinsky Theatre, Saint Petersburg. From its first performance, the ballet was universally hailed by contemporary critics as one of Marius Petipa's choreographic masterpieces, particularly the scene from the ballet known as *The Kingdom of the Shades*—one of the most celebrated pieces in all classical ballet. By the *fin de siècle*, *The Kingdom of the Shades* scene was regularly extracted from the full-length work as an independent showpiece, and it has remained so to the present day.

Dancers entered the large studio, a historical rehearsal hall with vintage black and white photos encased in dust-covered antique frames hanging on lath and plaster walls, wooden floorboards aged by thousands of ballet steps, and white ballet barres, the paint worn off by years of hand-holding. A perfect ambiance for Gabriela to share her story. She was slight of frame with graying hair pulled softly back with a barrette (no ballerina bun anymore) and gentle gazing eyes. Gabriela spoke broken English, but her friend Elizabeth Kendall, a New York City dance critic and nonfiction writer, would translate. Dancers scattered themselves in front of these honorable speakers, some sitting on the floor while others sat on benches or chairs. The director of the ballet school introduced Gabriela and said that all questions would be translated by Ms. Kendall. A young dancer raised her hand and asked the first question: "Ms. Gabriela, why did you start ballet?"

With eyes gazing not at the dancers but at the distant past, Gabriela gave a startling answer. "You do not want to know war." Without hesitation, she continued with personal details of living as a young girl during the 1941 grueling siege of Leningrad (Saint Petersburg since 1991) during World War II. All healthy people, like her father, enlisted to help fight the invading German forces, and he died in battle. The Nazis almost completely encircled Leningrad by early September 1941 as a brutally cold winter fell upon the besieged city. Supplies of food, water, and heat dwindled while starvation and death enclosed upon the city. Gabriela recalled eating sawdust bread because of the extreme food scarcity. Almost completely encircled, Leningrad's one supply and evacuation lifeline remained—Lake Ladoga. The Russians had previous experience building ice roads, and in November 1941, the construction began for an ice road across Lake Ladoga.

During that bitterly cold winter of 1941–42, the coldest winter in one hundred and forty years, Gabriela, with her mother, grandmother, aunt, and cousin, escaped their besieged Leningrad by crossing Lake Ladoga. They were the last convoy of people to cross the ice road that winter. The dangerous evacuation, amplified by the German bombardment of this "River of Life" and the vicissitudes of freezing weather, blustery winds, and snow-covered ice, amplified her family's fear of making it to the other side. Only three years old at the time, Gabriela retained vivid memories of that frightening journey across the ice. They journeyed by truck, and she remembered seeing the truck in front of them break through the ice and sink. Her truck went around the gaping hole in the ice and made it across the frozen lake.

Welcoming strangers greeted them with warm soup from a big pot, needed sustenance for their starving bodies and emotional relief from their fear. They waited for the train that would take them eastward to safety in Perm, a town deep in the Ural Mountains, where many writers, actors, and artists were also relocated. Once onboard the crowded train of strangers, Gabriela and her family sat together with fellow travelers. When one of the strangers learned that they had survived the siege, a woman put a loaf of bread in Gabriela's hands. When Gabriela held the bread, she began to cry because some crumbs had fallen off—crumbs, precious food not to be wasted.

After an arduous month of train travel, Gabriela and her family arrived at their temporary home, but temporary meant five years. As a young child, Gabriela remembers dancing and playing with her cousin to pass the time. There was a ballet school there, and she took some lessons. The nine-hundred-day siege of Leningrad ended in January 1944.

The citizens began to rebuild and reclaim their city and their lives. Gabriela and her family were homeward bound by train, arriving in Leningrad in 1947. They, too, began to reclaim their lives. For Gabriela, she would continue dancing, but this time, serious ballet training. Accepted at the esteemed Vaganova Academy of Russian Ballet, Gabriela reclaimed her life in Leningrad with ballet.[87] From Saint Petersburg along the Neva River to Saint Paul along the Mississippi River, a Russian ballerina's intriguing stories were translated by her friend as questions flowed from aspiring young ballet dancers. She took them on a balletic journey, starting with her life-threatening truck ride over an ice road to ultimately reaching stardom and being honored with the highest title of *prima ballerina assoluta*.

Take a step back in time to 1952, on another hot summer day at 1680 Grand Avenue. Mr. Andaházy paused while teaching ballet in his Saint Paul studio. Was it the musical score that the pianist just played, a student's comment, or noticing his wife walk in that triggered a memory? Similar to Gabriela Komleva's answer, "You do not want to know war," Mr. Andaházy's pause flashbacked to his own story of war and displacement. He shuddered and then lectured the dancers saying, "How lucky we were to be working hard to create beauty."[88]

Lóránt Andaházy was born in April 1914 in the Hungarian High Tatra range of the Carpathian Mountains, a natural border between a dual monarchy of the two states of Austria and Hungary. At Lóránt's birth,

Franz Josef, of the nearly six-hundred-and-fifty-year-old Habsburg dynasty, ruled as the emperor of Austria and king of Hungary. The Austro-Hungarian Empire extended from Switzerland to Russia with eleven nationalities and multiple religions. Lóránt entered a world filled with political tensions and increased nationalistic pressures. The June 1914 assassination of Archduke Franz Ferdinand—nephew of Franz Josef and heir to the Austro-Hungarian Empire—in the Bosnian capital of Sarajevo was both catalyst and a cause that ignited World War I in August 1914.

As a global war raged, Lóránt, with his brother and sister, lived an idyllic life on their Andaházy estate, shielded from the horrors of war. As a young boy, Lóránt received equestrian training from the Cossacks. His

Lóránt Andaházy's birthplace estate in the Hungarian High Tatra range of the Carpathian Mountains. Courtesy of Marius Andaházy.

father was a great horseman, and their horse, it is told, could come into the dining room and eat from their hands. His godmother, Princess Sefried, youngest niece of Emperor Franz Josef, would often visit the Andaházy estate for vacation, reveling in the natural bliss of the High Tatra Mountains. The Old World's ambiance of fiery Hungarian dances at the harvest, passionate music from roving gypsies, and pastoral scenes of shepherds and their sheep on mountaintop meadows, made an indelible mark on Lóránt's character.[89]

World War I, the Great War, ended on November 11, 1918, and with its ending, so too did the Austro-Hungarian empire and the Habsburg monarchy. Treaties signed with both Austria (1919) and Hungary (1920) made them successor states, and each saddled with "the sins of the parent Dual Monarchy."[90] Hungary's borders were redefined, and the ensuing disintegration of the Hungarian estates in 1920 forced the Andaházy family to leave forever their noble estate in the High Tatra range of the Carpathian Mountains.

Lóránt, only eight years old, along with his mother, grandmother, and older brother and sister, emigrated penniless to the United States in 1922 on the SS *Finland* to Ellis Island. They journeyed to Cleveland, Ohio, where other Hungarians had settled. Lóránt's father stayed behind with hopes of regaining his estate. Underlying this noblesse oblige, the strong bonds of a love affair kept him tethered to Hungary. With the imperial dynasty dissolved and the growing nationalist movements among its diverse population, noble lineage no longer held

esteem or power in Hungary. Despite efforts to have his estate returned to the family, an association with the former imperial nobility was not recognized. Lóránt's father passed away in Budapest, never reuniting with his family in America.

From wealth and noble heritage, the Andaházy family met poverty in Cleveland, Ohio. Lóránt and his brother were sheltered in a boys' orphanage and his sister in a girls' orphanage. Their mother worked cleaning homes and could only see her sons and daughter on Sundays for a visit. The Andaházys adopted the United States as their new home and became American citizens, fully embracing the New World institutions that grounded them in democracy, freedom, and opportunities. Lóránt's Hungarian birth name became Americanized to Lorand when they passed through Ellis Island. In 1985, during a visit back to Hungary, he obtained a copy of his birth certificate and discovered that his name was spelled Lóránt. He then asked his son, Marius, to change all references to his name with the correct Hungarian spelling with accent marks.

Lóránt graduated from high school with athletic success. He became an award-winning gymnast, competed in track-and-field events, and eclipsed others in equestrian skills. For three consecutive years, from 1934 to 1936, he won the Ohio State gymnastics championship.[91] At one track-and-field practice, he quickly climbed up rope ladders knotted together and strung between two high poles, with a platform on top of each pole. He reached one platform and made a one-arm handstand on it, and then like trick riding, he switched the handstand to his other arm and balanced.[92] During summer vacations, Lóránt spent time at horse shows and exhibitions, heralding back to his Hungarian roots. He excelled in trick riding, dressage, and horse jumping. He could raise himself to a handstand on the saddle while the horse trotted in circles. Lóránt would then amazingly stand on one arm then the other.[93] At the Great Lakes Exposition in 1936, he achieved a rating as "one of the finest horsemen in the country."[94]

Lóránt's athletic interests also led him to formal ballet training in 1933 with Serge Nadejdin, a graduate of Saint Petersburg Imperial Ballet School, a former director of the Theatre Imperial Alexandre, and a contemporary of Anna Pavlova. Nadejdin was a close friend of Michel Fokine when they both attended the Imperial Ballet School, and he was one of two friends who attended Fokine's wedding. For twenty-five years, he directed the Serge Nadejdin Imperial Ballet School in the Hippodrome Building in Cleveland.

In the autumn of 1935, Léonide Massine's American premiere of *Choreartium* was on the playbill at the Metropolitan Opera House in New York.[95] This ballet employed a large cast that included Anna Adrianova.[96] Lóránt decided to watch a rehearsal for the ballet *Choreartium* and saw a beautiful dancer perform the "Girl in Blue" role. He passionately became enamored with "that iridescent, almost mythical ballerina."[97] The performance of Massine's *Choreartium* drew him in, completely captivated by the stunning

Lóránt Andaházy. "Andaházy Ballet Borealis Souvenir Pamphlet." Created for the December 6, 1961, performance at the University of Minnesota Northrop Memorial Auditorium. Photography by Constantine of Hollywood. Courtesy of Marius Andaházy.

beauty of dazzling costumes, gorgeous sets, and Massine's choreography set to Brahms's Fourth Symphony.

More determined than ever, Lóránt continued ballet in order to pursue the ballerina. Under Nadejdin's tutelage, and with Nadejdin's Russian connections, plus his virtuosic athleticism, Lóránt was accepted into the de Basil's Ballets Russes company in 1936. He received documents detailing where he needed to meet the company, what to bring with him, and what his dancing stipend would be. Documents were signed, sealed,

Anna Adrianova (far left) in the Ballets Russes production of Massine's *Choreartium*. A young Shirley Bridge (Anna Adrianova) when she first danced with the Ballets Russes. Dance Collection of the New York Public Library, Astor, Lenox and Tilden Foundations. Photography by Maurice Seymour.

and Lóránt headed confidently to meet "that girl he was going to marry." Lóránt's decision to attend a de Basil's Ballets Russes performance changed the course of his life—unyielding like a river cascading down from the high mountain peaks of the Tatra Mountains. Classical ballet takes root in Minnesota because of an intriguing love story and a marriage between Lóránt Andaházy and the beautiful "Girl in Blue."

Anna Adrianova in Massine's *Choreartium*. "Andaházy Ballet Borealis Souvenir Pamphlet, 1961-62." Photography by Constantine of Hollywood. Courtesy of Marius Andaházy.

SCENE 3
Anna Adrianova (stage name) née Shirley Bridge

Shirley Bridge was born in December 1917 in New York City, and her first artistic influences began as a young child at a vast New York City atelier of her maternal grandfather, Douglas Volk. A teaching artist and working artist in the late 1800s and early 1900s, Volk was renowned for his figure and portrait paintings, especially those of Abraham Lincoln. She spent hours imitating the poses she observed in his paintings. Shirley lost herself with total enjoyment in Volk's atelier—the smells of oil paint, watching Volk's fingers hold a palette of colors, touching the soft ends of his paint brushes, and hearing Volk's musings about the people he painted stirred within her an affinity for art—an affinity force that forever connected Shirley's artistry to the time spent with Volk. Years later, Shirley would stake her roots in Saint Paul and Minneapolis, Minnesota, where decades earlier, in 1886, Volk and his artist wife, Marion Larrabee, helped to found the Minneapolis School of Fine Arts.

From New York City, Shirley's doctor father and homemaker mother moved the family to Rochester, New York, where they settled and established deep tap roots. Shirley's artistic influences from Volk opened the door to enthusiastically embrace another art discipline and another artist: ballet and Enid Knapp Botsford, who trained under Luigi Albertieri, an artistic descendant of Enrico Cecchetti. As a young ballerina in the early 1920s, Botsford danced in New York City and was selected by Anna Pavlova to train at her London studios. She may have remained there, but an appendicitis attack in 1922 brought her home to Rochester, where she remained and, for decades, ruled as the queen of dance in Rochester.

Shirley trained fervently with Botsford, learning the Cecchetti Method and developing a technically strong foundation in classical ballet. In 1933, as a sophomore in high school and shy of sixteen years old, Shirley convinced her parents to let her take the train by herself to New York City and attend the American debut performance of Col. Wassily de Basil's Ballets Russes de Monte Carlo at the St. James Theater. An impresario, Sol Hurok, brought the company to the United States with astounding success. Léonide Massine's presence, as chief choreographer with fifty-five of the Diaghilev ballet's costumes and decor, "now offered a different viewpoint on the matter of heritage

. . . His new ballets, notably three works set to established symphonies by Tchaikovsky, Brahms, and Berlioz, offered the opportunity for an amalgamation of sundry dance styles."[98]

What would become a life-changing birthday present, Shirley traveled to New York City. When the performance was over, she audaciously went backstage, found the

Les Sylphides. Premiere at the Northrop Memorial Auditorium, August 1952. "Andaházy Ballet Borealis Souvenir Pamphlet, 1952." Courtesy of Marius Andaházy.

director, and said that she would like to audition for the company. They told her to come back the next day, and she planned on it, never informing her parents that she was going to audition for the Ballets Russes company.

Léonide Massine directed the audition the next day with Col. Wassily de Basil, impresario Sol Hurok, and Fokine also attending. Massine asked her to perform any piece of choreography that she knew. Shirley knew one variation from *The Sleeping Beauty* that her ballet teacher had taught her. She asked if there would be music for her dancing, and the flat answer was no pianist, no music. Nevertheless, Shirley danced. After she finished, Massine said, "Fine. Can you show us a second piece?" Shirley replied that she created her own choreography to *Persian Market*, a piece of classical music by Albert Ketèlbey in 1920, for orchestra with an optional chorus. She performed her work, and immediately upon completion, Shirley heard, "Very nice. How soon can you leave with the company?"

Her fluid grace and creative energy gained de Basil's approval and Massine's interest with her excellent technique. Shirley's success even surprised her. She was the first American girl to be accepted by the company, and they asked her, "Are you still in high school?" She answered, "Yes, but I can get out of it." She left the St. James Theater effusively happy, screaming so loudly that she lost her voice.

Back at home, Shirley began the battle with her parents to allow her to join the company. They acquiesced but said she needed to finish her geometry and home economics classes in the next six weeks during her sophomore year in school. With an intrepid spirit, Anna replied that she knew geometry had value in life, but "why did she need to know how to bake biscuits!" Her son, Marius, later would say that his mother made great biscuits.[99] The telegram arrived confirming her selection into the de Basil's Ballets Russes company; her parents signed the documents, launching Shirley's ballet career. With Shirley's debut dancing the role of prima ballerina in *Les Sylphides* at London's Convent Garden, "choreographer Michel Fokine labeled her as the 'perfect Sylphide.' Later this same ballet was to become a 'hallmark' of her own Andaházy Ballet."[100]

As a young company member, Shirley was asked to change her name to something that sounded more European. At first, Shirley chose Dominie Bogardis, an old Dutch ancestor's name. Extensive touring in the United States by the de Basil's Ballets Russes company had brought esteemed attention to Russian-influenced ballet, and de Basil thought it would be advantageous to have a more Russian-sounding stage name for Shirley. So, in 1934, she became Anna Adrianova. In some Ballets Russes books, Dominie Bogardis appears as a separate dancer, but Shirley-Anna-Dominie is one and the same. Anna's parents hesitatingly supported her decision to join the Ballets Russes company, although they never agreed to her name change. Shirley's deeply held affinity for ballet never left her, and neither did her Russian name. In Minnesota, most dancers did not

even know her birth name; she remained forever Anna Adrianova or Mrs. A.

The impresario Sol Hurok managed and financially supported de Basil's Ballets Russes American tours. These taxing one-night tours to many American cities established ballet as an institution and became one of Hurok's most extraordinary achievements. "The company and orchestra traveled in eleven Pullman cars, with a special train for scenery and costumes . . . The company performed in all sorts of places, from school auditoriums to professionally equipped theaters." In October 1935, the company's season at the Metropolitan Opera House in New York ended and was followed by an incredible cross-country tour of twenty-five thousand miles continuing into 1936. Anna valiantly endured the physical strain of performance, averaging three hundred performances a year.[101]

Massine recognized Anna's exceptional qualities of movement and was equally impressed by her ability to "invent steps spontaneously to music, responding to the style, mood and rhythm of the piece . . . "[102] Knowing that Massine liked her creative spirit and how she could "spontaneously invent steps," Anna approached Massine one time when their train was snowbound in Oregon. She had an idea about a possible new ballet to César Franck's Symphony in D Minor. They had a long and interesting discussion about this idea, and he expressed interest in collaborating with her. Even though the Symphony in D Minor ballet never actualized, Massine's affirmation of her choreographic ideas and skills gave her confidence to one day be a choreographer. In Minnesota, her choreographic acumen would come to fruition.

Anna knew that further study and training would develop her artistry to an even more prominent level. In 1938 she requested and was granted a one-year leave of absence from de Basil's Ballets Russes to study in Paris under Mathilde Kschessinska, who had reigned supreme for twenty-five years in Russia. A contemporary of Petipa, Cecchetti, Nijinsky, Pavlova, Fokine, and numerous other illustrious artists, Kschessinska was renowned as the first Russian ballerina to perform thirty-two *fouéttes en tournant* in the third act of *Swan Lake*. The arrangements for Anna's leave of absence were made by Arnold Haskell, *London Times* critic and publisher of

Kschessinska's memoirs, assisted by Victor Dandré, the husband of Anna Pavlova. In 1921, Kschessinska married the Grand Duke André of the Romanov family, cousin of Nicholas II. She became Princesse Romanovsky-Krasinsky, and her admiring students called her *Chère Princesse* or *Petite Princesse*.

Anna spent one year under the guiding influence of *Chère Princesse* ". . . impressed by her ever-creative spirit, by the dramatic or lyrical feeling with which she imbued even the most technical of exercises."[103] Twenty-two years later, in the summer of 1961, Anna visited Kschessinska for one month in Paris. The night before Anna returned to America, Kschessinska told her, "I find you one of the most qualified of my pupils to teach like me and to perpetuate

A 1935 photograph of Mathilde Kschessinska in Paris, given to Shirley Bridge (Anna Adrianova Andaházy) in 1961. "Andaházy Ballet Borealis Souvenir Pamphlet, 1961–62." Photographer unknown. Courtesy of Marius Andaházy.

my tradition . . . *Très, très bien—j'approuve.*" Kschessinska nurtured Anna's passionate dedication to ballet and improved her personal artistry and technique. Anna carried the spirit of Kschessinska and dancing with de Basil's Ballets Russes to teaching at her own school—an artistic lineage passed along in Minnesota.

Anna's bedrock enthusiasm and dedication to ballet never lessened. For five years, Anna toured internationally to Monaco, Spain, France, England, Germany, Italy, Mexico, Cuba, the United States, Canada, and Australia with the de Basil's Ballets Russes. She garnered acclaim for the verity and plasticity of her movements. Her salient qualities of poise, fluid grace and musicality, clarity of technical strength, and an alluring personality distinguished her from the other dancers in de Basil's Ballets Russes.

Anna Adrianova in Nijinska's *Les Cents Baisers* with the de Basil's Ballets Russes.
Courtesy of Marius Andaházy.

SCENE 4
Les Ballets Russes (1934–1945)

Anna Adrianova, "this elusive and inspiring dancer artist,"[104] and Lóránt toured and danced together from 1936 until 1938 before Anna's Parisian sabbatical. When Anna returned to de Basil's Ballets Russes in 1939, technically and artistically stronger, she danced leading roles in *Les Sylphides*, *Choreartium*, *Aurora's Wedding*, *Symphonie Fantastique*, *Protée*, and *Les Cents Baisers*.

World War II began sweeping across Europe with devasting fury, and de Basil's Ballets Russes looked to other continents to bring the company. He also changed the company's name to Col. W. de Basil's Original Ballet Russe de Monte Carlo. In 1939, Anna and Lóránt continued dancing with the company until the end of the year when de Basil's Original Ballet Russe de Monte Carlo planned to leave for Melbourne, Australia. Anna needed to take another leave of absence because she was approaching a nervous breakdown. Anna rested in America; Lóránt danced in Australia. Their courtship over miles of touring with de Basil's Ballets Russes to Australia, New Zealand, the United States, Canada, England, France, Mexico, and Cuba sealed their unique relationship that would endure for almost fifty years.

Lóránt's career with de Basil's Original

Lóránt Andaházy's leap in *Schéhérazade*. "Andaházy Souvenir Pamphlet, 2000." Photography by Constantine of Hollywood. Courtesy of Marius Andaházy.

Ballet Russe de Monte Carlo apexed with his portrayal of the Golden (Favorite) Slave in the Fokine/Rimsky-Korsakov ballet *Schéhérazade*. When he starred as the Golden (Favorite) Slave, he wore Nijinsky's costume.[105] Critics from New York City to Melbourne, Australia compared him to Nijinsky's 1910 stellar performance of this role. Pitt Sanborn of the *New*

York World-Telegram wrote, "Andaházy a marvel as Favorite Slave . . . never, it seems safe to say, had *Schéhérazade* enjoyed here so enthralling a presentation . . . and that is said without forgetting the superlative performance, years ago, of Nijinsky as Favorite Slave," and an Australian critic singled him out saying, " . . . there seemed to me to be only one figure of outstanding, nay colossal, conspicuousness: Andaházy . . . not only his virtuosity as acrobatic dancer, but also his ability for varying his expression, of his face, of his body, of his movement . . ."[106] Lóránt also garnered acclaim for his interpretation of principal roles in *Polovtsian Dances* from *Prince Igor*.

Almost a year later, in October 1940, the de Basil's Original Ballet Russe de Monte Carlo found itself back on the western shores of America with four performances in Los Angeles. Lóránt and the "iridescent, almost mystical ballerina," Anna, began touring again in the United States. During a break after five performances in New York, Anna and Lóránt headed to Anna's childhood home in Rochester, New York. Delighted to see her but surprised to meet Lóránt, Anna's parents did not approve of him. He had three faults: he was a Hungarian foreigner, a dancer, and a Roman Catholic. Contrary to her parent's wishes, they eloped to New York City and were married on February 1, 1941 in the "Little Church Around the Corner," near Fifth Avenue. Established in 1848, this church has long been a favored church for artists, actors, and vaudeville performers. Anna and Lóránt continued touring as a couple, and her parents only learned of their marriage in a newspaper article about Col. W. de Basil's Original Ballet Russe de Monte Carlo.

International tensions were rising and strained. The treaties that ended World War I left countries divided and bitter, doomed to establish a lasting peace. Political and economic uncertainties also provoked a rise in right-wing Nationalist parties, the most heinous of them being the Nazis in Germany. At the height of Lóránt's career in de Basil's Original Ballet Russe, his dancing stopped with the bombing of Pearl Harbor on December 7, 1941, and the United States declaring war. The glory days of Lóránt and Anna dancing together in de Basil's Original Ballet Russe de Monte Carlo ended.

With the first draft, he joined the United States Army in 1942. Anna returned home to Rochester, New York, to bear their first child. Lóránt's assignment duty sent him to World War II's European theater. It was ironic that Lóránt, a stellar dancer in theaters around the world, found himself fighting in a wartorn "European theater." World War I forced Lóránt's family to leave Hungary, and World War II called him back to Europe. Lóránt's athleticism, physical agility, and strength, which served him so well in the Ballets Russes theaters, also served him well in World War II's European theater. Lóránt believed that his athletic and ballet training saved his life many times during the war.

In Normandy, he led his men down a narrow road lined with tall hedgerows. German soldiers ambushed them and opened heavy machine gunfire. Lóránt's ability to leap over the hedgerow saved his life; many others did not survive. Commanding the Armored Reconnaissance Unit in the 33rd Infantry Regiment, he oversaw the combat of this armored unit in Northern France, Normandy, Rhineland, Ardennes, and Central Europe. His company was the first to set foot on German soil. As a stalwart leader, under his command, his unit liberated prisoners from the Nordhausen-Dora concentration camp. He later stated, "I took the first German town away from Hitler, although deeply saddened to witness such inhumanity."[107]

With World War II raging, Anna learned that Tatiana Semenova, a de Basil dancer whom she had met and who also had studied under Kschessinska, formed a group called the Foxhole Ballet in coordination with the United Service Organizations (USO). It was the first classical dance unit organized to entertain the troops overseas. Anna made the bold decision to join the Foxhole Ballet in 1944 and went to Europe in hopes of finding Lóránt.

For two years, Anna danced with the Foxhole Ballet in both the Mediterranean and European theaters. Foxhole Ballet dancers, many accustomed to cross-country train travel, rode dangerously in the gun turrets of B-24 and B-25 bombers. Their performances, called Camp Shows, raised curtains in North Africa, Sicily, Italy, and "fortress Europe" with many front-line battle areas for their

Lóránt Andaházy (second from right) and soldiers in front of their vehicle revealing the insignia Lóránt created "Regina Pacis" (Queen of Peace). This was the only vehicle that made it through the entire war. Courtesy of Marius Andaházy.

stages. They may not have been the biggest names in show business, but they were headliners for the war-weary soldiers.

When these dancers decided to join the Foxhole Ballet and bring entertainment and a bit of home to the soldiers, they understood that they were taking a risk. While performing in Rome on a bomb-damaged stage, a weak board broke and Tatiana Semenova, the Foxhole Ballet founder, fell through it with serious damage to her left knee and a compound fracture in her right arm. Her Ballets Russes career ended in war-ravaged Rome, and twenty-eight performers from the many various Camp Shows perished during their service. As artists and entertainers, they knew that the show must go on.[108]

At each Camp Show, the Foxhole Ballet danced with poise, technical strength, and beauty. Soldiers sat in front of the makeshift stages, basking in a welcome break from a fatiguing war with its dangers, horrors, and death. At each Foxhole Ballet performance, Anna danced with enthusiasm, hoping to hide the desperate look in her eyes as she searched each soldier's face for a glimpse of her husband. Anna met Lóránt's general, and he told her that Lóránt was on the front lines. Before victory was declared in Europe in 1945, when the Foxhole Ballet was performing in Germany, at last Anna found Lóránt. His general, impressed by Anna's courage to defy wartime dangers and continue her search for her husband, arranged for them to have a second honeymoon at a repurposed castle turned into battle headquarters. Reunited once again, but in a ravaged European theater

Anna Adrianova's gift from Lóránt, a compact engraved with the names of all the cities where the Foxhole Ballet performed. Courtesy of Marius Andaházy.

that disrupted and ended their Ballets Russes careers.

Lóránt entered as a private and came out as a captain. A wounded soldier and highly decorated, he received the Silver Star, Bronze Star, Purple Heart, and the European Theater of Operations ribbon with five battle stars. Lóránt's army chaplain and friend, Rev. John Buchanan, invited Lóránt and Anna to settle in Saint Paul, Minnesota. World War II became their swan song to dancing with de Basil's Original Ballet Russe de Monte Carlo. A bold "Yes" to Rev. Buchanan's invitation included their personal "Yes" to building a ballet program in this Midwestern state.

In 1945 these two windswept Ballets Russes dancers made Saint Paul their home, bringing with them the spirit of Col. W. de Basil's Original Ballet Russe de Monte Carlo and its ballet lineage and tradition. Alexandra

(Sandy) Klas recalled how her Aunt Frances Boardman, longtime reporter and music critic for the Saint Paul newspapers, ". . . helped many immigrants who were fleeing Europe and settling in Saint Paul during and after World War II. All were talented artists. Among them were the Andaházys, whom she helped start their ballet school."[109]

A United States Army officer arranged for them to meet. Seated together on the tank, lower left. (Location in Europe, date, and photographer are unknown.) Courtesy of Marius Andaházy.

Variation:
Andaházy School of Classical Ballet
(renamed from the original, Andaházy Borealis Ballet School, ca. 1965)

A poleward blue September morning sky, with a lingering warmth of summer days, greeted ballet dancers in 1995, heading to 1680 Grand Avenue to begin the new ballet season. A few people gathered at the locked door, murmuring in hushed, concerned voices, reading and re-reading a small sign posted on the inside of the glass-paneled door: "The Andaházy School of Classical Ballet is formally closed." Shocked. Disbelief. No previous notice. A ballet school tethered to an almost fifty-year history—gone.

Arriving in Saint Paul in late 1945, Lóránt and Anna Adrianova Andaházy, accomplished Ballets Russes dancers, brought with them an extraordinary experience of dancing and working with some of the best artists of the twentieth century, such as Massine, Fokine, Danilova, and Dolin. They found a home on the second floor of 1680 Grand Avenue in Saint Paul with their two young sons, Lorand (1942) and Zoltán (1947). Lóránt's fellow war buddy, Donald (Don) Smolik, owned the building and wanted to help support their efforts at bringing ballet to the Twin Cities. In June 1949, when the grocer, Herman Marten, occupying the main floor, decided to leave 1680 Grand Avenue, the Andaházy family settled in a home in Saint Paul on Macalester Avenue and signed a lease for the second-floor space, and the newly named Andaházy Borealis Ballet School. On the main floor of the building, Don and Marjorie Smolik started one of the first Ace Hardware stores.

From 1947 to 1954, Mr. Andaházy (Mr. A) taught at Breck High School and became a senior counselor of horseback riding and gymnastics for two of Breck's summer camps in Steamboat Springs, Colorado. "Many students from Breck benefited from Mr. A's teaching," stated Breck alumnus Stanley S. Hubbard.[110] In addition to teaching at Breck, Mr. A also taught ballet with Mrs. A at their school. In October 1948 and January 1949, both Lóránt and Anna Andaházy had the opportunity to join the national touring production of the *Carousel* musical in Detroit, Michigan, and New York City. Their two young sons traveled with them, and a friend and dancer, Bill Hayes, ran the ballet school in their absence.[111]

The Andaházy ballet school and satellites had a formidable presence in the Twin Cities from 1947 to 1995. Directed by both Lóránt and Anna Andaházy, the instruction specialized in the Imperial Russian classical style, with its strong influence from the principles developed by Enrico Cecchetti's work in Russia and through Cecchetti's own involvement with the Diaghilev's Ballets Russes. They sought to develop a unity of style to achieve the highest technical and artistic standards. They taught with affirming words of encouragement and gave necessary corrections in a respectful and kind manner. All student levels received quality instruction and attention. One student, Gary Good, was impressed by Mr. A's jumping. He said, "When he did a *révoltade*, his foot was three inches off the floor. He turned and moved gracefully. He landed without a sound. It was amazing to watch."[112]

At Central High School in 1949, an Andaházy student encouraged her friend, Pat Garland, to come with her to the Andaházy ballet school. Pat had danced in Chicago as a young person before her family moved to Saint Paul, but she wondered if they would accept her—a black dancer. "You see, in Chicago at that time, if an African American student showed up at an elite downtown school expecting to enroll for classes, that student would be told very quickly, 'Yes, you can take classes here, but you will have to take individual classes.' So, in April 1951, my mother brought me to the Andaházy's studio. That was the beginning of my eleven years with them." Pat Garland remembered "the way they taught the beauty of extending movement, holding balances, and achieving things that you didn't think possible . . ."[113]

The Andaházys attracted students of all ages, sizes, skin color, and religious affiliations. What mattered most to them was the ability to dance and the desire to train in classical ballet. Eventually, the 1680 Grand Avenue space became their only studio. One student said, "The school was a magical place—a place where we students scarcely noticed aching limbs, bleeding toes, or broken hearts because we were enthralled with the excitement of pursuing and witnessing

ideals of beauty all instilled and exemplified by our beloved teachers."[114]

The Andaházys augmented their core curriculum by inviting nationally and internationally renowned ballet dancers and teachers to come and share their stories and their teaching. Their school garnered recognition as an excellent classical ballet school and grew in size. Even though the school was officially closed in 1995, Marius held the last International Summer Intensive Course in June and July 1996.

Patricia Garland as the Maiden of the Fields in *Slavonic Scenes*, 1961. "Andaházy Ballet Borealis Souvenir Pamphlet, 1961-62." Photography by Constantine of Hollywood. Courtesy of B. Patricia Jemie.

Variation:
Andaházy Ballet Company
(originally Andaházy Ballet Borealis)

"In the specialized sphere of the dance, the de Basil Ballet, which, by virtue of world war [World War II] and accelerated social change, seems to be farther back in time than is actually the case, [it] has proved to possess this kind of eternal life."[115] Both Lóránt and Anna Adrianova Andaházy, as carriers *of this kind of eternal life*, passed on to their students and company dancers an understanding of how the beauty of their art has staying power that towers over the woes and challenges of time. As charismatic ballet artists, they carried the spirit of the Ballets Russes throughout the Twin Cities and its metropolitan area and Greater Minnesota. Their touring also took the dancers to Rochester, New York, Washington, D.C., and Portugal.

The following events compiled by Jane Keyes, a former Andaházy dancer and school secretary, provide a glimpse into understanding the depth and breadth of the Andaházys' lasting influence—a sharing in ballet's eternal life.

In 1951, the Andaházys entertained Lucia Chase, founder of American Ballet Theatre (ABT), and Alicia Alonso, a former dancer with ABT and founder of her own ballet company in Cuba, her home country. The Andaházys, committed to hosting renowned dancers and teachers from beyond their studio walls, made these efforts a priority for the benefit of their ballet students as well as to stay connected to the ballet world at large. Another luminous event occurred in 1951—the debut of the Andaházys' company, Ballet Borealis, with the Twin Cities premiere of *Aurora's Wedding* at the Gillette State Hospital. In 1953, Andaházy dancer, James (Jim) Keyes, danced for a season with the Ballet Alicia Alonso in Havana, Cuba.

Aurora's Wedding. Jane (Harrington) Keyes as the Hummingbird Fairy and James (Jim) Keyes as one of Three Ivans. Photography by D. C. Dornberg of the *Pioneer Press*, 1958. Courtesy of Jane Keyes.

92

Jaffne Kayesh, stage name for James/Jim Danforth Keyes. *St. Paul Dispatch*, October 2, 1953. "I remember this picture hanging in the St. Paul studio always . . . When I took class, I felt like he [my dad] was watching me." Alicia Brooks Keyes, daughter. Photography by John Miss. Courtesy of Jane Keyes's pictorial biography of James (Jim) Keyes—*Mom, tell me about my dad.*

Finale, *The Sleeping Beauty, Act III* 'Aurora's Wedding.' "Andaházy Ballet Borealis Souvenir Pamphlet, 1961-62." Courtesy of Marius Andaházy.

Anna Adrianova as Zobéide (lower right) and Lóránt as the Golden Slave (upper right) in *Schéhérazade*. "Andaházy Ballet Borealis Souvenir Pamphlet, 1961-62." Courtesy of Marius Andaházy.

When the Ballet Russe de Monte Carlo came to town in March 1952, Mr. A. danced in *Schéhérazade* at the Minneapolis Lyceum Theatre. One evening during the week's stay of the Ballet Russe, the Andaházys entertained the company at their 1680 Grand Avenue studio. The party lasted all night. Five years later, when the Royal Ballet of London came to the Twin Cities, the Andaházys hosted another party at 1680 Grand Avenue and were honored with the presence of Margot Fonteyn. The Andaházys' company performed at the Mayo Civic Center Auditorium in Rochester, Minnesota, in 1953. They danced with the Rochester Symphony Orchestra: *Les Sylphides*, *The Snow Maiden*, and *Slavonic Scenes*. In 1955, the company performed with Herman Hertz

and the Minneapolis Symphony: *Les Sylphides*, *Spectre de la Rose*, *Cargo of Lost Souls*, and *Slavonic Scenes*.

In November 1970, Anna left her life as a dance artist to become a postulant in the Poor Clare Monastery of Our Lady of Guadalupe in Roswell, New Mexico. The nuns generously housed her and opened their monastery spaces to Anna for her spiritual needs and choreographic musings. During her six-month sacred sabbatical, she coached and taught *Los Seises* to the Franciscan Sisters. Imagine that! Mrs. A. returned home in April 1971 refreshed, renewed, and ready to teach again.

The Andaházy Ballet Company traveled beyond America's borders to Portugal with

Anna-Marie Holmes, internationally known for her excellent knowledge of the classical repertoire and her ballet teaching expertise. Anna-Marie and her ex-husband, David Holmes, were the first North Americans invited to dance with the Mariinsky Theatre in Saint Petersburg, Russia.

The Andaházys, their dancers, sets, and costumes traveled to Portugal in August 1973 with a twenty-four-day performance schedule in five cities. Rehearsals blended with sightseeing, relaxing by the pool, and performing a varied repertoire. The company had six performances of *Swan Lake, Aurora's Wedding, Schéhérazade,* and *Les Sylphides.* The next touring schedule took the company to Rochester, New York, in May 1974. Two performances sponsored by Enid Knapp Botsford, Mrs. A's first teacher, included *Les Sylphides, Black Swan,* Pas de Deux, and *Schéhérazade.* The Andaházys were pleased and proud to have their youngest son, Marius, dance with them.

Schéhérazade. Leah Abdella as an Odalisque (standing), Linda Purdy as an Odalisque (kneeling on the left), Rebecca Rigert as a Hindu with an Urn (kneeling on the right), Karen Paulson Rivet as a Wife (reclined on the right). "Andaházy Souvenir Pamphlet, 2000." Photography by Constantine of Hollywood. Courtesy of Marius Andaházy.

The Final Bows of Lóránt and Anna Andaházy

An unexpected letter arrived in April 1982 announcing that Lóránt and Anna were being honored with an award from the Franciscan International Organization for selfless dedication and contribution to the classical arts while still raising a family. With the heartbreaking return of Anna's cancer, life gifted them with this pleasant surprise. The Andaházys could not be present at the award ceremony, so Anna created a ballet, *St. Francis and Lady Poverty*, instead of giving a speech. This was the last ballet Anna Andaházy created but could not finish; with Anna and Lóránt's request, Marius finished it.

At the Upper Midwest Faith Gathering in 1982 at the Minneapolis Auditorium, the Andaházy Ballet Company performed *St. Francis and Lady Poverty* to a sold-out audience. Anna was limping, and her family suspected that the cancer must have metastasized. She continued to get worse, but at Thanksgiving in 1983, Anna rallied—a life-journey-end rally. She declined rapidly, and on December 1, 1983, Lóránt and his sons all held hands in a circle and prayed her off. As Marius later shared, "It was so, so difficult."

Emotionally and physically more than difficult, Lóránt and Marius moved forward, taking care of both the ballet school and the company. Marius continued teaching at the Andaházy School of Classical Ballet, and he also took a teaching position at the Visitation School in Mendota Heights, Minnesota. In February 1986, Lóránt was staging *Los Seises*, and Marius noticed a very bloodshot eye. The family called 911, and Lóránt went by ambulance to Fairview Southdale Hospital. Lóránt seemed very agitated and preferred to go to the Veterans' Hospital. He had had a light stroke. At the Veterans' Hospital, the staff concurred that Lóránt needed an angiogram.

During the angiogram procedure, the doctor punctured Lóránt's aorta but was unaware. Marius taught ballet that evening and strongly felt that he needed to go visit his father. When he entered Lóránt's room, Marius noticed his father writhing in pain. He went to the nurses and told them about the pain, but they made light of it and said that occasionally some pain followed an angiogram. The night drew on; the doctors and staff realized that he was bleeding internally and proceeded with emergency surgery in an effort to save Lóránt's life. Marius stayed by his side throughout the night until the morning, talking to him and telling him how much he loved him. Marius understood and believed that his father could still hear him. Lóránt Andaházy met his Maker and saw Anna again on February 19, 1986.[116]

Portrait of Anna and Lóránt Andaházy. "Andaházy Ballet Borealis Souvenir Pamphlet,1961-62."
Photography by Constantine of Hollywood. Courtesy of Marius Andaházy.

Spartacus, Pas de Deux with Marius Andaházy and Antoinette Peloso, guest artist from the Metropolitan Opera Ballet, New York City. Choreography after Yuri Grigorovich, staged by Andrei Tremaine, Los Angeles. "Andaházy Souvenir Pamphlet, 2000." Courtesy of Marius Andaházy.

Coda: Artists' Stories

Marius J. Andaházy: Artistic Director of the Andaházy Ballet Company and the Andaházy School of Classical Ballet (Interviews 6/14/21; 8/28/21; 9/13/21)

Marius is the youngest of Lóránt and Anna Adrianova Andaházy's three sons and the one who continued the artistic directorship of the Andaházy Ballet. He trained assiduously for nine years under his parents. He also studied on scholarships with the School of American Ballet (the official school of New York City Ballet) and American Ballet Theatre School—both located in Manhattan. The 1970s and '80s also afforded Marius invitations to train during eight different North American tours of Moscow's Bolshoi and Leningrad-Kirov ballets. Among the youngest of all dancers participating in the 1969 Moscow First International Competition for Artists of the Ballet, Marius performed the *Nutcracker*, Grand Pas de Deux on the main stage of Moscow's Bolshoi Theatre partnering Linda Raetzel (née, Finholt).

At that time, he observed some of the teaching principles and exercises of the legendary Soviet ballet pedagogue Agrippina Vaganova. As early as 1971, after multiple guest appearances in Buffalo, New York, under the direction of Kathleen Crofton, Marius implemented the Vaganova ballet training into his work.

In 1974, the Royal Swedish Ballet arrived in Minnesota during their North American tour. The Andaházy School of Classical Ballet hosted the company's daily training and rehearsals. The Scandinavian company's ballet master at the time, Frank Schaufuss, invited Marius to train daily with the company. Marius was asked to submit his résumé with the intention of joining the company. In October 1975, Marius received a formal invitation to join the Royal Swedish Ballet. Four years as a member of the Royal Swedish Ballet gave him the opportunity to take three years of master classes with the Bolshoi's prima ballerina, Olga Lepeshinskaya, who was the company's resident-guest ballet mistress in Stockholm. With the Royal Swedish Ballet, Marius performed in major capitals of Europe and Scandinavia. Performing on the ancient Odeon of Herodes Atticus, beneath the Parthenon in Athens, is especially memorable for him.

While with the Royal Swedish Ballet, Marius had the opportunity to present one of his own choreographies, Vivaldi Concerto (created initially for the Andaházy Ballet Company). The accolades for Vivaldi Concerto led to the commissioning of a tour de force *pas de deux*. This ballet, *Appassionato*, was performed at the University of Minnesota's Northrop Auditorium in July 1980. Local critic, Catherine Taylor, stated that its choreography "showed mastery of the language of classical style in its beautifully whole conception and essentially modern, no-frills manner." (*St. Paul Dispatch*)

His tenure in Sweden also led Marius to his future wife, Krisztina Simonffy, whose family, like Marius' father, hailed from Hungary. They were married in 1982 in Assisi, Italy, and in 1988 made River Falls, Wisconsin, their home, where they raised four children.

As a principal dancer, Marius performed leading roles in many of the great classics, including *Swan Lake, Les Sylphides, Graduation Ball, The Nutcracker, Schéhérazade*, and *Le Spectre de la Rose*.

From 1990 to 1996, Marius established the International Summer Intensive Course of the Andaházy School of Classical Ballet, bringing notable teachers and pedagogues to the Twin Cities community. Dormitories were provided. Local and foreign students benefitted from instructors who were acclaimed prima ballerinas, such as Alla Sizova and Gabriela Komleva of the Mariinsky Theatre. Closing programs were performed on stage at Visitation School and at the Hennepin Center for the Arts.

Marius accepts invitations as a guest artist and lecturer at ballet schools, academic institutions, churches, and civic events locally and nationally.

He is a fount of charismatic charm, humor, and grace. Marius embodies an unre-

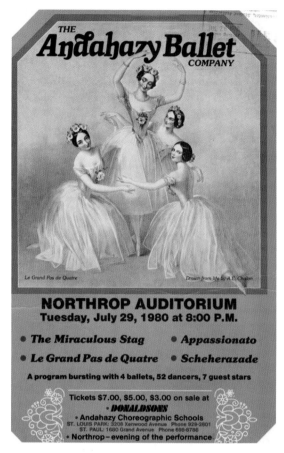

Andaházy Ballet Company. Souvenir program cover created for the July 1980 performance at the Northrop Memorial Auditorium. Courtesy of Marius Andaházy.

strained zeal for passing on the legacy he inherited from his parents and the brilliant dancers of the twentieth century. In addition to his artistic inheritance, he also has preserved a repertoire of forty-eight ballets complete with choreography, orchestral scores, backdrops, costumes, performance playbills, photographs, and other memorabilia.

From 1984 to 2021, Marius directed the Department of Ballet at the Visitation School in Mendota Heights, Minnesota, an esteemed academic preparatory school with a commitment to Salesian spirituality and the classical traditions.

In June 2020, Marius was asked to give the keynote address to the graduating seniors. He chose to share a quote by St. Francis de Sales: "Try to carry out your tasks cheerfully; but if you cannot do it cheerfully, at least do it courageously." (From *Letters of Spiritual Direction*). At the end of the 2020–21 academic year, Marius retired after thirty-seven years of teaching ballet at Visitation. The entire school, faculty, and staff surprised him with a heartwarming send-off for his nearly forty years of taking ballet's torch of eternal life and passing it on. It took grace and substantial grit, but he succeeded.

Stanley S. Hubbard: In Support of Ballet
CEO of Hubbard Broadcasting (Interview 7/19/2021)

Kari Hubbard Rominski, Executive Director of the Hubbard Broadcasting Foundation, has been a supporter of ballet for over twenty years. The executive director of Saint Paul City Ballet would meet Kari for lunch or coffee, and then after a friendly conversation, the financial needs of the ballet would be discussed, and the ballet would send the Hubbard Broadcasting Foundation a grant request. Kari always would say that her father, Stanley Hubbard, would ask when she gave him the grant proposal, "Are the Andaházys still involved?" For over twenty years, this business relationship became more than "just business" but also a pleasant and casual collegial friendship. At a lunch with Kari, the author asked if she could meet her father and interview him for any interesting stories about Mr. Andaházy. The request was made and an interview granted. During the interview, Mr. Hubbard shared his most salient memories of Lóránt Andaházy.

In the lobby of Hubbard Broadcasting, Mr. Hubbard met the author with a personal greeting and apologized for being late. He opened the lobby door and escorted her to the stairway leading one floor up. With a light and quick step, Mr. Hubbard led the way up the stairs, down a long hallway with wooden walls and a soft yellow glow of lighting. It looked like a step back into the 1950s. Mr. Hubbard walked briskly for his age, looking pleasantly confident in his business casual. They entered his office, greeted Cathy, his executive assistant, and pointed to where the interview would take place. He was unassuming, gracious in all ways, and made sure the setting was comfortable for the interview.

The author sat down at one end of the large, wide conference table while Mr. Hubbard settled down across from her. With a smile and a business-like tone in his voice, he asked, "What do you want to know about Mr. Andaházy?" She slid across the table an article from the *Ramsey County History* magazine titled "Stanley Hubbard Remembers." He quickly glanced at the article with a reminiscing nod, smiled, and then with a wink, Mr. Hubbard said, "What else would you like to know?"

The author replied, "Whatever you remember most."

"I remember him so well, and I can visualize him right now. He was a short guy and ram-rod straight. Why he liked me, I don't know." First of all, I was a junior and senior in high school, Breck High School, when I first had Captain Andaházy. He was a professor of military science and tactics; we called it PMST (Professor of Military Science and Tactics). Andaházy was a tough, no-nonsense guy, and fair-minded. We all looked up to him. I graduated in 1951, and at that time, Breck was located fifteen minutes north of the Twin Cities, where Bethel University now stands. Many students and I called Breck "the dump on a hump."

Author: "Did you know that he was also a ballet dancer besides being a US Army and World War II veteran?"

"Yes. He told me the story of his first day in the army when he went to the mess hall for dinner." He approached a table where two sergeants were already sitting. He sat down, and one of them asked him what he did before he enlisted. Andaházy said that he was a ballet dancer. They laughed, and one of them stood up and made fun of him, pretending to do a pirouette.

Andaházy was at basic training, and one time they had to go through an obstacle course, and one of the obstacles was a structure of two tall poles, each with a platform on top, strung with netting between them. The soldiers had to climb up to the top of the netting and then over to the platform and stand on the platform. It was a race to see who could get to the top of the net and over to a platform. Andaházy was the first one to the top, and on the platform he did a handstand and stayed there balancing. A colonel saw him and shortly thereafter sent him to officers' training.

Author: "What else did he do during World War II?"

"He commanded his unit, and they were the first to cross the Rhine and enter Germany; unfortunately, most of the men in his unit were killed. His unit was the first to liberate a German concentration camp."

Author: "Do you have another story about Captain Andaházy?"

"My senior year, he made me Sergeant Major of the corps. That meant I only reported to Captain Andaházy; I did not answer to other officers. I don't know why he liked me, but I'm glad he did."

The interview was short, and Mr. Hubbard, being quite humble, said that a friend of his, Mr. Fletcher Driscoll, knows so much more than he does. Perhaps Stanley Hubbard had more he could share, but perhaps he had a full schedule at work that day. He had been on the Andaházy Board of Directors for several years, and for over thirty years, Hubbard Broadcasting stored all the Andaházy company's props, sets, and costumes.

Mr. Hubbard escorted the author back to the lobby as he had escorted her in. As they walked down that long hallway to the lobby, she shared with him a story from her father's life as an army soldier in Europe during World War II. The interview ended as it had begun—pleasantly sharing personal stories.

Elizabeth Kendall:
Writing Professor at New York School University, Creative Nonfiction (Interview 6/4/2021)

The author reached out to Elizabeth Kendall in 2021, hoping for an interview to confirm some information about Gabriela Komleva, ballet mistress at the Mariinsky Theatre. It was a delightful reconnection, and many anecdotes about Gabriela were confirmed.

After graduating from Radcliffe-Harvard in 1973, Elizabeth came to New York as a dance critic and ballet historian. She has written five books and is presently writing a book on Balanchine. She began as a modern dancer in a class at Radcliffe, and because of modern classes, she was required to take ballet. From that time, her interest in ballet became her focus.

Elizabeth first traveled to Russia in 1978. She never took a course in the Russian language; she said she learned it by ear. In January 1990, she was sent to Russia by *The New Yorker* magazine to write about the Dance Theatre of Harlem, which had been there since 1988. Elizabeth was waiting at the Mariinsky for the director, Oleg Vinogradov, who was supposed to meet her for an interview about the Dance Theatre of Harlem's artistic

Elizabeth Kendall. Courtesy of Elizabeth Kendall.

residence in Saint Petersburg. The director never showed up for their meeting, but Gabriela Komleva happened to walk in where Elizabeth was waiting. They had a brief conversation, and Gabriela invited Elizabeth to her home to watch a video of the Dance Theatre of Harlem. Later, Elizabeth went to tea with Gabriela, and they became friends.

Also in 1990, Elizabeth spent every day at the Kirov, but one day she was going to another theater north of Saint Petersburg—the Petrograd side. Elizabeth's ticket put her in a theater box and she saw Fanny Elssler dance her famous "cachucha." Even though Elssler was retiring, she performed magically. Once Elssler put her costume on, entered the stage, and began dancing, she became a Spanish dance artist performing in Russia.

From the 1990s to 2010, Elizabeth traveled back and forth to Russia for eight summers. In 2000, Elizabeth took a course at the Modern Dance History Conservatory, across the hall from a class taught by Gabriela; and from 2006–2013, she researched facts and information for her book *Balanchine and the Lost Muse*.

Elizabeth shared with the author the following facts about Gabriela's young life in Russia during World War II, her ascendence as a *prima ballerina assoluta*, and her friendship with Minnesotan dance artists.

September 1941: During the nine-hundred-day siege by the Nazis of Leningrad (Saint Petersburg), getting food into the city was a near impossibility. One ice road across Lake Ladoga, called the Road of Life, enabled food to come in and people to leave. The Russians built and erected pilons under the ice to support the weight of trucks.

Gabriela was three years old, and with her mother, grandmother, aunt, and cousin, were on the last convoy out of Saint Petersburg in the winter of 1941–42. (Father as a naval officer, had died—assumably fighting the Nazis.) The trucks were being bombed, and the truck in front of them sank after being hit. Her truck went around the big ice hole, and the evacuees reached the other side where they found Russians with a pot of warm soup waiting for them.

On the train to Perm in the Ural Mountains—about thirty days travel—one of the travelers learned that they had survived the siege of Leningrad, and she put a loaf of bread in Gabriela's hands. A starving Gabriela began to cry because some crumbs had fallen. Gabriela and her family lived as displaced persons for about five years in Perm. A Leningrad teacher was there and taught dance (artistic gymnastics), and Gabriela passed her time dancing. During that time, her cousin, unfortunately, contracted tuberculosis and died.

The family returned to Leningrad in 1947. At nine years old, Gabriela was accepted to the Vaganova Academy of Russian Ballet. So began her ballet training and what would become her career as a ballerina. Gabriela's performance in the role of Nikiya in the ballet *La Bayadère* was stupendous. Gabriela totally believed in the realness of that part; she delved into that world on the stage. Elizabeth remarked, "Seeing that depth of faith in these roles, we realize it's a kind of art we may never see again. Steps and drama were infused."

Gabriela loved being in Saint Paul, Minnesota, because it gave her more privacy by not being noticed all the time. As a *prima ballerina assoluta*, fame gave her constant recognition. She stayed in a "munchkin" home in the Lake Nokomis area, and she loved swimming in the lake. When Gabriela taught ballet in Saint Paul during one of Marius's Summer Intensives, a most memorable moment occurred when Marius asked her to do a variation from the ballet *Flames of Paris*. She never had danced it and was not sure if she could remember the choreography. Gabriela took only a few minutes to think about the choreography, and then she performed the whole variation.

Elizabeth accompanied her friend Gabriela Komleva, ballet mistress of the Mariinsky, to Saint Paul, Minnesota, in 2002. Gabriela was here from Saint Petersburg as part of a Masters Series for ballet students at Saint Paul City Ballet. Elizabeth had just published a book, *American Daughter*, one that she gave as a gift to Saint Paul City Ballet. The greater gift of lasting value was the melding of Russian and American friendship with Gabriela, Elizabeth, and Minnesotan ballet students.

Upon invitation, Gabriela, a much-loved master ballet teacher, returned to Saint Paul for master ballet classes during the summers of 2002 to 2004. In 2005, Karen Paulson Rivet, an excellent ballet teaching artist for Saint Paul City Ballet, along with the school director, traveled to Saint Petersburg and visited Gabriela. In 2008, Saint Paul City Ballet organized an excursion of twenty-two ballet students and adults to Saint Petersburg. The students had an opportunity to take a ballet class from Gabriela Komleva. They also had a customized tour of the Vaganova Academy of Russian Ballet. The adults and students toured Saint Petersburg with a Russian tour guide who vividly made Russian history come alive with a myriad of interesting stories. Attending a ballet performance at the Mariinsky Theatre was one of the many highlights of the trip.

Gabriela and her husband, Arkady, are still living in Saint Petersburg. During the 2020 pandemic, they both contracted Covid-19 but, fortunately, have regained their health.

Elizabeth Kendall's short curriculum vitae:

"I'm a nonfiction writer who's explored several genres of this interesting catchall category: narrative history, research-based memoir, and a more fanciful kind of memoir.

My fifth and newest book, *Balanchine and the Lost Muse*, is maybe my favorite. It sent me deep into Russian archives to find out how the great dance-maker Balanchine discovered his art during the crazy years of the Russian revolution. And to find out if his young, gifted ballerina friend was murdered, and if so, why. I grew up in St. Louis. I live in New York City. I teach literature and writing to the very interesting students at Eugene Lang College of New School in Greenwich Village."

Joseph Savino (Jo) Trained with the Andaházys, Dance Artist with the Ballet Russe de Monte Carlo, Founded a ballet school and company in Saint Paul, National and international dance artist and teacher (Interview 7/22/2022)

A Saint Paul native, he started ballet training with the Andaházys, and as he became technically stronger, Jo left Minnesota. He danced first with Mia Slavenska and Freddie

Five Moons (from left): Maria Tallchief, Marjorie Tallchief, Rosella Hightower, Moscelyne Larkin and Yvonne Chouteau. Oklahoma's five Native American ballerinas who became trailblazers during the twentieth century, performing with world-renowned companies, becoming artistic directors, and founding schools. Courtesy of Oklahoma University School of Dance.

Franklin, who co-founded the short-lived Slavenska-Franklin Ballet in New York City. It was Freddie Franklin, a principal dancer with the Ballet Russe de Monte Carlo, who encouraged Jo to join the Ballet Russe de Monte Carlo. When the Ballet Russe de Monte Carlo performed at the Northrop Auditorium in 1954, Jo performed the principal role, the "Poet," in *Les Sylphides*. While dancing with the Ballet Russe, Léonide Massine often chose Jo and Rochelle Zide-Booth as *pas de deux* dancers.

Jo's dancing took him to four continents, and he danced and performed with several prima ballerinas. He partnered with three of the five Native American ballerinas, the five "Moons," who achieved national recognition defying racial barriers and achieving success in the ballet world. Jo became close friends and a dance partner with Rosella Hightower, and he also partnered with Yvonne Choteau and Marjorie Tallchief.

Jo returned to Minnesota in 1971 and founded the Jo Savino professional performing ensemble, naming it Saint Paul City Ballet. He also established the Classical Ballet Academy located at the base of the formidable Ramsey Hill. The architecturally stunning former German Bethlehem Presbyterian Church, designed by the local architect Cass Gilbert and finished in 1890, became the Academy's home base. It is listed on the National Register of Historic Places.

When Jo was setting choreography for his company's performance of *Giselle*, he needed extra dancers. He asked the Andaházys if Janet Smith could dance in *Giselle* for his production. Mrs. A said, "No," but Janet boldly decided to leave the Andaházys and perform in the production. She stayed with Jo's company and became one of his strongest dancers and teachers.

With his connections with the Ballet Russe, he brought Freddie Franklin to Saint Paul to set the ballet *Coppélia* on Jo's company. The company performed throughout the Twin Cities, in Granite Falls, Minnesota; in Menomonie, Wisconsin; and in Fort Dodge, Iowa. Jo also expanded his curriculum and hired Phil Alesso to teach tap to his student dancers. In 1985, Jo Savino left Minnesota, but he continued dancing and guest teaching both nationally and internationally.

Jo Savino, *Photo Studio*. Jo Savino's Classical
Ballet Academy, Saint Paul, 1970s. Photography
by Leland Wyman. Courtesy of Joseph Savino.

The Firebird (*L'Oiseau de feu* by Fokine), 1978. Jo Savino's Saint Paul City Ballet.
Janet (Hansen) Smith as the Princess. Courtesy of Maryann Smith Johnson.

Loyce Houlton, Choreographer at Work. The Contemporary Dance Playhouse Program, ca. 1966. Courtesy of John Linnerson. Photography by Myron Papiz.

ACT TWO

A Dancer's Twilight Tales (Loyce Houlton's Memoirs)

Volume One (1925–1972)

The Age of Aquarius

Minnesota Dance Theatre Company Dancers, 2005.
Courtesy of Erik Saulitis, photographer.

What is My Pedigree?

In Loyce Houlton's memoirs, *A Dancer's Twilight Tales, Volume One*, she begins with "On October 27, 1986, I was successfully fired from the Minnesota Dance Theatre (MDT) and School that I had founded . . . The company history and publicity materials had already been rewritten to eliminate my name from the paragraphs. It was almost as if I had never been there . . ."

Even though her self-esteem had plummeted, Loyce knew that she needed to move forward and imbibe in life. She wanted her loving and supportive husband, four beautiful children, and four sweet grandchildren to know of her twenty-five years of joy, challenges, and working in the art she loved—dance. The Board of Directors' decision to erase and change history would fail. Loyce Houlton's creative force remained, lingering in the wings, ready to step back on stage at the right time.

With a bold grit and a graceful salutation to all the memories of the people and dance artists she collaborated with in the past, Loyce listened to her friend and dance critic from her New York University days, Doris Hering, who encouraged her to write a book. Loyce took her advice and began writing her memoirs, *Twilight Tales*, as she called up the voices of her past.

In the dance world, some people spoke of a dancer having a pedigree. When asked what her dance pedigree was, she laughed inwardly at the thought of describing herself as a cat, dog, or horse. Nor did she hail from a wealthy, well-established family. Loyce grew up in northern Minnesota, in the small town of Proctor, about nine miles from Duluth. The town was divided both economically and ethnically, and her family lived on the "wrong side of the tracks." Her parents worked hard and made sure that Loyce and her two sisters had education, culture, and music.

Carmina Burana, ca. 2004. Minnesota Dance Theatre, choreography by Loyce Houlton (1976) and restaged by Lise Houlton, Artistic Director and co-directed by Lise Houlton and Dominique Serrand, in collaboration with Bradley Greenwald. Courtesy of Erik Saulitis, photographer.

SCENE 2

Beginnings

At kindergarten age, Loyce's mother enrolled her in piano lessons in Duluth—the big city. During her piano lessons, she heard thumping sounds coming from the top floor of the Lachmund building. One day, she quietly sneaked up there, looked through the window, and saw a large room, a piano and pianist, and an elegant, older woman teaching dance. Loyce, enticed by the sights and sounds of the dance studio, convinced her parents that she wanted to dance; she danced and learned ballet and tap for several years until that fateful day when her dance teacher moved to California. No more tapping and pink ballet slippers.

During the Great Depression, her family and friends endured the wiles and woes of finances, work, and food scarcity. Loyce imitated her older sisters when they put on records and danced to what was in vogue at the time, like the Charleston, the Bunny Hug, and the Castle Walk. This was Loyce's education in dance—"no pedigree, but one heck of a lot of fun."

Loyce graduated from high school with honors, awards, and acceptance to Carleton College in Northfield, Minnesota. She concentrated on literature and dance—modern dance. What a surprise for Loyce to learn that no tap or ballet shoes were needed, only her bare feet; a liminal appreciation for modern dance took root. Her teacher, Eleanor King, brought New York City and the Humphrey-Weidman technique based on breath and fall-and-recovery to the college and its small town south of the Twin Cities. King left the next year and headed back to New York City. Loyce decided to concentrate on her academics and improve her scholastic average. She began dancing again during her junior and senior years with Nancy McKnight Hauser, an excellent teacher and a devotee of Hanya Holm and Mary Wigman. Two years with Nancy Hauser became Loyce's resolute decision to embrace modern dance with its barefooted, new movements for the back, arms, and torso. Those two years were filled with ebullient growth and a broadened understanding of movement. After graduation, Hauser and Loyce remained friends; they both carried different dance aesthetics but a respect for each other's work.

New York City, with its vibrant and diverse dance scene, gave Loyce an intense desire to move out East and attend New York University. NYU required two years of a foreign language for admission, which Loyce did not have; resolute, she dug her heels in, stayed in Minnesota, and enrolled in first-year German at St. Scholastica, a small, private Benedictine college only eleven miles from her hometown of Proctor. Immersed in German, Catholic liturgy, philosophy, and the mystics became the silver thread woven into her future choreography of *Carmina Burana*. Aware of Loyce's dance background, the sisters at the college asked her to teach a dance class. She became friends with one of her dance students, Bird Steele, and learned that Bird's mother taught modern dance in New York City.

A serendipitous friendship became another thread woven into Loyce's dance education. Bird Steele's mother, Bird Larson, grew up in Mora, a small rural town in Central Minnesota, and graduated from a Minnesota state teacher's college with a degree in physical education. After college, Larson followed the dance muse and went to New York City and then to Europe, where she took classes at the Isadora Duncan School. She also eagerly learned about Rudolf Laban's invention of dance notation and Émile Jacques-Dalcroze's eurhythmics—connecting music, movement, mind, and body.

When Bird Larson returned to New York City, she opened a dance studio, sharing what she had learned abroad with her students. She also taught physical education courses at Elmira State Teachers College (Elmira College) and included modern dance in her classes. Both her studio and an awareness of her dance teaching on the collegiate level inspired other colleges to consider adding dance to their physical education departments.

After Loyce's German endeavors in Minnesota, she returned to New York City, her mecca for the arts, and at last, a dream came true. Under the director of NYU's Dance Department, she finished her master's thesis on "Bird Larson, the First Technician of American Modern Dance." Loyce became a dance "bum" and moved from one modern dance teacher to another as her technical understanding of modern dance was expanded and deepened. She also took many classes at the Martha Graham studio, watching and learning how to motivate her movements with a curved back and released torso. Louis Horst, one of her influential teachers at NYU and Graham's longtime mentor, also became one of her dearest friends.

Louis introduced Loyce to Nina Fonaroff, a former Graham dancer who started her own company. Louis and Nina also taught classes at the Neighborhood Playhouse. Louis paid for Loyce's ballet classes at the Balanchine school so she could garner more muscle cell memory for classical ballet technique, and at the same time, also paid for Graham classes, encouraging Loyce to learn both. Loyce danced professionally with Eleanor King, Nina Fonaroff, and with members of the New Dance Group.

Loyce decided to give up her dream of joining a company like Martha Graham's or George Balanchine's New York City Ballet—besides, she was in her mid-twenties. She set her sights westward and back home to Minnesota. Another dream waited there for her, Bill Houlton, home from his naval duty during World War II and starting pre-medical school. Loyce loved dance; it sustained and nourished her emotionally. She knew that the fiery flame of dance would always flicker within her, and someday its blaze would flare again.

Variation:
The Contemporary Dance Playhouse
(Taking the Plunge; Raring to Go!)

Married and settled in an apartment near the medical school in the 1950s, Loyce's "hiatus from dance was filled with the joy of two beautiful sons . . . and keeping up a lively correspondence with friends from New York City, like Louis Horst . . . "[117] During Bill's residency in anesthesiology, they moved to an old section in Minneapolis called Prospect Park. That house forever became the Houlton home and home to a daughter and another son.

When her daughter, Lise Houlton, was four years old, Loyce invited neighborhood children to their home for creative dance classes. Her foray back into the dance world began with a backyard production of *Peter and the Wolf*, the Sergei Prokofiev version. Her children and their neighborhood friends danced to the jubilant praise of the parents. So pleased, the parents rented a local school's gymnasium to perform *Peter and the Wolf* for the community; and thus, Loyce's official entry into the Twin Cities dance scene.

From the world of neighborhood and children, Loyce began teaching a modern dance class at the University of Minnesota. Her hope was to inspire them with what she had learned in New York City and a sense of the creative process. By the end of the first year, they had raised enough funds to send students to Connecticut College for a six-week summer session with stellar dance notables, such as Jóse Limon, Martha Graham, and Louis

The Contemporary Dance Playhouse, Program Cover, 1962. Visual artist unknown. (1962-1969 were years of incredible accomplishments. It was destroyed by arson in 1969.) Courtesy of John Linnerson. Photography by Erik Saulitis.

Horst. Loyce's classes increased in popularity in the second year at the university, and they were asked to do lecture-demonstrations. By the end of her two years of teaching modern dance, the university had the largest Orchesis, the official dance organization of colleges in the United States.

Loyce went on to teach dance at Macalester College in Saint Paul. Classes were taught in a small studio in the women's physical education building, and rehearsals were anywhere that had room and space

117

David Voss. Photography by Myron Papiz, ca. 1966. Courtesy of the University of Minnesota Libraries, Performing Arts Archives.

available. One day in 1961, a beautiful young student dancer came to her and said, "Mrs. Houlton, I was walking in Dinkytown . . . and saw stained glass windows on the second floor of this interesting building. It's above a dry cleaner's . . . it is for rent."[118]

Loyce and her student went there immediately and saw the space; it was perfect. She told the owner that she would like to rent all of the upstairs, but unfortunately, another dancer also wanted to rent the space. The owner, Mr. Chandler, said he would make a decision and get back to Loyce soon. Two days later, Mr. Chandler offered Loyce the rental contract, saying she could take the premises beginning June 1, 1962. The Contemporary Dance Playhouse began with a nucleus of Loyce's University of Minnesota and Macalester College students. (Years later, Loyce discovered that the other dancer was Nancy Hauser who wanted to rent the space.)

That summer, a staff of many volunteers took charge of the artistic and business aspects of running The Contemporary Dance Playhouse: Artistic Director Loyce, eleven dancers, accompanist, technical director, secretary, archivist, hostess, maintenance and cleaning, cooking, and bookkeeping. A summer schedule of classes had been printed, and somehow more than just friends and neighbors learned about the Playhouse. Word spread fast that Dinkytown held a hidden splendor of art, and soon requests were made for lecture-demonstrations.

In 1962, Beth Linnerson, the sister of the Playhouse's gifted technical manager, John Linnerson, founded a children's theater in a poor section of Minneapolis. Beth asked Loyce if the Playhouse would perform for The Moppet Players. Without an inkling of hesitation, Loyce said, "Yes," and *Madeline's Christmas* was performed on The Moppet Players' tiny stage. With standing-room-only for some of the performances, *Madeline's Christmas* was a resounding success.

The next year Beth invited the Playhouse dancers back. Loyce chose an Amish-themed story called *Shoo Fly Pie*, a visual winner. John Donohue of the Children's Theatre Company designed the scenery. The same children danced in *Shoo Fly Pie* that danced in *Madeline's Christmas*. This year the adult company members also danced in the show, and like the year before, it received accolades from

Don Morrison of the Minneapolis newspaper. The Contemporary Dance Playhouse grew, evolved, and made its salient mark of excellence in the Twin Cities. Its reputation had spread beyond Dinkytown's neighborhood streets and storefronts. The collaborations with the University of Minnesota further expanded their reach.

The first years of the Playhouse were abundantly filled with excitement and new collaborations. Both James Lombard, director of the Northrop Auditorium (now Northrop at the University of Minnesota), and Frank Bencriscutto, band director at the University of Minnesota, gave the Playhouse many performance opportunities, which led to new choreographic works. One work with the university's band, *Apotheosis*, toured with the band and seemed to have a haunting effect on audiences since it was a time when nuclear holocausts were on people's minds.

On another occasion, a dance called *Metamorphosis* was created, and the music was composed by David Voss, a dancer-composer. The uniquely designed costumes had hoods to the waist and tubular material to the floor from which the dancers would emerge. A dancer, Katherine (Kathie) Goodale, could not escape from her costume despite punches and gyrations to get out. She received bravos from the audience for her extraordinary solo performance.

Loyce Houlton in rehearsal at The Contemporary Dance Playhouse, 1964. Photography by Myron Papiz. Courtesy of the University of Minnesota Libraries, Performing Arts Archives.

The Contemporary Dance Playhouse was a barefooted company with a barefoot artistic director and choreographer. Bob Dylan's words to his song *The Times They Are A-Changin'* aptly described the changes happening at the Playhouse, but classical ballet seemed to be rising like a rosy-fingered dawn on a new day with new directions for Loyce's vision.

Variation:
The Russian-Ukrainian Connection

The stars of the Bolshoi Ballet, arriving in the fall of 1963 on an extended tour of Canada and the United States organized by Sol Hurok's organization, would premiere in New York City with Asaf Messerer's new work, *Ballet School*. The plans to stop at every major city in the United States included the Twin Cities, and requests went out for children to audition for a role in the ballet. The University of Minnesota asked if they could use Loyce's portable barres and her best accompanist for the audition at Coffman Union's ballroom and if the Bolshoi could use The Contemporary Dance Playhouse for classes and small ensemble rehearsals.

Loyce froze still for a few moments. They are known as a barefoot studio; could her young students handle a ballet audition? Although the children's program had a strong dual program of classical ballet and contemporary dance, the children had experienced a different ballet style when Loyce hired a Ukrainian teacher. He was impatient, hot tempered, and hit the children lightly when he felt they were doing a movement incorrectly. At that point, Loyce said "nyet" to this teacher, and he was not asked back. However, Loyce did not say "nyet" to one of the most important individuals in her life—the Playhouse's photographer, Myron Papiz, a Ukrainian of great artistic sensitivity.

Loyce's ballet teacher approached her when the notice went up. She suggested that two of their students could handle the audition: Mary Joan Gregorian and Lise Houlton. Decision made. Of the two hundred students who auditioned, twenty-seven were chosen to perform with the Bolshoi, and Mary Joan and Lise were among those who would dance. At rehearsal the next day, Loyce sat with two other teachers who had come with their students: Lorand Andaházy Jr., a teacher at the Andaházy Borealis Ballet School in Saint Paul, and Bud Johansen, director of Rochester Ballet and former dancer with the Andaházys. They were both taking copious notes to know what to review with their students. Loyce thought maybe she should also take some notes, but she did not. She confidently knew that her two students would remember the new choreography.

In June 1964, the Royal Ballet of London came to Minnesota with Rudolf Nureyev on the roster of dancers. The University of Minnesota again asked Loyce if the company could use her studio for classes and smaller ensemble rehearsals; Northrop at the University would be used for rehearsing the ballets. Of course! When Loyce first saw Nureyev step into their studio, she stared in awe at this Russian superstar. Extending her hand to greet and welcome him was a blur; she only remembered an electric flash that penetrated her hand. They talked briefly about taking him on a tour of the Cities after the rehearsal. Nureyev kindly declined. He would like most of all to see the Mississippi River and the statue of Hiawatha and Minnehaha.

After rehearsal, a reporter from the Minneapolis *Star Tribune* chauffeured both Loyce and Nureyev to see the Great Mississippi River and to visit Minnehaha Falls, flowing from some late winter snowmelt. They dined at the Sheraton Ritz for lunch, and in one lull in the conversation, Loyce asked Nureyev what he thought of the American dance scene. Nureyev swiftly stated his appreciation for Martha Graham and that he felt Glen Tetley's *Pierrot Lunaire* as one of the finest ballets he had seen. His quick response surprised Loyce but resonated well within her psyche. Tetley's career began with Hanya Holm, and later, he was a member of Martha Graham's company. After the Royal Ballet left town, Loyce felt that her life "was made richer not only by the beauty of the Royal Ballet repertoire but by the extraordinary gift of off-stage time with a young Russian

defector . . . All the stars were winking and blinking at me, and my Russian Connection was gaining momentum."

Summertime 1965, Loyce hired a new ballet teacher versed in the Cecchetti method for ballet. Enrico Cecchetti became a teacher for Diaghilev's Ballets Russes dancers, and he also taught Anna Pavlova. Learning ballet from the Cecchetti method, Loyce's students would have a historical link from their new teacher to Diaghilev, to Pavlova, and to Cecchetti—a ballet lineage. To further

American Ballet Theatre, New York. Summer 1968. Madame Pereyaslavec (Madame Perry) with Lise Houlton, student. Photography by Myron Papiz. Courtesy of the University of Minnesota Libraries, Performing Arts Archives.

enhance the students' technical strength, an excursion to a Cecchetti one-week seminar in Lansing, Michigan, was planned, registration for classes sent in, fees paid, and airplane tickets purchased.

Once on Michigan State University campus, Loyce and her teacher and dance students discovered that the classes would be taught by the famous Madame Pereyaslavec. Loyce intrinsically knew that this was a Russian-Ukrainian connection. When Madame Perry (as people called her) entered the studio for the first ballet class, she exuded a regal charisma with a dramatic flair. She spoke briefly with the accompanist, and out of the mouth of this petite woman came a loud, bold, commanding voice: "First position, please." Madame Perry's demonstration of the movements was flawlessly beautiful. The suppleness of the port de bras and the torso reminded Loyce of how Martha Graham's whole body would flow and soar.

At an afternoon tea reception for Madame Perry, Loyce had an opportunity to tell her how much she enjoyed watching her teach the class. Madame Perry then shared how her inspiration came from Agrippina Vaganova. In her day, Vaganova "possessed neither good looks nor influential protectors, so she was given the official status of ballerina only in 1915, one year before her retirement from the stage."[119] She then became a superior teacher, and her method grew beyond Russia with worldwide approval. Her student dancers became a new galaxy of luminous Russian stars. At the end of the seminar, Madame Perry asked to speak quietly to both Loyce

and Lise. She gave Lise a picture of herself and wrote, in Russian, some words in the corner of the photo. Back in Minneapolis, the words written on the photo were translated, and this is what Madame Perry wrote: "Dear Lise, One day you will be a ballerina. Love, Valentina Pereyaslavec."

Welcome to Minneapolis, Madame Pereyaslavec and Valya, ca. 1969. Photograph by Myron Papiz. Courtesy of the University of Minnesota Libraries, Performing Arts Archives.

In a playbill from 1966, Loyce says in its foreword, "Our school had to be inclusive—not exclusive—and like ballet, modern dance would be a part of the total curriculum . . . My dream was and is that the students who study at the Playhouse School will be so versatile that they can perform equally well in bare feet, in slippers or en pointe as the choreography or repertory demands." Loyce also wrote the following description of The Contemporary Dance Playhouse in its 1966 Performance Program:

The Contemporary Dance Playhouse School for training students of all ages in all areas of dance—ballet, modern, and contemporary techniques, adagio, folk, mime, and repertory.[120]

The Contemporary Dance Theatre, the residence of adult and children's performing companies, presenting full-length contemporary dramatic ballets, concerts, lecture-demonstrations, and master classes.

Six years after Loyce, in her own words, "took the plunge" and took hold of the premises above a dry cleaner's store, she dared to take another risk: the thrust stage of the Guthrie Theater. Donors and friends Markell Brooks and Muriel Pesek leased the Guthrie Theater one night in 1968 for the Playhouse company. The program included four works by Loyce: *Opus from the Inside Out*, music composed by Paul Fetler, a friend; *Audition* to a nocturne by Antal Doráti, former conductor of the Minneapolis Orchestra; *Images of Love*, to a Ravel string quartet; and, *The Killing of Suzie Creamcheese*, music by Frank Zappa and the Mothers of Invention by a local group called Noah's Ark. An extended standing ovation occurred that memorable night at the Guthrie Theater. Memorable as well for a decision made to change their name to one that resonated with their school and company's widespread recognition: Minnesota Dance Theatre (MDT).

Madame Pereyaslavec at the Playhouse, ca. 1968. Class with The Contemporary Dance Playhouse students. Photography by Myron Papiz. Courtesy of the University of Minnesota Libraries, Performing Arts Archives.

Martha Graham. The movement of fabric was always of prime significance in Graham's dances, and it is shown in this photograph. Barbara and Willard Morgan photographs and papers, Library Special Collections, Charles E. Young Research Library, UCLA.

Variation:
The Legacy of Martha Graham

In the early 1960s, the Walker Art Center brought two principal Graham dancers, Bertram Ross and Mary Hinkson, to teach Graham classes at the Minneapolis YWCA. Loyce considered Bertram a Greek god and Mary a goddess—both dancers were muses of great inspiration. Loyce envisioned Graham's company, consisting of devoted Greek Olympians, but as Graham would say, they were acrobats of God. Loyce strongly felt that her classes at the Playhouse and the company's basic training in ballet with the Vaganova approach to movement blended well with Graham movement techniques. Loyce registered Lise for the first workshop, and she signed up as an observer.

Whether it is ballet or the Graham technique, Loyce believed that an excellent teacher totally understands the body and its center of movement and passes that understanding to the students. "A Graham class always starts with half an hour of floor work. The floor serves the same purpose as the ballet dancer's barre; it eliminates the problem of balance . . . "[121] With help from the floor or barre, dancers begin to strengthen their centers from where the movements emanate.

In August 1968, Loyce's company dancers and advanced students traveled to New York City to experience Madame Perry's classical ballet classes at American Ballet Theatre and with Mary Hinkson at the Graham School of Contemporary Dance. Loyce put into action what she believed was necessary for her students to become versatile dancers: ballet and modern dance. At that time, ballet was considered European and modern dance American. Loyce continually melded them both together in her teaching and choreography.

Loyce also invited Madame Perry and her accompanist, Valya, to Minneapolis, and they stayed at the Houlton home. Loyce's company and advanced students improved by leaps and bounds with Madame Perry's sensational classes and the inspirational accompanying by Valya.

In the mid-70s, Loyce was ill with neuropathy, and the board agreed to have a Graham teacher substitute until Loyce recovered. Ethel Winter, coming from both a ballet and a Graham background, agreed to leave New York City for a seven-week course at Minnesota Dance Theatre. A perfect fit for MDT's dual ballet and contemporary programs. In 1975, Graham's company brought seven works to the Twin Cities and performed on the Northrop at the University of Minnesota's stage. One afternoon before a Graham performance, Loyce observed a rehearsal. She heard Martha Graham loudly reprimanding the dancers saying, "You do not look like you have been trained by me . . . You look like ballet dancers!"[122]

Loyce stated, "In spite of the tempestuous schism swirling between modern dance and ballet in New York and Minnesota, she felt that even then a combination of these and the resulting symbiosis would be the dance of the future. To her, this symbiosis was still the ideal foundation for the dancer of the twentieth century."

MDT company dancer, 2012.
Courtesy of Erik Saulitis, photographer.

Variation:
The Spectre of Robert Joffrey

In the 1960s and '70s, Minnesota Dance Theatre's students and company experienced the spectre of Robert Joffrey through the presence of three women who knew him well: Françoise Martinet, the teacher; Rochelle Zide, the régisseuse; and Nicole Sowinska, the dancer. Each of these women gave MDT a link to Joffrey and the extraordinary person he was: accomplished dance artist, superb teacher, and an astute businessman.

Françoise Martinet came into the lives of The Contemporary Dance Playhouse in 1967 because her fiancé, Michael Moriarity, had just signed a contract with the Guthrie Theater. As a classical ballet teacher and member of the Joffrey Ballet who toured the United States, her *je ne sais quoi* enamored all to her. Françoise taught not only the company and advanced dancers but also children.

During Françoise's four-year tenure with MDT, she ardently participated in all areas of MDT including lecture-demonstrations, choreographic work, and rehearsal assistant for *Nutcracker* Fantasy roles and the premiere of *Little Match Girl*, created for MDT's first Adventure in Music performance with the Minnesota Orchestra. Lise, in her first leading role, captivated the audience. John Sherman of the *Minneapolis Star* wrote, "the bewitching little star of the piece was twelve-year-old Lise Houlton who danced a long and complex role with unfailing skill and marvelous self-possession . . . "

A mere beginning, the *Little Match Girl* was followed by excellent and sometimes breathtaking works that took the stage: *The Three-Squared Circus* with a *très beau pas de trois* (very beautiful dance of three) called "The Dazzling Princess Czo Chu," choreographed by Françoise; and *Nutcracker Fantasy*. The skilled and cooperative Northrop stage crew made much of the magic happen on stage. John Linnerson (a.k.a. St. John), Loyce's technical director since the 1960s said, "All the union stage workers loved Loyce; we made her vision happen, and it was fun."[123]

Françoise Martinet, Summer Dance at The Contemporary Dance Playhouse. Courtesy of Judith Brin Inger. Photography by Erik Saulitis.

Françoise Martinet encouraged Loyce to have a classical piece set on the company, and when she excitedly suggested *La Fille Mal Gardée*, staged by Fernand Nault, for the Joffrey Ballet, Loyce agreed. They called Nault in Montréal to get permission to stage the ballet. He could not come to stage it and recommended Rochelle Zide-Booth to be the régisseuse. In fact, when Rochelle and Nault discussed it, Nault actually gave Rochelle all the rights to the ballet. As he told Rochelle, "I'm too busy with other projects, and I don't care to stage *La Fille Mal Gardée* anymore."[124]

Rochelle Zide-Booth (Chellie) danced with the Ballet Russe de Monte Carlo from 1954 to 1958 under Sergei Denham. A petite dancer, but with a memory like an elephant, so when anyone was injured or ill and had to be replaced, Rochelle was the go-to girl because "Chellie knows it." Denham kept saying that Chellie was "the best little girl they'd ever had."[125] She also danced for the Joffrey Ballet. During her tenure with the Joffrey, Rochelle danced several roles in *La Fille Mal Gardée*, including the lead role of Lisette. She was available for one week in the summer of '68 to teach MDT the one-hour ballet.

La Fille Mal Gardée, a comic ballet, shares the distinction of being one of only two eighteenth-century ballets that are still in a company's repertoire. However, it has changed since its premiere in 1789. When one "sees an original ballet production today, it tends to be a restoration, pieced together from old notations, photographs, memories, written accounts, the reading of tea leaves, and inventive channeling of the past."[126] *La Fille Mal Gardée* was linked to the program for the Adventure in Music series at Northrop for the 1968–69 season. The director of the music series did not think that the title of the ballet would sell in the Twin Cities, so Loyce agreed to change the title to *The Overly Protected Daughter*.

Rochelle arrived to set the ballet, and MDT quickly experienced Rochelle's brilliance as a human anthology of music and choreography. Staging the ballet went smoothly; she was a blue ribbon régisseuse. A veritable smart and classy ballerina, modern dance did not ring Rochelle's bell, but Loyce explained that at MDT, they dance *contemporary, not modern*. Rochelle believed that "a pointe shoe in ballet was what the barefoot was to modern dance." Loyce asked Rochelle if she would like to see some of her choreography. Rochelle agreed. After the dancers presented Loyce's contemporary works, a long, uncomfortable silence fell on everyone. Finally, Rochelle blurted out: "Look, Lady. What are you doing here in Minneapolis? . . . You must go east to New York."[127] Loyce was stunned by her comment; those words were not expected at all. Unable to attend the rehearsals of *La Fille Mal Gardée* between the summer and its February premiere, Rochelle wrote a letter to Loyce thanking her for keeping *La Fille* well-rehearsed without her presence as the régisseuse. She also wrote, "You made me see dance in a new and very beautiful way—contemporary, innovative, yet based so strongly in Dance . . . "[128]

One more dancer with the spectre of

Joffrey would grace the MDT studio—Nicole Sowinska. She studied with Joffrey for five summers in Seattle, and then a terpsichorean pull drew Nicole to New York City, and she danced for two years in Joffrey's company. Nicole inspired Loyce and became a focal point for some of her best choreography. Nicole also encouraged Loyce to put her contemporary visions en pointe, and she worked on setting en pointe some of the more diffi-cult pieces of choreography. A true give and take developed in Loyce and Nicole's creative endeavors.

Loyce considered Françoise, Rochelle, and Nicole three fantastic and unsung women. They passed on to Loyce's dancers what these three women had learned from dancing with Robert Joffrey. For Loyce, these links to the spectre infused some of her greatest creative growth.

La Fille Mal Gardée, A happy and comic ballet where the heroine manages to marry the man she loves. "Ribbon Dance" with Rochelle Zide-Booth as Lisette, in the lead female role, and Gerald Arpino as Colas, in the lead male role in the Joffrey Ballet production. Courtesy of Rochelle Zide-Booth.

Cedar Village Theater. Photographer unknown. Courtesy of the University of Minnesota Libraries, Performing Arts Archives.

Variation:
A Resident Theater of Our Own

A quest to find a performance space of their own led Loyce and John Linnerson to search nooks and crannies all over Minneapolis to find the right space. Attracted to the Cedar-Riverside neighborhood near the University of Minnesota, Loyce and John found possibilities in the old Cedar Theater. On a frigid January day in 1969, they signed the lease for the Cedar Theater, thrilled to have a space to call their own for performing, but a space that needed major facelifts in all areas of the building and disinfecting and cleaning everything. With their own theater, naming it the Cedar Village Theater, they could present concert dance seasons, expand their repertory, and give emerging choreographers a space to present their works.

A renovation team of four collaborators—John Donohue of the Children's Theatre; Karlos Ozol, a technical and lighting expert; and St. John and Loyce—began planning. Volunteer parents, dancers, students, and anyone else who believed in this vision joined in as the Blue Jean Brigade. Their mission: all the dirty work. Everyone pulled up their sleeves and worked heartedly and hard all January with its share of frigid weather, icy roads, and snowfalls. The grand opening on March 15 had already been scheduled and announced, and one month of renovation and scrubbing passed quickly with much more left to do. With only a month and a half left to prepare for a scaled-down version of *La Fille Mal Gardée*, hosting two dance companies from New York City, and using the grant money for the grand opening—they needed a miracle.

Serious comments were made about renovating this old theater for the arts. The entire Cedar-Riverside area in the 1960s resembled a small Greenwich Village in New York City or Haight-Ashbury in San Francisco. Don Morrison, a freelance writer for the newspapers, said, "The old Cedar Theater has operated for more than twenty years as a place of public assembly. But when the dance troupe presented its remolding plans, inspection officials decreed that a sprinkling system must be installed—at a cost of $2,000."[129] Despite setbacks and unexpected financial hurdles, much renovation had been accomplished, and February was almost over. Now to the main priority—making a proscenium stage—March was coming in like a lion.

Like the royalty of centuries past, Markell Brooks and Muriel Pesek continued as generous queens of friendship and funds in support of the renovation. They opened their homes and hosted fundraisers. Donors eventually gave $86,000 in support of the Cedar Village Theater. The chamber theater of Loyce's dreams became a reality—"resplendent in sophisticated black. Its diamond clusters would be the dancers."[130] Curtains would raise on March 15, 1969.

A successful grand opening received a positive review in the *Star Tribune* by Allan Holbert, who wrote, "Last night the members of this bright and vital young company took off their overalls, donned their tights, and put on a sometimes rough but always stimulating show . . ."[31] Loyce and her company had only Monday to take a rest—the usual dark Monday when theaters are closed after a performing weekend—because Tuesday, Anna Sokolow's company would arrive to perform on the Cedar Village Theater's stage. Glen Tetley's company would arrive soon after. Sokolow's company of dancers arrived noticeably fatigued from all their touring, and Anna seriously wondered if they were capable of performing. With rest and dinner at the Houlton's home, and delightful dinner at a donor's home another night, their energy bounced back—or perhaps their performance adrenaline—and they performed beautifully.

Immediately after Anna Sokolow's company left, the Glen Tetley company arrived. Glen and Loyce both embraced and lived in two dance worlds—classical ballet and modern, but the word "contemporary" was preferred by both. Like Anna's company, they were tour-exhausted. Relaxation, good food, and conversation were a welcome relief from the arduous travel.

The program they brought to the Cedar Village Theater was a rare program for the Twin Cities: *Embrace Tiger And Return to Mountain*, and Glen's own works, *Pierrot Lunaire* and *Mythical Hunters*. Glen later set *Mythical Hunters* on MDT. At that moment, Loyce's "crystal ball had not yet revealed" that one day she would be in New York City attending a performance of the ballet *Pierrot Lunaire* on the stage of the Metropolitan Opera with Rudolph Nureyev dancing the role of Pierrot and Lise Houlton dancing Columbine, en pointe. Lise one day would become the muse in Glen's extraordinary choreographic life.

JACK MITCHELL
NEW YORK

Pierrot Lunaire. Choreography by Glen Tetley, music by Arnold Schoenberg, and photography by
Jack Mitchell, New York. Photograph given to Loyce Houlton from Glen Tetley with the inscription,
"With much love and appreciation to Loyce and The Contemporary Dance Playhouse."
Courtesy of the University of Minnesota Libraries, Performing Arts Archives.

Graduation Ball. Minnesota Dance Theatre, 1970. Choreography by David Lichine. Photography by Myron Papiz. Courtesy of the University of Minnesota Libraries, Performing Arts Archives.

Variation:
The Miracle of Lichine

In the fall of 1969, Loyce imagined a new work for her company, David Lichine's *Graduation Ball*. He was Russian-born but lived and trained in the Russian School in Paris. He joined de Basil's Ballets Russes and danced with some of the great ballet legends—Danilova, Massine, and Balanchine. He married Tatiana Riabouchinska, one of the three "baby ballerinas," a term invented by the English dance critic, Arnold Haskell, to describe three young dancers of the Ballets Russes de Monte Carlo in the early 1930s. (The others were Irina Baronova and Tamara Toumanova.)

Would this world-renowned dance artist and choreographer come to Minnesota? Loyce boldly called the Lichine studio in Los Angeles, and a few days later, David returned her call. Was it cold in Minnesota? Where would I live? David stated his fee and said he would come. Thrilled to hear Lichine's openness to setting his work on her company, Loyce said she would get back to him with details and a confirmation of his fee. Loyce had to find a way to cover his large fee and all the production costs. Her two queen benefactresses, Markell Brooke and Muriel Pesek, averred to cover his fee as well as production costs.

Once in Minnesota, David began his first class by walking around the room, smiling, and asking the dancers questions. The company, both nervous and excited to meet him, relaxed and smiled at his unusual way of starting class and casting the roles with humor and quick wit. David's rehearsals were tough and demanding, requiring grit and stamina. Some movements were repeated over and over again to arrive at the quality and aesthetic he envisioned. David often spoke of Anna Pavlova because she encouraged him to dance—after demonstrating his naturally high jumps for her. Pavlova got him started in his dance career and urged him to give up his greatest love—football.

One board director, Edward Holmberg, was "urbane, witty, sarcastic, good-looking and devoted to the arts."[132] Edward spoke Italian, which endeared him to David, and when Edward came to watch rehearsals, it delighted David to visit with him. David accepted invitations to dine with the Holmbergs, and a friendship developed. David christened him Prince Edward VII, which forever became David's term of endearment for Edward.

The details for the production were well underway, and David enjoyed working with the company. He approached Loyce to see if he could set another work on the dancers for the second half of the program, and he would do this second work, *La Création*, for no cost. The ballet represented the birth of an idea and the crucial role of the choreographer. David needed a gifted child to dance the birth of a choreographer's idea. Two children were selected—Tina Swenson and Stephanie Karr-Smith. In the midst of rehearsing *Graduation Ball*, *La Création*, and *Tenderplay* (a ballet by Michael Uthoff), David approached Loyce with his desire to set *Le Rencontre* on the company, again for no additional fee. *Pourquoi pas?* Why not? David might have said if Loyce had hesitated. MDT was on a roll.

In March, on the day of the premiere of *Graduation Ball*, Loyce received a call from the Sheraton Ritz that David had left a letter for her. She knew that no amount of her pleading and coaxing would convince David to stay for the premiere of *Graduation Ball*; he felt it was being left in Loyce's excellent care. His letter sincerely affirmed Loyce and her company, writing: "You have a wonderful company, with beautiful dancers . . . There are lots of ideas in the sky and on the earth, and you have them in the palm of your hands . . . I love your school, and I hope that one day I will return." Love, David Lichine

Graduation Ball at the Northrop with the Minnesota Orchestra attracted an audience of 4,500 and rave reviews from the critics. *La Création* premiered the next month at the Cedar Village Theater, but it had a lukewarm response from both the audience and the reviewers. However, the curtain closed on *Le Rencontre* with thunderous applause; the audience loved it.

The company performed *Le Rencontre* many times, and in one of Loyce's preshow visits to the lobby to observe the people coming in, she approached two young women who had bought their tickets and one for their German Shepherd dog. Loyce told them, "You cannot take the dog into the theater," and they answered, "He has never missed a show." After the performance, these two ladies approached Loyce and told her, "*Le Rencontre* is his favorite—he really liked it the best."

Late one June evening in 1972, Loyce answered the phone, and a strange voice asked, "Is Mrs. Houlton there? I have an important message for her." "This is she speaking." "The message is . . . I will never return. I love you and goodbye . . . David." Then the telephone went dead, and Loyce then knew that David had called to let her know that he was dying. David Lichine died on June 26, 1972, in Los Angeles. He is best remembered as one of the stars of the de Basil's Ballets Russes from 1932–41 and 1947–48.

Loyce and her husband flew to Los Angeles in 1984 and went to visit the Lichine Studios. To their surprise, Mrs. Tatiana Riabouchinska Lichine was there. A kind and gracious woman, she told us how David had been quite ill before his death. We did not stay long. The studios were empty because many students from the Lichine Studios were rehearsing for the opening ceremony of the 1984 Olympics. That same day, we saw the premiere at Grauman's Chinese Theatre for the Minneapolis star Prince in his first motion picture, *Purple Rain*.

In reflecting about David Lichine, Loyce wrote: "We knew the Boy-Man in his twilight. We understood his dreams and his deceits, his naïveté and his sophistication. That, in the midst of the dying of light, there was such a burst of light when he was with us—that was the miracle of Lichine."

Russian Ballet: David Lichine in *Protée*. Credit: Private Collection © Look and Learn/Bridgeman Images.

THE
DANCING TIMES

A REVIEW OF DANCING IN ITS MANY PHASES

With which are incorporated "THE AMATEUR DANCER"

and "DANCING & THE BALLROOM"

| New Series No. 464 | MAY, 1949 | Monthly One Shilling |

John Kriza

in the American Ballet Theatre's production of *Billy the Kid*.
On another page Miss Lillian Moore writes of the reorganisation
of Ballet Theatre, so popular with English audiences during its
season at Covent Garden in 1946.

John Kriza in the American Ballet Theatre's production of *Billy the Kid*. Composed by Aaron Copland.
Credit: Lebrecht Music Arts/Bridgeman Images.

Variation:
Early Alliances with the Stars of ABT

One evening, Madame Perry called Loyce. She knew and supported Loyce's efforts at building a young, vibrant, and sustainable company. She told Loyce that she had a good teacher, Scott Douglas, who is no longer dancing with American Ballet Theatre, and perhaps Loyce could use him as a master guest teacher.

Scott Douglas, from being a classical danseur, was now dancing in the new company of Glen Tetley. Once again, a thread would be woven in the dance loom through Holm, Graham, Joffrey, Tetley, and Douglas to Loyce's dancers.

Scott came to MDT with incredible experience performing in many ballets by several widely acclaimed choreographers. Scott had three excursions to Russia, was sociable, and was a gourmand with good food and drink; plus, the dancers adored him. Scott at first had doubts about coming to Minnesota to teach the "Dinkytown Dance group," but once here and in class, those thoughts soon evaporated. Like so many people unfamiliar with Minnesota, especially the Twin Cities, they are often stupefied when they come here and discover the vibrancy of its art and culture.

Two years later, the University of Minnesota's Adventure in Music series planned to have an all-American program and approached Loyce to see if she would choreograph an Americana ballet or dance.

She remembered briefly meeting John Kriza, who came to her production of *Graffiti* at the Cedar Village Theater and also saw him in the American Ballet Theatre's performance of *Billy the Kid*. An artistic sleuth, Loyce tracked down Johnny Kriza, who was teaching in the Dance Department at Indiana University in Bloomington. John agreed to set *Billy the Kid* on Loyce's company only if Lucia Chase, who owns the rights to the ballet at American Ballet Theatre, would give permission to Johnny to set it on Loyce's company. The stars aligned, permission was granted, and MDT continued its stride forward.

Johnny taught the company class three mornings a week, and during class, he began to prepare the dancers for Billy's rehearsals. Like Scott Douglas, he taught with kindness and affirmed the unique talents each of them had—and not to be apprehensive but to expect miracles. One time, Johnny noticed that a competitive energy had sprouted between two dancers. He came over to them and quietly told them, "Look—there are no small parts, only small artists."[133] In April 1972, MDT took the stage at the Northrop with *Billy the Kid* to a resounding audience reception. The ballet was a tremendous success, and Johnny was thrilled.

A few weeks after *Billy the Kid*, Loyce and her dancers went to the Mid-States Regional Dance Festival in Kansas City. Anton Dolin, who had staged *Pas de Quatre*, gave the keynote speech at the final dinner. He mentioned Loyce's *pas de deux* in her ballet, *Wingborne*, which was created in honor of MDT's loyal benefactress, Markell Brooks, shortly after she passed away. His words bestowed deep admiration for *Wingborne* and Loyce's artistic excellence. Anton Dolin called this barefooted work performed by Lise Houlton and Andrew Thompson "the *grand pas de deux* of the twentieth century."

Johnny Kriza. He staged Eugene Loring's *Billy the Kid*, with music by Aaron Copland, for MDT in 1972. Permission was granted from Lucia Chase, owner of the rights to the ballet at American Ballet Theatre. Courtesy of the University of Minnesota Libraries, Performing Arts Archives.

Variation:
Jacob's Pillow—Tomorrow, Spoleto!

In the 1970s, Loyce's creative genius rolled out a wave of choreographic works for the company. She also embraced the stellar works of other choreographers: Anton Dolin (*Pas de Quatre*), John Kriza (*Caprichos*), Brian Shaw (*Les Patineurs, Façade, Act III of The Sleeping Beauty*), Rochelle Zide-Booth's Ballet Russe version (*Raymonda*), and Merce Cunningham (*Winterbranch, Canfield*).

In 1971 and '72, Loyce and MDT were invited to perform at Jacob's Pillow in the Berkshires in western Massachusetts. When Ted Shawn, the founder and creative energy of Jacob's Pillow, introduced MDT at their first performance in the Ted Shawn Theatre at Jacob's Pillow, he spoke glowingly about Loyce and the company with these words, "from far away—from Minnesota—there came a woman who could envision dance beautifully without benefit of swans, and she was developing a language for dance that was distinct and creative."[134]

Next stop—Spoleto, Italy! Scott Douglas invited Loyce and company dancers to Italy, where Glen Tetley and Scott Douglas were in residence. Loyce said an immediate "yes" to the invitation. In Spoleto, the company could learn Glen's *Mythical Hunters* and then perform it in the beautiful Teatro Nuovo. Once again, the thread linking dancers with creative geniuses of the past would be woven.

Jacob's Pillow. A dance center, school, and performance
space in Becket, Massachusetts, in the Berkshires.
Courtesy of Erik Saulitis, photographer, 2021.

Minnesota Dance Theatre company dancer, Andrea (last name unknown), ca. 2005. MDT's
Loyce Houlton's Nutcracker Fantasy (annual marketing piece). Lise Houlton, Artistic Director.
Courtesy of Erik Saulitis, photographer.

Volume Two (1962–1986)

The Age of Aries

Loyce Houlton's Nutcracker Fantasy (annual marketing piece).
Lise Houlton, Artistic Director; Matt Jensen, Dance Artist, ca. 2005.
Courtesy of Erik Saulitis, photographer.

SCENE 1
Nutcracker Fantasies

In the early '60s, The Moppet Players approached Loyce, asking her to stage another Christmas dance drama for their December show. Loyce had been listening to holiday music, and her creative energies were already forming thoughts about a holiday dance, like little holiday elves ruminating about her brain. After purchasing the complete Minneapolis Orchestra's recording of the *Nutcracker Ballet* conducted by Antal Doráti, Loyce played the music over and over again for herself and her children. She read the fascinating E. T. A. Hoffman's tale, *The Nutcracker and the Mouse King*. Hoffman's story is darker than the version that reached the stage in 1892 Russia, and Marius Petipa chose to follow the lighter adaptation of the tale written by Alexandre Dumas, père. This version included themes from the music, notated by Tchaikovsky, and colorful illustrations by Warren Chappell.

An intoxicating Nutcracker spell absorbed Loyce's creativity, and she became drawn into Tchaikovsky's gorgeous music, although she typically leaned on contemporary composers for her choreography. She seriously questioned how she, a barefooted choreographer, could tackle a classical ballet. She wanted to develop a Nutcracker story with a symbiosis of her dance sensitivities—classical ballet blended with contemporary dance. Could she do it, and would the audience like the result? Finally, Loyce told herself, "What the heck? I'm resolved to do my own version of the Nutcracker."[135] She never imagined that one day her local Nutcracker would be considered by many the gold standard of Nutcrackers.

On a postage-stamp-size stage, 12 x 14 feet, with twenty-two performers, *Nutcracker Fantasy* would entertain the audience at The Moppet Players' holiday show. Loyce planned, plotted, and had fun imagining how she would choreograph the story. First, she decided that David Voss, a leading dancer in the company, plus the class accompanist, school assistant, and resident composer, would be perfect as Godfather Drosselmeyer, a pivotal role in the production she imagined. David would dance, "his eyes twinkling with capricious humor, cavorting through the magical shenanigans of Drosselmeyer." From the ballet's opening scene at the home of Judge and Frau Silberhaus to the dual with the ferocious Queen Rat and the Nutcracker, and then the mystical traveling to the Land of Sugar Candy adorned simply with a gossamer billowing of chiffon material, the first *Nutcracker Fantasy* gave intimations of the original story and a larger production to come.

Minnesota Dance Theatre company dancer, ca. 2005. MDT's *Loyce Houlton's Nutcracker Fantasy*, Lise Houlton, Artistic Director. Courtesy of Erik Saulitis, photographer.

After the premiere opening of the *Nutcracker Fantasy* at The Moppet Players Theatre, Allan Holbert of the *Minneapolis Tribune* wrote: "Want to get Christmas spirit in one easy step? . . . Take your children to the *Nutcracker Fantasy* at The Moppet Players Theatre . . . this is one of the best things that has ever happened to the famous ballet."[136] This would be the tone of reviews for the next fifty-plus years. Each year, as confidence grew in staging this classical ballet, Loyce kept enhancing numerous aspects of her Nutcracker and added more balletic choreography to various scenes. As she enhanced her Nutcracker, more accolades and audience numbers were added each year.

One summer in the mid-60s, Richard Cisek, general manager of the Minneapolis Symphony (now the Minneapolis Orchestra), called Loyce and asked if her company would perform the *Nutcracker Fantasy* with the orchestra at Northrop that December. Loyce's immediate response was, "I don't think so. . . . we are too small . . . the children are too tiny . . . we would look lost on that large auditorium stage." And then he added, "Think about it please . . ."[137] Loyce did think about it. She gathered a creative team together and presented her team's thoughts and vision to the Northrop staff. They gave

146

a thumbs up, and *Loyce Houlton's Nutcracker Fantasy* continues to delight large sold-out audiences to this day.

During the 1960s, Loyce also choreographed several pieces for Christian liturgical services and directed and staged three operas. She wrote the libretto for a teenage opera by composer Paul Fetler called *Sturge Maclean*. When the cast sang the final number, "Last Time," lyrics by Keith Richards and Mick Jagger of an emerging rock group known as the Rolling Stones, a howl of approval erupted from the high school audiences.

In 1969, The Contemporary Dance Playhouse caught fire. Nearly all of it burned down, and the top floors of the MDT studios were destroyed. It seemed to have been arson, but nothing was ever confirmed. MDT lost their grand piano, all their early costumes, videotapes, phonograph records, and invaluable piano scores. Loyce said that the total loss was overwhelming, but most importantly, it was empty at the time, and no one was there. It was the birthplace of The Contemporary Dance Playhouse, now the Minnesota Dance Theatre, and the emotional loss could not be estimated by dollar value.

Chronicles. Andrew Thompson with MDT. Choreography by Loyce Houlton. Photography by Paul R. Hagen. Courtesy of the University of Minnesota Libraries, Performing Arts Archives.

SCENE 2

Interims

Minnesota Dance Theatre headed to Kansas City to perform and support the Midwest Regional Dance Festival, an organization promoting efforts to affirm regional dance companies. Loyce had galvanizing conversations, sharing success stories to hard-fought battles. A broad range of people, from dancers to artistic directors, from technical directors to accompanists, and from school directors to dance critics, believed that the Midwest does not need to be a clone of New York City, Europe, or Russia. At the festival, Lise Houlton and Andrew Thompson performed *Wingborne*, and a review of it appeared later in *Dance Magazine* with a full-page photograph. The critic, Rose Ann Thom, wrote, "Miss Houlton like a butterfly emerging from a cocoon . . . Just as we begin to muse on the beauty of a lift, it has vanished. Each movement flows into the next, leaving the viewer a little sad for having lost it so quickly."

The 1970s brought MDT more artistic collaborations with other artists and organizations. Being local and busy, MDT added to the vitality of the Twin Cities arts community. Two invitations to perform at Jacob's Pillow were fantastic opportunities for MDT to see and engage with other dancers and their works. The invitations from Jacob's Pillow's director affirmed that great dance happened in Minnesota, showcased by the choreographic works Loyce created and the excellent technique and versatility of her dancers.

MDT approached a salient mark: ten years of dance, and in Loyce's terms, ten years "of indescribable hard work and moments of great pleasure." Time to celebrate a Decade of Dance and perform repertory from José Limón's *La Malinche* to Marius Petipa's *Raymonda*. *The Nutcracker Fantasy* had helped grow the school by seven hundred students. Looking back, Loyce said, "We had been lucky in love and lucky in sponsorships."[138]

In the midst of winter, the Decade of Dance gala had a smashing success at The O'Shaughnessy Auditorium (now The O'Shaughnessy) on the campus of the College of St Catherine (now St. Catherine University), where Loyce had taught dance. With Muriel Pesek's unswerving allegiance to MDT, she organized Italian fundraising dinners preshow; other volunteers sold tickets to the dinners and the gala performance. All dinners and all tickets for the concert were sold out. Would people cross the great Mississippi River to attend the gala? The river's geographical divide separated Saint Paul and Minneapolis culturally with their distinguishable personalities.

Loyce knew that people came to their Cedar Village Theater from Saint Paul, but would people from Minneapolis go to Saint Paul? Or would December's icy and snowy weather be a good excuse not to go? For that one night, nearly two thousand people came, including these prominent dancers: Eleanor King, her first modern teacher, from New Mexico; Martha Hill, her professor at NYU and head of the Juilliard Dance Division, from New York City; two teachers from the Graham Company also from New York City; and Ted Shawn sent a congratulatory note from Jacob's Pillow. All in all, it was a stupendous success and celebration.

Chronicles. Frances Machala and Ronnie Holbrook with MDT.
Choreography by Loyce Houlton. Photography by Myron Papiz.
Courtesy of the University of Minnesota Libraries, Performing Arts Archives.

SCENE 3
Unforgettable Women

In the summer of 1974, Loyce had reached a low point. Pain-filled sieges from diabetic neuropathy limited her mobility, and her beloved Cedar Village Theater was not faring well. Even though the programs and premieres at the theater were popular, the performance income did not cover all the expenses of rent, utilities, and maintenance. During this angst-filled time, Loyce's friend, Eleanor Steber, an American opera diva also known to Loyce's family as an "Improper Diva" because of her colorful limericks, visited. Eleanor offered to do a benefit concert at Cedar Village Theater. She convinced Loyce to have her company also perform at the benefit. Loyce's *Twisted Tree* intrigued Eleanor, and she wanted Loyce's company to perform it for the benefit.

That night after the benefit performance, Eleanor said, "Loyce, you must do *Knoxville: Summer of 1915*. I will sing it."[139] Eleanor had already recorded the music, and she wished to sing it while Loyce's company performed. In the creation of *Knoxville: Summer of 1915*, Eleanor and Loyce spent many luscious hours with the prose poem in the preamble of James Agee's Pulitzer Prize-winning book, *A Death in the Family*. Eleanor commissioned Samuel Barber to compose music to this prose poem. Agee's words, a dream-like depiction of an evening in the American South, spoke strongly to Loyce. Eleanor's singing would "sweep Loyce back to 1915 and into the world of 'strawberries, pasteboard and starched milk' . . . or 'streetcars raising their iron horns.'"

Knoxville: Summer of 1915 premiered as a special event for America's two-hundredth birthday. Stunning reviews for *Knoxville* came out from newspapers on both sides of the Mississippi, declaring it "triumphant," "an outstanding work," and "regional brilliance."[140] Loyce said that many called *Knoxville: Summer of 1915* an American gem. The bicentennial year was a headliner year for Loyce and MDT. Loyce created two exquisite works that remain in MDT's repertory—*Knoxville: Summer of 1915* and *Carmina Burana*. (In March 2022, MDT celebrated its sixtieth season at The O'Shaughnessy in Saint Paul with a program titled *Early Spring—Masterworks Old & New* with *Knoxville: Summer of 1915* on the program.)

Another prominent and unforgettable woman, who graced Loyce's home and the MDT studios, was Margot Fonteyn. A promotional campaign for her autobiography brought her to the Twin Cities. Margot attended the morning company classes, and after each class, Loyce and Margot chatted.

A *pas de deux* from *Le Corsaire* performed by Margot Fonteyn and Rudolf Nureyev, 1962.
Photography by Leslie Spatt (London).

Margot always had a piece of chocolate at that time. One morning Margot told Loyce that there were hundreds of dancers who could lift their legs higher than hers. Loyce saw that "Her naturalness and lack of egotism was part of her endearing personality . . . She was a vision of artistry and verified it constantly with her demeanor and dress."

Dayton's book division was included in Margot Fonteyn's autobiography campaign. Mike Raskin, the vice president of the Dayton-Hudson Corporation and a go-getter on MDT's board of directors, invited Loyce and her husband to a special autographing dinner party at his home in North Oaks. Margot asked Mike to also invite Lóránt and Anna Andaházy to the dinner. Margot knew them well from their performing and touring years as professional dancers with the Ballets Russes. The Houltons, the Andaházys, and Margot Fonteyn were chauffeured together by limousine to the Raskin family home. The conversation during the ride covered pleasant and fascinating ballet reminiscences. The dinner was scrumptious, and the table conversation delightful. Margot was quite fatigued, so they decided to head home earlier than planned. The Houltons, Margot, and the Andaházys were chauffeured homeward, holding onto indelible memories of dinner with an unforgettable prima ballerina.

Variation:
Shatterings

In 1974 many exquisite works emanated from Loyce's stream of creative energy, but these triumphs were vexed by eradicable shatterings. A crazed man entered MDT's Cedar Village Theater and exploded two Molotov cocktails—one in the middle of the stage and the other up in the technical booth near the projectors. Both blew up but caused minimal damage. Again, like the fire at The Contemporary Dance Playhouse, no one was there. The arsonist was found and arrested. He explained that by destroying the theater, he would stop anti-religious and sinful movies and dance.

Loyce also lost her two favorite muses: leading dancers Lise Houlton and Dana Luebke; MDT endured more negative reviews than positive; and the board of directors made the decision to give up the Cedar Village Theater—their valued performing space—for fiscal reasons. The standard of excellence for a nonprofit board of directors is fiduciary responsibility, which includes raising funds necessary for operation. Loyce's board of directors were not able to acquire the additional sources of revenue needed to keep the Cedar Village Theater.

When the Playhouse burned down, MDT's school had moved to a Masonic temple located at Fourth Street SE and Central Avenue in a depressed area near downtown Minneapolis. The two-story building with Masonic architectural beauty had plenty of open spaces, a two-story auditorium, and three magnificent studios that could double as small theaters—a much-needed space since they no longer had the Cedar Village Theater for performances. One of Loyce's favorite board members, Mike Raskin, informed her that another Masonic temple on Hennepin Avenue in downtown Minneapolis had "For Rent" notices on the building.

Loyce did not feel that they needed to move, but with her husband, Bill, and St. John, they decided to look at the space.

Variation:
Escapades in HCA and in Germany

This old Masonic temple on Hennepin Avenue had a sense of largesse and grandeur, but it was disgustingly filthy and "derelict," as Loyce said, yet they could see through the disastrous mess to the possibilities of ample studio and performing space. Raskin's timing was perfect! Soon another owner bought the Masonic building on Fourth Street. "Wham! MDT was kicked out of their studios."[141] Thus began another move to another space. The temple needed renovation, restoration, and sanitation efforts. Hearkening back to when Loyce took possession of the Cedar Theater, MDT once again channeled their grit and efforts to make a new home for their art.

A headline in one newspaper said, "Masonic Temple gets New Life," and the city garnered funding for its part in the temple getting a new life. During the whole renovation process, Loyce's creative energies never stopped. St. John asked her one time, "Do you ever sleep? Not much was her reply."[142] With the brilliant restoration of this building on the corner of Sixth and Hennepin completed, the city christened it the Hennepin Center for the Arts. Loyce pondered, "Where are other artists?" The rent had escalated, making it difficult for many artists to rent studios there. Ah, evanescent space . . . the forever-need and quest for artists.

In their own space, and with the financial success of Loyce's *Nutcracker Fantasy*, the MDT Board of Directors approved an invitation from the artistic director of the Deutsche Oper Ballet for Loyce to choreograph a new work based on the Tristan and Isolde legend, a famous medieval love-romance with Celtic roots. Loyce enjoyed working with professional companies and looked forward to this artistic and educational exchange of ideas. Loyce traveled to West Berlin and set the choreography for the work she named *Tristan*. The premiere at the Berlin Oper Haus received bravos, applause, and booing. Loyce learned that "the highly charged German audiences" would give equal amounts of bravos and boos.

155

Concerto Barocco. Michelle Haugen and Erin Thompson (left to right). Choreography by George Balanchine. Music by J.S. Bach. Photography by Dan Seifert. Courtesy of the University of Minnesota Libraries, Performing Arts Archives.

Variation:
An Arduous Journey to Balanchine

When Loyce rehearsed with Nina Fonaroff's dance company in the Balanchine School studios in New York City, at rehearsal breaks she would sometimes go and watch Mr. Balanchine rehearse his company in the larger studio. Loyce was fascinated with Balanchine's rehearsal process. She tucked away many moments of what she saw for later ruminations; later became imagining works by George Balanchine, of Russian heritage, in MDT's repertoire.

Ever reaching beyond its studio walls and open to all kinds of possible collaborations, MDT became part of the University of Minnesota Art Gallery's plans for a major exchange of Russian visual and performing arts, with invitations sent to MDT and other institutions to participate. She saw how a Russian exchange of art would be the turnkey for the Balanchine Trust to approve MDT's desire to stage a Balanchine ballet.

After a journey to Moscow and Saint Petersburg, as part of her preparation for MDT's involvement with the Russian Cultural Exchange, Loyce was on a creative roll and MDT had just been declared a Twin Cities major arts organization. Timing is everything, and Loyce's request for the ballet *Concerto Barocco* from the Balanchine Trust was affirmed, and this ballet would be taught to the MDT company by a Balanchine associate. When the Northrop's curtain raised on opening night for *Concerto Barocco*

George Balanchine, renovator of American ballet, ca. 1950s. Courtesy of Bridgeman Images.

and revealed a black scrim and dancers dressed only in white tunic rehearsal costumes, lights, and tights *à la Balanchine*, the audience applauded spontaneously—a perfect opening to Bach's Double Violin Concerto in D Minor and the quintessential Balanchine choreography from 1941. In the late '70s, three other Balanchine ballets requested, granted, taught, and learned by her company eventually took the stage in Minneapolis. *Allegro Brillante*, *Serenade*, and *Four Temperaments* added exceptional works to the MDT repertoire.

"Swan Lake Minnesota," *Twin Cities Reader*, June 13, 1984.
Courtesy of the University of Minnesota Libraries, Performing Arts Archives.

Variation:
Extraordinary People

"In the midst of new friends, old friends and collaborations, there came upon me a handsome young prince . . . Peter Markle."[143] Markle had been commissioned to select a Minnesota artist and film the person in a series called "Encounters with Minnesota Artists." For several weeks Peter and his crew worked inconspicuously following Loyce and her dancers in the studios, rehearsals, and theaters. Peter's camera and lens were his eyes absorbing the creative process of Loyce and MDT. He constantly remained by Loyce. The result: Reality firsthand.

Mike Steele reviewed the film *Loyce* in the morning *Tribune*, ". . . Scenes of Houlton working hard in the studio, creating contemplatively at home, teaching in the school, running her dancers through rugged rehearsals . . . all expose an equally vulnerable but determined and tough lady pursuing a vision."[144] In *Loyce*, there were no extra processes like background lighting or technology tricks. The film exposed both the grace of dance and the grit to do it.

Another filmmaker, Kenneth Robins, approached Loyce for his vision of *Swan Lake, Minnesota*, destined to be an out-of-the-usual classical production of *Swan Lake*. It would be MDT's first television work. With some recent bad press and the board taking a vote to fire Loyce because she was "unfundable," the board's majority did vote to keep her.

Loyce then approached *Swan Lake, Minnesota* with a will to persevere.

The scenes for the film were shot in the wildest of venues for a ballet shoot: a chicken coop at a farm commune, an eroded barn overgrown with weeds and bushes, and a TV talk show with Houlton's four dogs. The dancers, Swan Ladies, performed in cow stanchions fluttering their wings, floating on inner tubes, and riding bales of hay on a conveyor belt. With Loyce's recent reproaches from her board of directors and some bad press, she had heightened apprehension the day of the private showing. At the end of the film, the MDT staff at the showing were stunned; the film went way beyond their wildest imaginings. *Swan Lake, Minnesota* was a smashing hit and positive reviews hailed from local newspapers to *Vogue* magazine to the *New York Times* to the *Wall Street Journal* to the *Christian Science Monitor*. To top it off, *Time-Life* named *Swan Lake, Minnesota* as one of the best video films of the year.

Another extraordinary person who came unbelievably into MDTs life at this time was Prince. He had chosen one of MDT's jazz teachers, Johnny Command, to teach movement and choreography to him and his group, The Revolution. Since Johnny was on the MDT faculty, Prince used the MDT studios for rehearsals. With Loyce's constant financial dilemmas, she decided to take a risk and ask Prince if he would do a benefit concert

Prince and Loyce Houlton. An MDT benefit event at First Avenue in Minneapolis, ca. 1984. Photography by Allan Beaulieu. Courtesy of the University of Minnesota Libraries, Performing Arts Archives.

for MDT. Miracle of miracles—he said, "Yes," and plans for the benefit event went into an energized high gear.

First Avenue was an obvious choice for the venue and for the group that would front Prince—MDT dancers, of course. For their show, Loyce chose two classical pieces that would be performed first, and to close the program, she received Prince's permission to use a song from his *Prince 1999* album. Loyce selected DMSR (dance, music, sex, romance), and one verse read, "All I want to do is dance/Play music, sex, romance." DMSR was the closing piece for the MDT dancers. Most of this song had inappropriate words for a general audience, but its rhythm and pulse drew increased excitement from the crowd, ready for the big act to follow.

When the curtains finally opened and Prince stepped out on stage, coiffed and costumed to the hilt in his high-heeled boots, the audience applauded without restraint. He began singing some songs he created and composed for his forthcoming movie, *Purple Rain*. Prince did not do anything outrageous, but he did dance sensually—like Nijinsky in *Afternoon of a Faun*. Unlike the Parisian audience when pandemonium broke out as the audience reacted viscerally with shouting, booing, and stamping feet to Nijnski's performance, the First Avenue audience cheered Prince again and again.

Prince exited the stage, but the continuous applause with shouts of "Encore" called him back. Loyce stepped up to the microphone and said, "He's not just a Prince—he's a King!" Prince ran to Loyce, and with a hug, she gave him a bouquet of roses and a single purple rose.

Variation:
Fini! (The Purge)

In 1985, Loyce made a humbling decision that she could no longer be the artistic director of MDT. She felt that she no longer had the funding pipeline needed to maintain the company and its repertoire at the level that already had been achieved. She selected a formal retirement date: June 1, 1987—covering MDT's twenty-five years of growth and glory, shatterings, and sadness. Loyce suggested that she sit on a search committee to find her replacement and that she would want to continue to teach and choreograph for the company. Loyce brought a potential search committee together at her home comprising the president of the board of directors, a board member (the loyal Edward Holmberg), the director of the school, the company's leading dancer, and St. John.

An ominous presentiment pervaded the meeting, and a mysterious undercurrent of hidden agendas seemed to flow under the strange ambiance. The idea of forming a search committee fell on deaf ears.

In October 1986, Loyce produced what would be her last MDT program. The varied program offerings were top-notch with a stellar lineup of guest artists: Jory Hancock from Pacific Northwest Ballet, Kevin MacKenzie and Martine van Hamel from ABT, and her daughter Lise Houlton. The audience attendance was pathetic, the preconcert receptions were miserable, decimating factors involved with the program, and

jaded critical reviews were written—such a contrast to MDT's history of remarkable performances and positive critics' reviews.

Soon after the disastrous program, on October 27, the Board of Directors summoned Loyce to a meeting that day. Loyce sensed a dark foreshadowing of change. She had coffee that morning with two friends from Pacific Northwest Ballet, Kent Stowell and Francia Russell. They asked Loyce how things were going for MDT. "Loyce answered flippantly, 'I think I will soon be fired.'"[145] Nor did Loyce know that these two friends were chosen to replace her. Were they aware of this? History remains silent. Loyce found out that her premonition was right-on. Sitting at the Board of Directors' meeting and facing many directors she did not know, they exhibited no spirit of leadership, enthusiasm, or openness. Loyce felt gagged from discussing her ideas. "An icy realization came over me. My art, my life at Minnesota Dance Theatre, was over. Somehow, they had removed me. I was fired."

After that painful and shocking day, Loyce decided on silence. In her silent retreat, unexpected phone calls came from other artistic directors who had been, as Loyce said, "decapitated from their companies . . . heads were flying off everywhere. It was like another French Revolution." John Linnerson, St. John, resigned in protest from the Board of Directors and expressed his rage in this poem on October 28, 1986:

Yesterday I became part of a mob, a democratic mob, that
Without delay or deliberation voted to save MDT from its founder Loyce Houlton.
It is a great power the mob has to deny time, the mob cannot wait
but demands an answer to the question NOW.
The mob sweeps everyone along, the vote is unanimous.
The strongest opposition is abstention.
Then comes confusion . . .

Loyce's charisma and creative force have influenced and shaped innumerable dance artists, musicians, theater personnel, donors, and audiences. Dance—Loyce's life-giving passion—boldly lives on through her family, as carriers *of this kind of eternal life.*

Katie Johnson, MDT company dancer from 2008 to 2018. Image used for MDT's school. Courtesy of Erik Saulitis, photographer.

Marcia Haydée and Richard Cragun with the Stuttgart Ballet in *Romeo and Juliet*.
Photography by Hannes Kilian.

Coda: Artists' Stories

Lise Houlton: Minnesota Dance Theatre, Artistic Director (Interview 7/9/21)

Lise spoke at length with fondness and admiration for her mother, and many of her mother's stories that she shared during the interview are mentioned in Loyce's memoirs, *Twilight Tales*...

For me, I wouldn't need a title. I am just happy helping dancers thrive and seeing the young ones fall in love with dance as a performing art. Our school was called The Contemporary Dance Playhouse—"contemporary" to be in the "now." The name was changed to Minnesota Dance Theatre to improve funding.

What I remember most as a little one is taking classes in Dinkytown at the Playhouse. We were not just inspired; we were fulfilled. David Voss and my mother taught such creative classes—full of imagery, learning and talking about music, doing locomotive patterns—a traveling barre across the floor. We were having so much fun and always excited for Saturday morning class, learning much without realizing it. David Voss had extraordinary talent, and he was a great colleague working alongside my mother, full of laughter, music, love, and joy. As Drosselmeyer, he was magical. Sadly, he died of complications from AIDS in the early '90s.

Another important dancer in MDT's history, and important to me, was Bobby Crabb, an early member of the company, and a great man, dancer, and partner. When I was thirteen years old, Rochelle Zide-Booth set the ballet *La Fille Mal Gardée* on us. I was Lisette and I danced with Bobby. He was often my partner in my youth, and I learned so much from him.

I have fond memories of three comments when I was at ABT in my first season: Antony Tudor came up to me and said, "You listen to everything I say." Confused, of course I listened to everything he said. And then Mikhail Baryshnikov (Misha) followed Tudor's statement and told me, "He just gave you a compliment." Tudor also once told Loyce, "I'm so glad you went through the pain of childbirth to give me your daughter."

I danced for the Stuttgart Ballet; Glen Tetley invited me to join. When I walked into the studio, I asked a friend who is this Marcia Haydée? In the corner this rather plain woman came out to dance the ballet *Voluntaries* and never had I seen such exquisite artistry and dance. She made magic, and I learned that she was Marcia Haydée, one of the great ballerinas of the post-World War II era. (She danced into the 1980s, and is still alive and working.) In the early 1960s, she and John Cranko laid the foundation of Stuttgart Ballet in Germany. For Glen Tetley, use of the back and torso were salient aspects of his choreography. He asked me when I first met him, "Do you remember when you were a bird?" I pass this thought on to my students and dancers. That question was invaluable information for Glen's aesthetic. If they understand it, God bless them. They will be better dancers.

I danced for Stuttgart from 1974 to 1976. When Glen Tetley and Scott Douglas transitioned out, I did as well and came home to have foot surgery, heal, and then dance as the Sugar Plum Fairy in my mother's Nutcracker.

Earthsong. Bobby Crabb and Lise Houlton. Choreography by Loyce Houlton. Photography by Myron Papiz. Courtesy of the University of Minnesota Libraries, Performing Arts Archives.

Loyce's memories of Lise:
Twilight Tales, Volume Two, 'Lise'

Lise was a quiet student. She always put herself in the back row of the class and the last line to travel across the floor. That choice bothered me because she was so excellent, but we were mother and daughter, and we both felt the pressure of it. Her beauty was there in her long neck, those delicate long arms and legs, and in her face. She had a charisma that touched all who knew her. Though her personality was quiet, her learning of choreography, its steps and movements, was at lightning speed.

By the time Lise was fifteen, it was off to Italy with the company. Featured in my *Terminal Point* and Michael Uthoff's *pas de deux*, *Serenata Danzante*, she took the stage in Jacob's Pillow and Spoleto, Italy. While in Italy, Glen Tetley taught her the principal female role in *Mythical Hunters*, with Scott Douglas there to coach and to add his intellect and care to Glen's magic.

It was in 1971 that Lise's career took a strong leap forward. Markell Brooks, our dear friend and longtime loyal patron, had died. I immediately called Lise and Andrew Thompson into the studio. In a burst of inspiration, we created *Wingborne*. It ultimately became my signature work. When I began creating *Ancient Aire* (the first act of my *Dream Trilogy*), I chose Lise and Andrew to portray the roles that would be so sculptural and austere yet filled with innocent sensuality and love. Lise's jasmine-scented young body gave the most artistic sensitivity to what was called "intercourse beautifully evoked on the cavernous stage of the Northrop."

Lise went to New York City to improve her classical training and then on to Germany and Stuttgart Ballet. Glen Tetley and Scott Douglas were holding the top reins in place of the brilliant John Cranko, who died suddenly. Not long after Glen and Scott left the Stuttgart Ballet, Lise came home. It was a gift of fate for me. Lise and Andrew danced in my *Romeo and Juliet* and in *Earthsong*.

Two weeks before a matinee performance of Sir Frederick Ashton's *The Sleeping Beauty, Act III* with the Minneapolis Symphony Orchestra and a promised full house at the Northrop, Glen Tetley called for Lise. He asked her to come and make her debut with American Ballet Theatre in his *Sphinx*. Martine van Hamel was slated to perform the role but had injured her ankle, and Glen wanted Lise to take her place. Anna Kisselgoff wrote in the *New York Times*, "To make a debut with a major company as a principal when one has not even been seen with it as a soloist is not an everyday experience."

Lise was offered a contract with ABT. She was promoted quickly through the ranks and danced mostly principal roles in the repertoire. For Lise's seven years with ABT, she was seen brilliantly as a principal dancer in several ballets by renowned choreographers, such as Antony Tudor, Sir Kenneth MacMillan, Glen Tetley, George

Balanchine, Mikhail Baryshnikov, and Lynne Taylor-Corbett. Lise was a virtuosa dancer. In 1985 Lise resigned from ABT; she foresaw a change in her ballet journey.

Loyce Houlton's twilight years faded into her passing on March 14, 1995, and Lise assumed directorship of Minnesota Dance Theatre.

Daniel Freeman: Musicologist, Accompanist, and Lecturer at the University of Minnesota since 1992 (Interview 6/15/21)

Daniel is an incredible musician and arts scholar. When conversing with him, he carries you away to a different place. You no longer feel Minnesota-grounded. Instead, Prague and Mozart greet you; you are on the grand escalier of the Paris Opéra; you have traveled back in history attending a Ballets Russes performance in 1952 Minneapolis; you are with Bill and Loyce Houlton in Spoleto, Italy, attending a performance at the Teatro Nuovo of *Mythical Hunters*.

Yes, Daniel is a consummate artist, brilliant, and completely charming. He has been a stellar accompanist for many ballet schools in Minnesota, primarily in the Twin Cities. Ballet students have enjoyed his accompaniment, and danced better because of it, at these studios: University of Minnesota, Classical Ballet Academy with Cheryl and Andy Rist, Ballet Arts, the Andaházy School of Classical Ballet, and Minnesota Dance Theatre.

Daniel's repertoire comprises a trove of marvelous classical music scores for the piano. He described three kinds of accompanists: 1) classically trained but too small of a repertoire for each of the ballet exercises; 2) improvising in one musical style; 3) and those who mix classical music with a varied repertoire of improvisation. Also, he understands that if accompanists use music that is rhythmically complicated, dancers may have trouble articulating the exercise with the music. Daniel also stated that it is difficult

Daniel Freeman. Photography by Gary Salazar. Courtesy of Daniel E. Freeman.

Daniel Freeman playing the piano in the Grand Salon of the French Embassy in Prague, 2014.
Photography by Christopher Schout. Courtesy of Daniel E. Freeman.

to accompany well when neither the teacher nor the students acknowledge that you are there. As the students enter the studio or rehearsal hall and acknowledge the accompanist, Daniel feels that it is a good beginning. When the teacher physically demonstrates a ballet exercise and verbally speaks the meter and counts, the accompanist can then choose the appropriate music.

Daniel tries to consistently project a positive attitude about the class—no matter what is artistically happening or not and to show respect for the teacher. Then the class accompanist will garner their own artistic reward. Whenever everything comes together in a ballet class the way that it should, there is an emotional rush that a pianist cannot experience in any other way. It is utterly unique and wonderful; the music moves through the dancers' bodies, then the dancers move.

Daniel had some of his most memorable and enjoyable experiences when he accompanied for Lise Houlton. When he first met her, he did not "know her from Adam." Daniel was quickly drawn into her sense of musicality for each exercise, at the barre or in center work. He saw that she set an emotional mood that accompanied each step. Lise's vivid way of describing the exercise and how they were to match the step was "inspirational and wildly erudite for him." His time spent accompanying Lise's classes endeared him forever to her and MDT. Every year during the holidays, the State Theatre will find Daniel and several of his friends gathered to enjoy *Loyce Houlton's Nutcracker Fantasy*. Daniel says he is always governed by sentiment and nostalgia. A veritable artist he is.

Andrew Thompson: Dance Artist, Ballet Teacher and Choreographer; and Jocelyn Lasban Thompson, Dance Artist, Colorado Ballet-Interim Artistic Director (Interview 9/15/21)

Andrew began his interview by saying, "I love to dance, teach, and choreograph. Given any chance, I'd do any of them." He continued his interview with clarity of dates and an incredible dance résumé.

Born in California, his family moved to Rochester, Minnesota, in 1961 when he was eleven years old. Once they settled in Rochester, his family learned of a ballet school directed by Bernard John Edward Johansen (Bud/Buddy Johansen). Johansen trained and danced with the Andaházys. He was a lead dancer in their company, Ballet Borealis, but when Marius Andaházy became the lead male dancer, Johansen moved to Rochester, Minnesota, and founded his School of Classical Ballet.

When Andrew's family arrived in Rochester in 1961, Johansen's ballet school was in his home, and his wife, Nancy, was the accompanist on their piano. Andrew's sister started taking ballet with Bud Johansen, and eventually the entire family began taking ballet—his mother (painter, singer, dancer) and all four siblings. Andrew wanted to quit ballet.

When Moscow Ballet arrived in Minneapolis in 1963, Andrew's sister and brother auditioned for the children's cast of Asaf Messerer's *Ballet School.* Andrew stayed home, reading a book under the backyard pine tree. His mother told him, "I'll make a deal with you: Try ballet for six months, and

if you still want to quit, I'll let you. I don't want you to make a decision that may change your life." During that time, "I got addicted."

Andrew's "addiction" to ballet took him to Minneapolis and Loyce Houlton's The Contemporary Dance Playhouse in the late 1960s. For eighteen years, he danced with MDT. He remembers Rochelle Zide-Booth and her brilliant classes and photographic memory. Rochelle was "seminal in my career," Andrew exclaimed. In the ballet *La Fille Mal Gardée*, Rochelle asked the men dancers who could jump well and do an *entrechat six*. Andrew executed that difficult step excellently and was then cast as the "Butterfly Boy." Other guest teachers—Françoise Martinet and Madame Perry—continued to ignite Andrew's desire to dance. He met Jocelyn at MDT where they began dating in 1977 and were married in 1984. Jocelyn quickly learned choreography and steps. Her career was launched after she took over a role for an injured dancer, and Loyce asked, "Who knows the part?" Jocelyn quickly answered, "I can do it!"

Andrew fondly remembers "the choreography for Loyce's Nutcracker . . . I loved creating magic as Drosselmeyer and becoming a Prince Charming as the Cavalier. Both roles were spectacular and so difficult . . . Loyce's Nutcracker is a work of genius." He also shared that some of their "forever friends" are still the MDT dancers. . . It was a great company, and it is a great sadness that it folded . . . We loved MDT and would have stayed there forever."

They did not stay in Minneapolis, but they did forever remain dancers, ballet teachers, choreographers, and guest teachers. Their ballet and contemporary expertise took them to several companies. As professional dancers, they became itinerant dance artists for a little over two years: Ballet Michigan, South Carolina Ballet Theater in its capital city, Columbia, which folded in four months, Delta Ballet in New Orleans, and then the Tampa Ballet in Florida. While in Tampa, they danced for Colorado Ballet, and for two years, they went between Tampa and Denver, finally settling in Denver. During their peripatetic lives, they had storage in three cities: Saginaw, Michigan; Denver, Colorado; and Tampa, Florida.

Andrew and Jocelyn made their home in Denver and danced with Colorado Ballet for eighteen years, from 1989 to 2007. They currently live in Las Vegas, helping care for Jocelyn's elderly parents. They continue to keep their "toes in ballet," teaching once a week in Las Vegas as guest teachers and Andrew as a guest artist in the International Youth Ballet's Nutcracker.

Deidre Kellogg: Dance Artist at Minnesota Dance Theatre; Co-founder of *The City Children's Nutcracker* (Interview 3/12/21)

The Saturday morning Creative Workshop remains in Deidre's memories as her favorite class when she was a young dancer, about ten years old. The class, combining ballet and contemporary, lasted two-and-half hours of energetic fun and imagination. It was a most intriguing children's class. Loyce told them she did not want gestures and imitations; she wanted the children to move to the "essence of the animal or object." Deidre remembers having fun becoming a ringworm or an amoeba.

Loyce would tell the dancers, "Leave your problems in your dance bag at the door." She wanted them totally immersed in the music, movement, and creative energy.

Some of the first company dancers stand out for Deidre. They were Marcia Chapman, David Voss, Susan Thompson, Becky Stanchfield, and Marianne Simons. As she got older, Deidre recognized the Mississippi River's cultural divide, but she totally enjoyed dancing at MDT and thought it was the best in the Twin Cities.

In 1991, Bonnie Mathis and Marcia Chapman moved Ballet Arts, their first school, located across the Hennepin Avenue Bridge, to the same building as MDT—the Hennepin Center for the Arts. Deidre placed her dance energies at Ballet Arts. She stopped her performing career when her multiple sclerosis got worse. Deidre continued teaching at Ballet Arts and was the head of its Contemporary Dance Department. In 1992, Kathy Thurber, a member of the Minneapolis City Council, approached Deidre with the idea of a city children's Nutcracker based on an Atlanta, Georgia, model. In collaboration with the Minneapolis Park and Recreation Board, Bonnie, Marcia, Deidre, and Kathy Thurber co-created *The City Children's Nutcracker*. As an outreach to children who do not have many opportunities to take dance or ballet classes, this project gave city children a chance to be in a holiday Nutcracker performance with avant-garde choreography and scenes. It had a successful ten-year run in the Twin Cities.

With Loyce's death in 1995, followed by Bonnie Mathis leaving Ballet Arts for Boston in 2005, there was a merge of Ballet Arts and Minnesota Dance Theatre to form a new organization called The Dance Institute. With this dramatic change, Deidre stopped her dancing career. The Dance Institute eventually became only Minnesota Dance Theatre—continuing MDT's long history, a professional company, and a vibrant school. Deidre also enjoyed working with competitive and elite figure skaters, teaching ballet off ice and choreographing programs on ice. She continued this work until her MS became too much of a deterrent—about 2013.

Patty Wolkoff: Early Years as an MDT Dancer
(Interview 10/5/21)

From Duluth, I traveled down to the Twin Cities in 1958 to begin my freshman year at the University of Minnesota. I met Loyce Houlton at the U of M and became involved in its Orchesis, a national organization of dance in collegiate departments of physical education. We took classes at The Contemporary Dance Playhouse. I performed in her first holiday show, *Madeline's Christmas*. I was cast as Santa Claus. Loyce and I would laugh because I was a Jewish girl playing Santa Claus.

We did modern dance, and Loyce would talk about her time in New York City with the Martha Graham School. She encouraged us young dancers to go to NYC and study Martha Graham's style. At the end of the school year, we would gather in the Playhouse kitchen and just talk. Her husband, Bill, was a modest man, Loyce's backbone and incredible supporter. Bill came to every performance, and together they raised their family in a "big home" in Prospect Park, Saint Paul. Franny, their live-in housekeeper, was an intelligent, beautiful soul. She also took dance classes from Loyce.

I am grateful for that time in my life and to have had the opportunity to meet so many people. I got to perform; I love performing. I loved learning about space, time, and movement. Viscerally, I can see Loyce in my memories. MDT and dancing for Loyce was my life.

With the Sunday *New York Times*, the first section I turn to is the "Arts" to see what people are doing in dance. My granddaughter danced at Saint Paul City Ballet—a beautiful, young dancer. She lives in Chicago now, working on her master's degree in Special Needs Education. But I told her, don't ever stop dancing!

Because of dancing, I developed a good work ethic, personal responsibility, and how to hold multiple perspectives at once.

Artist Charles Gilbert Kapsner, *River IV*, 11 x 14 inches, oil on cherry wood panel, 2016.
Mill Park in Little Falls, Minnesota, looking east across the Mississippi River to the
Laura Jane Musser Estate. Courtsey of the Saulitis Family.

Entr'Acte:
Both Sides of the
Mississippi

Bonnie Mathis in *Madrigalesco* by Benjamin Harkarvey, ca. 1968.
Photography by Marcus Bleckman. Courtesy of Bonnie Mathis.

SCENE 1
Ballet Arts Minnesota

Bonnie Mathis: Dance Artist, Co-founder of Ballet Arts Minnesota (Interview 8/3/21)

When Bonnie Mathis was seventeen years old, she attended the Juilliard School of Dance in New York City. Inspirational teaching artists during her tenure at the Juilliard were Antony Tudor, Maggie Black, and José Limón. She performed as a principal dancer for American Ballet Theatre and as a soloist with the Harkness Ballet in New York City. With the Harkness Ballet, she toured the United States, France, Monaco, Lebanon, and North Africa. Bonnie also performed with many modern dance companies, namely the Lar Lubovitch Company, the Paul Taylor Company, the Paul Sanasardo Company, and the Norman Walker Company and went on to perform with the Nederlands Dans Theater in Holland.

Bonnie brought this exceptionally broad experience as a principal dancer and teacher to Minnesota and became actively involved in the Twin Cities dance community from 1982 to 2005. She taught at Minnesota Dance Theatre for seven years while also teaching at the University of Minnesota. Bonnie vividly recalls teaching an early morning ballet class at the university. She would go into the dark gymnasium and turn on "those gas lights that made an explosive sound." Then slowly, the lights burned brighter, revealing dancers' bodies curled into a fetal position on the hard, cold floor." Class started at 8:00 a.m.—too early for student dancers who may have been up late with studies. Later they had a studio with mirrors, but still a hard, cold floor.

Bonnie Mathis. Photography by Marcus Bleckman. Courtesy of Bonnie Mathis.

In 1986, after Loyce Houlton was "dethroned," as Bonnie stated, she continued teaching at the interim school, Northwest Ballet, along with Marcia Chapman. Bonnie and Marcia joined forces in 1989 and co-founded Ballet Arts Minnesota. Their school, located across the Hennepin Avenue Bridge from downtown Minneapolis in the St. Anthony Main neighborhood, grew quickly.

Eventually, they needed more space, and in 1991 they relocated Ballet Arts to downtown Minneapolis, annexing their space to the Hennepin Center for the Arts. They created an amazing Nutcracker, *The City Children's Nutcracker*, which premiered in 1990 in collaboration with the Minneapolis Park and Recreation Board. Kathie Goodale helped establish this Nutcracker, and she and her husband even danced in the first act. Bob Goodale served on the Ballet Arts Board of Directors. *The City Children's Nutcracker* spoke to the importance, need, and value of ballet outreach in the community. It included dancers from the University of Minnesota, the local dance community, guest artists from Dance Theatre of Harlem, the Greater Twin Cities Youth Symphony, and choreographers such as Danny Buraczeski, Lirena Branitski, and Danny Ezralow.

Bonnie established Springboard Dance, a program where dancers made arrangements with their schools to attend academic classes in the morning and then ballet classes in the early afternoon. That gave the advanced dancers at Ballet Arts an opportunity to work with local and nationally known choreographers and perform their works. In addition to teaching and coaching dancers, Bonnie also created many dance concerts in Minneapolis, supported by grants from the Minnesota State Arts Board. In 1990 she received a Jerome Foundation Travel-Study grant to observe the San Francisco Ballet training and outreach program in the public schools. Bonnie also taught at the Kaatsbaan International Dance Center for the first fifteen years of its Extreme Ballet Program. In 2005, Bonnie joined the Boston Ballet to direct the Boston Ballet II and facilitated their performances in the Boston area and abroad until 2009. She is presently enjoying the consistent blue skies and warm sunshine in Tucson, Arizona.

SCENE 2
James Sewell Ballet

James Sewell: Co-founder, Artistic Director
(Interview 2/22/21)

James Sewell, a young competitive gymnast winning world championships in his early teens, took his first ballet class at the Children's Theatre Company and was hooked. His gymnastic training translated well into ballet, and he took twenty classes a week in Minneapolis. Two years later, James went to New York City, the epicenter of professional ballet companies. At seventeen years old, James attended the American Ballet Theatre's summer program in New York City. ABT invited him to join their Ballet Repertory Company; he accepted the invitation and stayed for one year.

James continued training in New York City for three years at the David Howard School of Ballet (the name changed to David Howard Dance Center in 1977). James attributes his time at David Howard's school for two major changes in his creative life. First, David Howard's belief that movement, instead of a linear shape that moves and then stops, is circular and keeps movement continuing without an end; and the second major influence was meeting Sally Rousse.

It seemed like the city gave James extra energy. He wanted to absorb as much choreography as possible. For two years, while

studying at the School of American Ballet, he was New York City Ballet's flower boy, the person who presents dancers with flowers on stage at the end of a performance. This responsibility allowed him to stay in the stage wings and see "up close and personal" the choreography. He watched Nureyev perform *Don Quixote* ten times, and each time there were subtle choreographic differences. James still clearly sees Nureyev "part-

Dancing with Chess Pieces. James Sewell Ballet. James Sewell in the foreground and Sally Rousse in the background. ca. 1995. Courtesy of Erik Saulitis, photographer.

ing his arms like the Red Sea" and making a completely new movement. James watched nearly every performance from backstage, and many of these found him next to George Balanchine. One time he asked Mr. B. if he would come and see some of his choreography. Mr. B said, "Yes. Talk to my secretary, and I will come and see it." Balanchine did not come. Lincoln Kirstein came in his place.

From 1978 to 1993, James spent fifteen years immersed in NYC's creative energy. He said, "I got what I needed in New York City, and I wanted to put it on our own dancers." When he arrived back home to Minnesota in 1993, "MDT had exploded, and with Pacific Northwest there was no model of a ballet company. There was a hole in the art scene, and I helped to fill this space in the Twin Cities." He started James Sewell Ballet (JSB). Sally was the equal developer and co-founder. "The company would not have existed without her brilliant dancing. All dancers, the artistic directors, and the executive director were all paid the same salary, and men were never paid more than women."

For six years, the JSB company used the studios at the Minnesota Opera Center and enjoyed a wonderful relationship with Kevin

James Sewell Ballet Company, 2012. Courtesy of Erik Saulitis, photographer.

Smith, the executive director of the opera. Then, in 2000, JSB moved to the Hennepin Center for the Arts, occupying studio 2B and developing the TEK BOX as a tool for studio rental and rehearsal space. James believed that the company dancers grew when they experienced other choreographers, and as they grew artistically, they came back to him as better dancers; "I saw fresh things happening with their bodies."

James's ten-year collaboration with the Reif Performing Arts Center in Grand Rapids, Minnesota, arose out of the Reif Center's need for advanced ballet instruction. James also had been questioning if he should have a school. Working with the Reif Center and their students gave James and his dancers the opportunity to teach students, help them choreographically, and give them the opportunity to work with professional dancers. One of the students at the Reif Center apprenticed with JSB for two years and became a company member.

Working with the Reif Center in northern Minnesota aligned with James's interest in touring and reaching people who did not like ballet or had never seen a contemporary ballet company. As a company of six to eight dancers, JSB can tour and push the boundaries of the art form using different music and contemporary themes. James believes showing something different from the traditional classic ballets, such as the *Nutcracker* or *Swan Lake*, "allows people to relate to ballet as a contemporary art form."[146]

The 2020 Covid-19 pandemic drastically challenged the world, as JSB had begun

Rachel Seeholzer with James Sewell Ballet, 2021. Courtesy of Erik Saulitis, photographer.

celebrating "Three Decades of Dance." They planned on touring twelve locations in Minnesota, bringing a repertoire with various works from the past thirty years. Covid stopped all the tours that were planned. And not to be completely crushed by it, they performed a "30th Anniversary Retrospective" in October 2021. As the curtain closed on their Saturday night performance, a murmuring of accolades was heard, such as, "That was unbelievably fantastic," and "I laughed, I cried, I smiled, I was enthralled." "Bravo, James Sewell Ballet!"

Sally Rousse: Fellow Candidate, Dance MFA, Dance Artist, Teacher, Choreographer, Curator, Writer, Advocate Certified in Brain Gym®, Reiki, Zena Rommett Floor-Barre® (Interview 7/10/21)

Sally grew up wanting to be the pristine, elegant, majestic classic ballerina like Margot Fonteyn. I grew up in Vermont, "not the ballet capital of the world." With seven children in her family, there was no extra money for ballet lessons, but her mother somehow made arrangements, and Sally began lessons when she was seven years old. "Ballet lessons were once a week, but it instantly became my identity; it all made sense to me." Sally started later than the other girls, but she was such a mimic that she did well and was thrown into the advance classes without knowing a lot of the basics. This experience made her an excellent ballet student.

When Sally went to the School of American Ballet in New York City, most of the dancers were from wealthy families—"...wealthier than I could ever have imagined. We were living nine people in half of a house, using food stamps." Sally said she never had a sense that they were poor, but looking back, "I can see that I had a frugal upbringing." She had to raise money to attend ballet school in New York City. She remembers that the other girls in the ballet school had several pairs of pointe shoes. She had one pair to get through the summer, and "they were dead in two days." Sally was fourteen when she had this experience.

Sally also struggled with one of the

Strutting with a Guitar. Sally Rousse with James Sewell Ballet, ca. 1995. Courtesy of Erik Saulitis, photographer.

Russian teachers during the summer session. Her accent was difficult to understand, plus Sally did not know all the correct ballet technique terms. "When this teacher said quickly, 'All do a *frappé en croix*,' she stopped the whole class and said to me, 'You do not know what *en croix* is?' I said, 'No.' She then kindly taught it to me and said, 'Now you know it.'" Sally felt mortified, and then she commented reflectively, "You do not try to become a scrappy, rogue ballerina; you just turn out that way."

Sally became an aesthetically strong and beautiful ballet dancer. She danced one year in Europe for the Royal Ballet of Flanders and continued dancing on and off in New York City for fifteen years. Sally met James Sewell in New York City while taking classes at David Howard's studio. Sally had been married when she met James; her husband had died after less than two years of marriage. James introduced Sally to *Four Last Songs* by Richard Strauss—a tender music about love and death—and Sally danced with it later in Belgium. This music helped her heal from the death and short-lived life with her husband.

James and Sally built and established a company in New York City. After only three years, they became known as "an elegant, quirky ballet company." Sally said that they really stood out and apart from other dance

One Hand Up. Sally Rousse with James Sewell Ballet, ca. 1995.
Courtesy of Erik Saulitis, photographer.

companies. Then James and Sally made a big decision and decided to leave New York City and head back to Minnesota, James's home state and home city of Minneapolis. Minnesota Dance Theatre and Loyce's company did not exist anymore. Mike Steele, the dance critic, told them, "You have to come back. There's nothing here."

When they moved back, they were both aware of the tensions that existed between various ballet schools, but they told each other, "We just have to be like Switzerland." And they were. Currently, Sally is in full-time graduate school (Dance MFA) while also teaching at Minnesota Dance Theatre and Lundstrum Performing Arts.

Coda: Artists' Stories

Eve Schulte: JSB Dance Artist, Choreographer, and Executive Director (Interview 6/25/21)

"I did not grow up wanting to be a dancer. I dappled in many things—a synthesis of athleticism, musicality, and theatricality." With this synthesis of movement-based experiences, Eve seemed primed for dance to find her. Once Eve started dancing, she found that dance-making always moved her brain: "I constantly want to learn and explore new things." Her dance career began with MDT in 2006 until 2009 when she joined James Sewell Ballet, which has been incredible, especially her interaction with so many people.

When George Sutton approached Eve, saying that he considered advocating for her as the next JSB executive director, Eve replied, "No way! Then I began to reconsider." Eve was thirty-three years old and said that she was "squarely in between dance-related careers." She did reconsider, and this is what James said about her in the executive director position: "One needs to be mobile and adjust quickly as an ED. Plus, Eve understands the ballet world. It's also good to have a woman as an ED, and Eve is youthful, understands the artistic work, and how to talk about it."

Ballet, she says, can be applied to so many other dance forms, and in any dance form, one needs to dance with the music, not to it. Eve recognizes that ballet has its history of white supremacy and being elitist . . . "but there are so many ways to also move people with being ballet trained." Eve speaks highly of MDT's training, calling it stellar ballet training that truly values both ballet and contemporary. And, quoting Loyce Houlton, "Bigger, better, more!" The MDT teachers that influenced Eve the most were Toni Pierce, Jennifer Bader, and Abdo Sayegh Rodríguez. "I do not consider myself a ballet artist, but it

Strobo. Eve Schulte with James Sewell Ballet, 2012. Courtesy of Erik Saulitis, photographer.

is the bedrock of my training. Now when I teach, I tell the students or dancers to send your roots into the ground so that your limbs can reach longer. I remember that from when I was ten years old." Eve believes cross-training can help ballet dancers "get on your leg in order to get off your leg, and vice versa."

Her personal goals are two: 1. Bringing more world-class choreographers to our local scene, and 2. Connecting more Minnesotans to dance. Contemporary ballet touches on all things that Eve loves—singing, physicality, theatricality, and working with tough subjects.

Tension. Penny Freeh with James Sewell Ballet, ca. 1999. Courtesy of Erik Saulitis, photographer.

Penelope Freeh: Dance Artist and Educator
(Interview 6/28/21)

Penny hails from Dayton, Ohio, where she trained and danced from 1978 to 1988. Penny said it had been the perfect place for her ballet training because of the incredible teachers in a nurturing environment where everyone's body type was accepted, and what each person could bring to the class was emphasized. Penny said that she became a dancer because she became confident in her own abilities.

In 1988, she graduated early from high school and began her dancing career as an apprentice with the Dayton Ballet Company. She then moved to New York City and continued training at the Joffrey Ballet School and landed a scholarship to attend The Ailey School. Penny states that she had ballet every day and her teachers valued what ballet could do to broaden the dancers' vocabulary, not only for ballet but also for modern and contemporary dance. As Penny reflected on her experience and time spent with the James Sewell Ballet company, she dreamed of being welcomed into a company that resembled her training environment. JSB was that company.

Penny is a versatile dancer. She dances in the contemporary landscape but can still wear pointe shoes for a different choreographic look. She holds tight to her ballet aesthetic and is rooted in its pedagogical syllabus. She now teaches young ballet students not to necessarily become ballerinas or danseurs, but to help them see how ballet can empower them in their dance—a reciprocity that also empowers her in her contemporary work.

In 2019, Penny completed her MFA in Dance at Hollins University; she also attended its study abroad program in Germany, concentrating on pedagogy. Then Covid-19 hit, but she stated that "retirement is not in my vocabulary. In many ways, I want to deepen the pedagogy I'm doing. I want to be part of a core faculty in a higher educational institution, but I do not want to lose my artistic endeavors. I want a good balance being a dance artist and a dance educator." Penny teaches ballet at the University of Minnesota and Saint Olaf College while maintaining a contemporary choreographic practice.

Pull-back. Penny Freeh with James Sewell Ballet, ca. 1999. Courtesy of Erik Saulitis, photographer.

L'Après-Midi d'un Faune. Andrew Lester as the Faune, 2007. Choreography by Phillip Carman for Saint Paul City Ballet. Courtesy of Louis Wendling, photographer.

Andrew "Drew" Lester: Performing Dance Artist, Visual Artist, Choreographer, and Teaching Artist (Interview 10/5/2021)

Andrew states that he was always an artist. He remembers when his father took him as an eleven-year-old to an audition in Brainerd, Minnesota, for Central Lakes Community College's production of *A Midsummer Night's Dream*. He made it, and the dancing scenes in the play sparked his desire to dance more. Andrew had an affinity for dance and movement, apparent to the theater's director, who told his parents about Andrew's natural talent for dance and performance.

In the early 1980s, Carlos Stroia established his ballet school in Little Falls, Minnesota. Andrew began dancing seriously with Carlos through high school and then continued at the University of Minnesota's dance program. While still finishing a BFA in dance, Andrew supplemented his ballet education at Saint Paul City Ballet with its Vaganova-based training. He became one of the founding dancers of Saint Paul City Ballet's professional company, and performed as Bob Cratchit in *A Christmas Carol, the Ballet*. He danced with them in several roles, also taught classes, and helped with some administrative details. Andrew said that his time at "SPCB was special, and it felt like a renaissance or reimagining of the Ballets Russes bygone era."

Andrew has performed with Ballet Minnesota, Continental Ballet, Twin Cities Ballet, and Stuart Pimsler Dance & Theater. His versatility made him an excellent dancer during his nearly six years with the James Sewell Ballet and his continued dancing for over a decade with Shapiro and Smith. His wife, Nichole, is a vocalist, writer, director, and producer. As dance, music, and theater artists, they completely support each other's endeavors.

Andrew said that he currently is dancing and teaching as a "mixed/contemporary" dance artist. Whether he is taking ballet or contemporary class or on stage performing, art pours out of every fiber of Andrew's being and soul. He breathes, thinks, talks, draws, and dances art. One person once spoke of him as being "the Nijinsky of Minnesota." Truth be said.

reimagining. Andrew Lester with Saint Paul City Ballet, 2010. Choreography by Ross Edwards. Ritz Theater in Minneapolis. Courtesy of Erik Saulitis, photographer.

Tributes. Cynthia Carlson and Andrew Rist with Minnesota Dance Theatre.
Choreography by Loyce Houlton, ca. 1978. Photography by Photos, Inc., Minneapolis.
Courtesy of the University of Minnesota Libraries, Performing Arts Archives.

SCENE 3
Classical Ballet Academy and Ballet Minnesota

Andrew (Andy) and Cheryl Rist established the Classical Ballet Academy in 1987, anchoring it in Lowertown, Saint Paul, a downtown older section. Similar to European cities, it has its small park surrounded by early twentieth-century buildings, home to artist lofts and studios, and to a local farmer's market, en plein air, replete with seasonal fruits, vegetables, and other tasty edibles. Affordable rents brought a hub of artistic energy, which was perfect for dance. The Rists established their ballet school on the cusp of the gentrification of Lowertown and the construction of a light rail with a terminal point there.

Andy and Cheryl were dancing with Loyce Houlton in 1986 when she asked Andy to consider a position as Avocational Director of Minnesota Dance Theatre. MDT at that time had serious challenges and hardships. Andy declined, and both he and Cheryl put their sights across the river to Saint Paul. Cheryl saw fertile ground for growth in Saint Paul. Jo Savino's Classical Ballet Academy had already closed when Savino left in 1986 to continue ballet and dancing in Guadalajara, Mexico. The Andaházys directed the only other classical ballet school on Grand

Avenue in Saint Paul, about six miles away, west of downtown. So, they set their stakes

Beethoven's 9th. Classical Ballet Academy, 2004. David Schmidt, Julia (Heggernes) Morrison, Garvin Jellison, and Allen Gregory (left to right). Choreography by Andrew Rist. Courtesy of Ballet Minnesota.

on Fourth Street, Lowertown, in 1987. Since Jo Savino's school did not exist anymore, they chose what had been the name of his ballet school: Classical Ballet Academy.

The first year the academy was open, they had a Nutcracker lecture-demonstration for 150 people in the nearby Galtier Plaza. Today their *Classic Nutcracker* is seen annually by ten thousand people at The O'Shaughnessy on the campus of St. Catherine University. In May 1988, the first Minnesota Dance Festival was staged at the Saint Paul Student Center Theater on the University of Minnesota, Saint Paul campus.

Classical Ballet Academy seeks to create a professional school dedicated to the pursuit of artistry in dance through quality education and training. It is the official school of Ballet Minnesota.

In 1990, Andy and Cheryl co-founded Ballet Minnesota, a nonprofit organization with its mission "dedicated to enriching lives by creating and sharing the artistry of dance through public presentation and education." Andy decided to take on the responsibilities of artistic director and choreographer. The inaugural performance of Ballet Minnesota was a tribute to Mayor George Latimer in the lobby of the Saint Paul City Hall. Ballet Minnesota continues to grow ever stronger, supported by four pillars of an annual season: a fall concert, their *Classic Nutcracker*, a Minnesota Dance Festival, and River Songs Summer Series.

Andrew (Andy) Rist: Co-founder, Artistic Director, and Choreographer for Ballet Minnesota (Interview 6/21/21)

"When I was a young boy, I knew there were two words that fascinated me: teaching and creating. These words seemed to always be in my consciousness. When I was in junior high, I dressed up like an old man once so people would think I had something to say. Teach and create. Two fascinating words that express and describe me well.

"I majored in chemical engineering at college, but it was not the chemical engineering that really interested me, it was the science behind it. I started dancing when I was eighteen because I was always interested in dance. I'm from Maine, and I started at a small dance school. The school was directed by a former gymnast who married a ballerina—both from Europe. They were good dancers, and I danced with them for about two years. I then went to the First Chamber Dance Company in Port Townsend, northwest Washington state, about two hours from Seattle. Cheryl and I met and danced there before we were both invited to go to Sacramento Ballet.

"During our time at Sacramento Ballet, Loyce Houlton was a guest artist. She was choreographing on the company one of her works. She invited us to consider dancing in her company. Cheryl was a better dancer than me, and she also received an offer to dance with the Dutch National Ballet; I did not. Cheryl declined the offer, and we both decided to go to Minnesota and dance for MDT."

Andy and Cheryl danced with Minnesota Dance Theatre from 1973 to 1987. Andy loved Loyce's contemporary work, which was a blend of classical ballet and modern: "It fed me. So that is what I do here at Ballet Minnesota. When I choreographed/restaged *The Rite of Spring*, it was more contemporary than ballet." During the tumultuous time, soon after October 27, 1986, when the board of directors fired Loyce Houlton, a merger was proposed between Pacific Northwest Ballet and Minnesota Dance Theatre. It was to be named the Northwest Ballet. The merger did occur, and the name chosen was the Dance Institute, but it proved to be a short-lived venture. "Cheryl and I decided to leave the Minneapolis dance scene and founded our own school in Saint Paul.

"I always wanted to have my own school, but as I became more and more advanced, I realized that no one would hire me to do what I wanted to do because I didn't have the credentials. I wasn't from ABT or a New York City ballet. I love to dance, but I got into dance to be a choreographer." In 2013, on the one-hundredth anniversary of the premiere of Nijinsky's *The Rite of Spring*, Andy's contemporary choreography for his *The Rite of Spring* received great applause, and one longtime supporter of Ballet Minnesota told Andy that it was "emotionally powerful." Ballet Minnesota's performance of *The Rite of Spring* was quite unlike its premiere

Robert E. Hindel. Bob has accompanied ballet classes for over forty years in the Twin Cities. He has composed ballets for both Marius Andaházy and Andrew Rist and is currently composing a musical about the life of Harriet Tubman. Courtesy of the Saulitis family.

Jim Arnold, Ballet Minnesota's mainstay production manager and set designer, ca. 1996. He was Ballet Minnesota's anchor of skill and reliance until his death in 2021. Courtesy of Andrew and Cheryl Rist.

in Paris in 1913 when pandemonium broke out. In Saint Paul, only applause and bravos descended on the dancers.

Andy prefers to work with original scores, and his *At the Museum* in 1994 to an original score by Robert E. Hindel hailed the beginning of many years of fruitful collaboration between Hindel and Rist. Several works have also been choreographed with original scores from collaborations with Charlie Maguire (the National Park Service "Singing Ranger") and the rock group Mock Duck. Andy authored his first book, *At the Museum:*

Adventures of the Ballerina Girls, published in 2010.

Fast-forward thirty years of Ballet Minnesota's creative energy to 2020–21 and the debilitating changes that occurred with the Covid-19 pandemic. Andy, always focusing forward with a positive look on what life may bring him, tackled the pandemic with a can-do attitude, choreographing *The Human Spirit in the Time of Covid*. Since theaters had restricted capacity, Ballet Minnesota had the performance filmed as a virtual performance.

Cheryl Rist: Co-founder, Classical Restagings and Costume Design for CBA and Ballet Minnesota (Interview 2/20/21)

During Andy's interview, he would say, "You must talk to Cheryl; she knows everything," and when Cheryl was interviewed, she was quite modest and asked if Andy had been interviewed. As a couple, their creative energies blended and played well together. They danced together for several years, established a ballet school together, and worked together to put Andy's choreography on stage with magnificent costumes and well-rehearsed dancers.

Cheryl states that she never had any other job other than dancing and trained under several stellar dancers and directors. She graduated from the Cornish School of Arts in Seattle, which had a classical ballet curriculum, and she had classes there with Robert Joffrey and Flemming Halby, a former Danish dancer. Cheryl attended Hanya Holm's summer intensives in Colorado Springs. In Minnesota, she studied and trained with Loyce Houlton and Frank Bourman. Cheryl trained in both the Cecchetti and Vaganova syllabi. Altogether, Cheryl trained primarily with ballet for eighteen years but also had excellent modern and contemporary training with Hanya Holm and Loyce Houlton.

Speaking of dancing with Minnesota Dance Theatre, Cheryl said, "I loved what I did, and when I was at MDT, I 'spoke' the art better with my dancing." Cheryl said that Loyce was so creative; they had a lot of work and a lot of dancing. She had her first baby and took only a brief hiatus from dancing. While dancing, Cheryl fell during a ballet lift and had a serious injury. Cheryl took another break from dancing. Healing took time, and when she regained her health during her second pregnancy, she came back to MDT. Instead of dancing, Cheryl worked in the costume shop, which was a union shop, and learned so much. She never thought she would be designing and making ballet costumes and tutus in the future. "I just had fun!"

Cheryl is well-known for costume design and construction. Reflecting on her "years and years of training," she feels that "knowledge is just pouring out of her." Ballet has been her career for thirty-seven years. Like Andy, she teaches many ballet classes and uses the Vaganova-based Russian method. Andy teaches more Cecchetti style, but Cheryl said that he must do certain movements the way she tells him—that is, the Vaganova method.

Cheryl feels that most of the ballet schools in the Twin Cities train their students in a contemporary or neo-classical ballet style. She believes that a solid ballet foundation opens a dancer up to doing other types of choreography. She and Andy strive to help their students "learn to love the work of the art, as they work hard."

Swan Lake. Ballet Minnesota. Restaged by Cheryl Rist, 2005.
Courtesy of Andrew and Cheryl Rist.

Coda: Artist Story

Cynthia Betz: Director of Development for Northrop at the University of Minnesota (Interviews 6/3/21 and 9/29/21)

Cynthia has spent much of her career as a balletomane—a ballet dancer for twenty years and arts administrator and organizational leader for about thirty-six years.

Her early training—and her sister Lisa Gray's training—began with the Rochester Ballet. Lisa and Cynthia, like so many others, were drawn to ballet. For her, "ballet seemed pure and beautiful; it looked magical." Cynthia trained with the Andaházys and danced in Jo Savino's company. From Minnesota, she went to Michigan and danced with the Grand Rapids Civic Ballet for four years.

Once back in the Twin Cities, she learned of CBA through Ruthena Fink at her dancewear store, Grand Jeté. She signed up for adult ballet classes with Andy and Cheryl and offered to help them with some of their marketing needs in 1990. Cynthia feels grateful that she was with Ballet Minnesota early on in its growth. She has given her support, expertise, and time to Ballet Minnesota since its inception in 1990, and at one time, as president of the board of directors. From 2004 to 2016, Cynthia remained active with Ballet Minnesota as the executive director. Presently she serves as an adviser to the board and the productions.

Cynthia believes her most memorable contribution to Ballet Minnesota was helping to create structure and operational foundation for actualizing Andrew Rist's artistic vision. She shared that Andrew's optimism fuels inspiration and motivation during the stage production of ballets and contemporary works. Cheryl Rist, director of Classical Ballet Academy, brought her phenomenal talents to costume design and restaging of the classics.

Ace Hardware Store, 1680 Grand Avenue in Saint Paul with second floor ballet studios for the Andaházys and Saint Paul City Ballet. Courtesy of Ruthena Fink.

SCENE 4
Saint Paul City Ballet

In late May 1996, when springtime was bursting with new growth and more daylight, Saint Anthony Park School of Dance was also bursting out of its current space on Energy Park Drive in Saint Paul. Growth was inevitable due to the charismatic personality and business acumen of the school's director, Sonja Hinderlie. One of her teachers, who trained at the Andaházy School of Classical Ballet, informed Sonja that the school had closed, but Marius Andaházy still held the lease for the studio space. A call to Marius with an invitation to dinner with Sonja and her teacher received a positive, "Yes, I'm interested, but I would like to meet Sonja and talk to her." Two other potential renters had already inquired about the space.

An evening dinner together at a local pie shop lasted three hours. Marius shared details of how a donor continued paying the rent after the school was closed, but that would be ending soon. He and Sonja had an extensive exchange of ideas about ballet and dance, which developed into an honest sharing of their philosophies of life and living. A pleasant dinner conversation led to a pleasant surprise with Marius's agreement to pass the keys onto Sonja and sublease the studio space to her. He asked her if she would like to see the studio at 1680 Grand Avenue. Sonja responded with a definite "Of course."

They drove separately to the Andaházy studio that Sonja had never seen. Marius parked next to the Wet Paint Art Supply store across from the Ace Hardware store on Grand Avenue in Saint Paul. He waited at the street level door of the hardware store, watching for Sonja and her teacher to arrive. For Sonja, it all seemed strange to be at a hardware store's door, but Marius explained that the studio space was on the second level. He opened the door to the wide swath of a blue, wooden staircase. At the top of the stairs, Marius opened a large, white door.

Sonja felt like she was Alice stepping through a door into Wonderland, and the time spent with Marius touring her through the spaces was indeed a time of wonderment with incredible stories of the Andaházy ballet history. Sonja could sense a sacred legacy in that space where the resilient floor boards supported dancers since 1949. He trusted that she would pass along the love of ballet as Marius and his parents had done for fifty-one years. Marius handed her the keys to the space. Holding the keys, Sonja's rite of passage had just occurred.

Plans began immediately to physically and administratively move Saint Anthony

Park School of Dance from Energy Park Drive to Grand Avenue in Saint Paul in early July. With the move to Grand Avenue, the "Park" was dropped from the dance school's name. The new studio spaces needed some cleaning and renovation. Renting scaffolding and buying new paint and cleaning supplies from the hardware store below were the beginnings of an excellent business relationship between the store and the school.

At the 1996 summer's end, a grand opening celebrated the new studio space for Saint Anthony School of Dance, and registration for ballet classes began. Wilor Bluege, one of the former Andaházy dancers and teachers, approached Sonja about a full-length story ballet that she had been creating based on a story she had written. Sonja listened to the music that Wilor had envisioned. One of Sonja's strongest traits is her openness to new ideas. She agreed to move forward with Wilor's fairytale ballet called *The Golden Bough*. The ballet, with choreography by artistic director Wilor Bluege and producers Sonja Hinderlie and the president of the Board of Directors, opened in November 1997 to a sold-out audience at The O'Shaughnessy on the campus of St. Catherine University.

Seated in the audience on opening night, the author overheard two fascinating comments right as intermission began: "I thought this was a little dance school above the hardware store," and, "This ballet is like what the Andaházys used to do." Kudos to the support of many professional artists, student dancers, parents, volunteers, and businesses that gave time, funds, and creative talents to make

Bluege's dream come true. With a large initial grant from the Boss Foundation and continued support from the Hubbard Broadcasting Foundation, *The Golden Bough* continued to be performed six times from 1997 to 2003. The 2003 performance took the stage in Saint Cloud, Minnesota, at the Paramount Theatre with another sold-out audience.

A domino of changes occurred when the board decided to establish a separate entity for the performing arm of Saint Anthony School of Dance. Incorporation in January 1997 was followed by an application for nonprofit status, and in June 1998 Saint Anthony Performing Arts Guild became a new nonprofit in Minnesota. The winds of change blew steadily and in August 2001 Sonja sold her school, Saint Anthony School of Dance, to the managing director. The ballet school honored its capital city and took the name Saint Paul City Ballet in 2002. Both the school and the nonprofit performing company continued to expand to a broader constituency and audience base—the catalyst that initiated aligning both the school and the performing company under the same nonprofit umbrella in 2006. With nonprofit status, the school became Saint Paul City Ballet School, and Saint Anthony Performing Arts Guild became Saint Paul City Ballet.

Wilor Bluege thought the name changes were excellent. As a prolific choreographer and a superb ballet and *caractère* teacher, Bluege continued until 2007 to set other classical ballets for Saint Paul City Ballet School. Under her artistic direction, ballet students danced in a restaging of Arthur Saint-Léon's lighthearted comic ballet *Coppélia*, with music by Léo Delibes. She also restaged excerpts of Marius Petipa's bold and brilliant *Don Quixote*, with music by Ludwig Minkus. In addition, Bluege choreographed for Saint Paul City Ballet a sacred dance work called *Agnus Dei* with music by César Franck.

Exponential growth occurred, and a professional company with contracted dancers became part of Saint Paul City Ballet in 2007. It developed into a strong institution with the broad support of donors, local businesses, and continued foundation support. Philanthropists Bruce Larson, Kathrine Hill, Ken Guddal and his wife, Marla Murphy-Guddal, were significant supporters in establishing Saint Paul City Ballet's professional ballet company.

Saint Paul City Ballet was known in the Twin Cities as a collaborative ballet company working with dance, theater, music, and visual artists. For example, one collaboration with a Minnesotan jazz composer and performer, George Maurer, led to a commissioned work called *Enticed* by Maurer and a performance of *Enticed*, along with other Saint Paul City Ballet works, at the Paramount Theatre in Saint Cloud, Minnesota.

Other ballet artists set other full-length ballets, and of special significance was an original ballet, *A Christmas Carol, the Ballet*, by artistic director, Karen Paulson Rivet. Its premiere in December 2004 at The O'Shaughnessy had an addition of an incredible guest theater artist: Gerald Charles Dickens, the great-great grandson of Charles Dickens, author of *A Christmas Carol*. With

Bruce Anton Larson (1940–2017). Fondly remembered as "The Kaiser" and "Bubba," he was a Saint Paul philanthropist, Europhile, and "Impresario" to Saint Paul City Ballet and Rivers Ballet. Courtesy of Erik Saulitis, photographer.

a resounding voice, he opened the ballet with one of its most memorable first lines: "Marley was dead, to begin with. There is no doubt whatever about that. The register of his burial was signed by the clergyman, the clerk, the undertaker, and the chief mourner. Scrooge signed it . . . Old Marley was as dead as a doornail." He also opened the second act of the ballet and ended it by repeating the famous last line, "God bless us, everyone." A *St. Paul Pioneer Press* writer called it a "sweet ballet." *A Christmas Carol, the Ballet* had an additional performance that December 2004 at the Paramount Theater in Saint Cloud.

With a deep chagrin for the dance community, Karen passed away in 2016. She had a "love for the classical art form of ballet and began her training with the Andaházy Ballet Company in Saint Paul. Karen became

A Christmas Carol, the Ballet. Saint Paul City Ballet, 2004. Claire Wojda as Tiny Tim and Royal Anderson as Ebeneezer Scrooge. Royal once said, "It was a pleasure and an honor performing in the ballet, which could not have happened without its generous donors, and the excellent choreography by the artistic director, Karen Paulson Rivet. Courtesy of Erik Saulitis, photographer.

a well-known, accomplished ballet mistress, performer, and choreographer. "Karen was an inspirational instructor for more than thirty-two years, loved by the many students she taught. Karen's gift of dance was a radiant gem to parents, company members, and patrons in the Twin Cities area."[147]

With uninterrupted growth and support, Saint Paul City Ballet established an outreach program in 2005. The philanthropist, Bruce Larson, supported this program which provided children's ballet classes at no cost at his Klub Haus on Rice Street. In partnership with the St. Paul Public School Community Education Program, adults could take ballet classes at the Klub Haus once a week for a minimal fee. Outreach also took Saint Paul City Ballet staff to northeast Iowa, where Sabrina Schmitt credits the longevity and success of her Iowa studios to Saint Paul City

Ballet staff whose inspiration and teaching instilled in her an appreciation for ballet that she passes on to her students.

Bruce Larson's support of Saint Paul City Ballet's outreach efforts continued until his death in 2017. The Germanic-American Institute in Saint Paul, under the direction of Jeanna Anderson, continued Bruce's adult outreach at the Haus's third-floor ballroom on Summit Avenue in Saint Paul under the name Rivers Ballet.

In partnership with the Landmark Center in downtown Saint Paul, another outreach program called Ballet Tuesdays began September 2009. In the stunning Cortile of the Landmark Center, Saint Paul City Ballet's professional company would perform excerpts of their current work at noon on the second Tuesday of every month during the academic year. Ballet Tuesdays remains a free event for

Outreach to West Union, Iowa, 2015. Sabrina Schmitt, owner of Expressions Dance Studio and Rivers Ballet dancers Eloise Berdahl-Baldwin, Rachel Hastreiter, Miller Balley, and their teacher (left to right). Photography Courtesy of Jennifer Murry.

all and continues today with the professional dancers from Ballet Co.Laboratory under the artistic direction of Zoé Henrot.

Each spring from 2010 to 2012, four artistic partners at Saint Paul City Ballet—Jennifer and Ross Edwards, Ted Sothern, and the author—produced full-length story ballets, including *The Sleeping Beauty*, *Cinderella*, and *Peter Pan*, to sold-out audiences at the E. M. Pearson Theater on the campus of Concordia College in Saint Paul. One artistic partner, Ted Sothern, had expressed interest in continuing his role as an artistic partner and helping to sustain and build the organization. He said, "I felt that during my tenure as an artistic partner at Saint Paul City Ballet, the organization was pursuing a niche in the Twin Cities of developing story ballets and continuing to build the professional company."

Germanic-American Institute, 301 Summit Avenue, Saint Paul. Dancers with Rivers Ballet: Kay Studer, Elise Honerman, Marlene Tupy (left to right), and Rachel Hastreiter (center and kneeling), ca. 2018. Courtesy of Erik Saulitis, photographer.

Coda: Artists' Stories

Rochelle Zide-Booth: Ballet Russe Dancer, Ballet Dancer with Robert Joffrey Ballet, Teaching Artist, and Régisseuse

If one could possibly describe Rochelle Zide-Booth, descriptions would include: Rochelle is an accomplished dance artist, ballet teacher, and a compendium of ballet history. One could sit down for hours and listen to fascinating stories about her travels and years with Sergei Denham's Ballet Russe de Monte Carlo or her personal experiences dancing with the Joffrey Ballet. Dancers taking an advanced ballet class from Rochelle leave the class artistically inspired.

Former Saint Paul City Ballet teacher Jennifer Murry studied ballet at Minnetonka Dance Theatre under the direction of Marianne Simons and then at Butler University, where Jennifer studied with Rochelle, one of her most influential ballet teachers. Jennifer kept in close contact with Rochelle, and when addressing her, Jennifer would call her Chellie. Jennifer once said, "Chellie is an outstanding teacher with both an incredible amount of skill and natural talent. Her mind predates the computer, and she's been in the right places with the right people at the right time. She is like the Babe Ruth of ballet. . .The only difference between Chellie and Babe Ruth is that Babe was not a nice guy, and Chellie is kind, loving, and a beautiful person inside and out."

Because of their friendship, Jennifer asked Rochelle if she would come to Minneapolis—again—and be the master guest teacher for a summer intensive at The Cowles Center for Dance & the Performing Arts. Rochelle's quick response to this invitation was, "Yes, it

Jennifer (Darcy) Murry as the Sugar Plum Fairy with Minnetonka Dance Theatre Youth Ballet Company's *Nutcracker*, ca. 1993. Choreography by Marianne (Greven) Simons, Artistic Director. Photography by Michelle Periolet. Courtesy of Jennifer Murry.

would be lovely to come back to Minneapolis. It has been years since I was there staging *La Fille Mal Gardée* for Loyce Houlton's company." In 2013 and again in 2014, ballet students "on both sides of the Mississippi" came to the Rivers Ballet Summer Intensive. Rochelle's choreography was challenging as she restaged *Classical Symphony* and sections of *Les Sylphides*. Challenging, yet forever memorable.

Rochelle wrote *Have Tutu, Will Travel*, her recently published memoirs detailing her dancing years with the Ballet Russe de Monte Carlo, the Robert Joffrey Ballet, and America Dances. The memoirs begin with her first ballet performance, and first encore, as a young child with The Harriet Hoctor School of Ballet in Boston. Rochelle wrote that the audience loved her, but more importantly, she loved them, and the dance hooked her forever.[148]

Rochelle's professional career began when she signed her first contract on her sixteenth birthday with the fabled Sergei Denham's Ballet Russe de Monte Carlo. A teenage prodigy, Rochelle immediately performed in solo and ballerina roles. In the spring of 1957, the Ballet Russe began its first season since 1950 at New York City's Metropolitan Opera House. The season began on April 21, Rochelle's nineteenth birthday, and continued through May 4. "In terms of attendance and intake, the April 21–May 4 engagement broke all records for an American ballet company at the Met, gross receipts amounting to $150,445."[149] Ed Sullivan happened to be in the audience and, enthralled with the performance, asked

Denham to have his company appear on The Ed Sullivan Show. Rochelle and the Ballet Russe de Monte Carlo performed the *Czárdás* from the ballet *Raymonda* for his show.

The next year, during the summer layoff and waiting to sign another contract with the Ballet Russe, she took a ballet class taught by Robert Joffrey at the American Ballet Theatre School. During the summer months, Rochelle continued studying with Robert Joffrey, and at summer's end, she "had turned from a very talented little girl

Rochelle Zide-Booth as Peep-Bo in the Ballet Russe de Monte Carlo production of Antonia Cobos's *The Mikado*, ca. 1957. Courtesy of Rochelle Zide-Booth.

into a mature dancer, and with great control …"[150] Her Ballet Russe colleagues, amazed at her new artistry, strength, and control, asked how she did that in one summer's time. Her response, "Bob Joffrey."

In 1957 Rochelle signed a contract with the Ballet Russe; Robert Joffrey Ballet also offered her a contract. Denham would not let her go, and she needed to refuse Joffrey's offer. In 1958 Rochelle joined the Robert Joffrey Ballet and would spend four years as a principal dancer, dancing lead roles in Balanchine ballets and amazingly, as she said, "seven other ballets created on me."

In 1961, Rochelle performed on Broadway with Jerome Robbins's Ballet: USA. Robbins wanted her to join his company for their US tour, but Rochelle declined, being contracted with the Robert Joffrey Ballet tour. Rochelle later explained that it was for the best that she declined Jerome Robbins's invitation. His company disbanded on the road when Robbins refused to take John Jones (a black dancer) out of the *pas de deux* with Wilma Curley (a white dancer) in his *N. Y. Export: Opus Jazz.*

As a mature dancer, Rochelle "was five feet two inches, dark-haired, pale-skinned, and her wide almond-shaped eyes summoned an *Arabian Nights* atmosphere. Fastidious, complex, scintillating, and energetic, Rochelle's dancing announced to many, 'Here is a ballerina.'"[151] A new ballet company was being formed for her as its prima ballerina when a severe injury ended her ballet performing career.

Unable to dance, she began an amazing *encore* to her ballet career, receiving the highest accolades for her work as: Ballet Mistress of the Joffrey Ballet and Boston Ballet; Artistic Director of Nederlands Dans Theater; Artistic Director of the New Zealand School of Dance; Director of Ballet at the Jacob's Pillow Dance Festival; Full-tenured professorship at Adelphi University; The first Fulbright lecturer to Czechoslovakia in Adelphi's one-hundred-year history, before the 1993 peaceful separation of Czechoslovakia into two new countries, the Czech Republic and Slovakia; Professor Emerita of both Adelphi and Butler Universities; Faculty of the Alvin Ailey American Dance Center; and lengthy teaching residencies in the Philippines, Israel, Hong Kong, and South Korea.

Rochelle has been honored by the governments of South Korea and Czechoslovakia. Especially honored in 2014 at a celebratory gathering in Pittsburgh, Pennsylvania, where she received the CORPS de Ballet International Lifetime Achievement Award for excellence in teaching ballet in higher education. Jennifer Murry and the author were invited as Chellie's guests.

Rochelle has been listed in 2000 Notable American Women, Who's Who of American Women, Who's Who in Entertainment, The International Who's Who of Professional and Business Women, and the *Jewish Women in America: An Historical Encyclopedia*. She is a dance and teaching artist par excellence, and her artist husband, Bob Booth, was her constant support and loving companion until his death in 2023.

Ted Sothern: Dance and Teaching Artist, former Artistic Partner of Saint Paul City Ballet, former Artistic Director of Hopkins Youth Ballet, and former Artist Director of Rochester Ballet Company (Interview 8/27/21)

Born and raised in Northeast Minneapolis, Ted's experience as a dance artist has a broad reach in Minnesota and beyond to New York State, North Carolina, Washington D.C., and the Far East in Japan. "I grew up here, and that's when I started dancing."

In sixth grade, Ted attended MDT's Nutcracker and became completely smitten by dance. Stephanie Karr-Smith and Toni Pierce danced for MDT. "I didn't know these people for another twenty years. Now I know them as colleagues in dance." To this day, Karr-Smith is still dancing as a guest artist

theatre dance place. Minneapolis, August 2021. Courtesy of Erik Saulitis, photographer.

at various schools and companies, and Toni Pierce founded a dance school in Saint Paul, TU Dance.

Ted began seriously dancing with Frank Bourman at Frank's school, Minnesota Ballet, located on North 3rd Street in Minneapolis in a building called 'theatre dance place.' Even today, a rusty sign above the 112 Eatery's front door, harkens back to his school like a ghost from the past. Bourman came to Minnesota with an outstanding ballet background. He received formative training in Los Angeles and continued training at the School of American Ballet. As a principal dancer, he performed with the Australian National Ballet, the Hurok Ballet Ensemble, and the Alicia Alonso Ballet Company. He was Associate Director and teacher at the New York Buffalo Theatre Company. In 1972, he accepted the position of Associate Director/Ballet Master of the Royal Winnipeg Ballet.

Loyce Houlton reached out to Winnipeg Ballet and hired Bourman to direct MDT's school in 1978. In a span of three years, Bourman's energy, expertise, and charisma grew the school. Ted's foray into dance began with Bourman at MDT, and his first jazz class taught by Larry Hayden at MDT. Ted was twenty-four at that time and believed that "Frank Bourman had his hand in training most anyone at MDT . . . "

Dance Artist, Ted Sothern, *Midsummer Night's Dream*. Boston Ballet 1988.
Photography by Bernie Ghardella. Courtesy of Ted Sothern

Bourman had a falling out with Loyce, left MDT, and established his school and company, Minnesota Ballet, in 1982. Larry Hayden came with him, and together they envisioned providing the Twin Cities with a ballet company of international standard that would enhance its cultural vitality. Bourman and Hayden had a falling out, and Frank Bourman went to Florida and kept dancing as a master teacher. Eventually, he ended up going to Boston Ballet because of Anna-Marie Holmes, his friend and an extraordinary dance artist and master teacher.

With Frank Bourman gone, MDT hired Bonnie Mathis as Ballet Mistress, and Ted went back to ballet training at MDT under Bonnie's direction, and as Ted stated, "For him, that was the only other option in the Cities." He was at MDT for only two and a half years when the MDT Board of Directors fired Loyce and made Bonnie Mathis the interim director. Ted decided at that point to leave Minnesota and went as an apprentice to Boston Ballet.

From Boston, Ted danced for The Washington Ballet in D.C. in 1988, and one of the "greatest things in my life" occurred during his time there. The ballet *Les Noces*, choreographed by Nijinsky's sister, Bronislava Nijinska, was being set by her daughter, Irina Nijinska. Ted exclaimed, "I loved it. We would be in rehearsals, and it was like I was in heaven. . . . a direct lineage . . . and I heard so many stories of the Nijinsky family, Pavlova, Diaghilev, and the Ballets Russes."

Ted continued auditioning and dancing in Europe. In the meantime, Loyce had entered the dance world again and was the choreographer for Ballet Michigan. Ted danced for her at Ballet Michigan at the Flint Institute of Music for two short seasons. That is where Ted met Stephanie Karr-Smith for the first time. She was Loyce's right-hand person who knew Loyce's choreography inside and out. Loyce had set *Les Patineurs* on the company, "the hardest choreography ever . . . adagio to grand allegro all on pointe shoes . . ." Someone was injured, and Stephanie Karr-Smith, who had not danced in six years, was given a pair of pointe shoes and danced the role beautifully. "She was amazing, and one could not take eyes off of her when she danced," Ted expounded.

He ended up in Chautauqua in 1990 because he needed to find work. He was hired to dance with the Chautauqua Dance Company, which paid dancers for seven weeks in the summer session. Barry, who had been on staff there for a number of years, first saw Ted with his backpack as he walked to a dance class, and he said to himself, "He's a dancer." Sure enough. He met Ted in ballet class, and from that point on, they continued dancing together whenever and wherever they went.

They danced together with Charleston Ballet Theatre in South Carolina, a sister school with Barry's Buffalo Ballet Theater. Ted and Barry also danced in Japan together for half a year with the Grand Diva Ballet out of New York, an all-male company performing classical ballets with a humorous twist. Ten years later, they moved to Minnesota full time. Barry taught at MDT, along with Karen Paulson Rivet, as MDTs primary teachers at that time. Barry also danced in Loyce's Nutcracker for six years as Drosselmeyer and worked at MDT for fifteen years.

As Ted reflected on his varied ballet career with several companies, he discussed his understanding of Loyce, MDT, and dance and ballet in the Twin Cities—personal and keen insights. Speaking about Loyce and MDT, Ted said her company was "musical, theatrical and worked together as a professional company. It received the lion's share of funding . . ." For Ted, Loyce was "way ahead of her time, talented, a genius . . . " When the company folded, the door opened, and many dance artists, like diaspora pieces of living art, spread throughout the Twin Cities, taking root and growing new schools and companies.

Claire Westby: Studio Manager of The Joyce Theater (NYC), Assoc. Prof. at NYU teaching ballet and contemporary for the BFA program, and former Dance Artist with Liz Gerring Dance Company (NYC) (Interview 11/1/21)

When Claire was seven years old, her soccer coach told her mother that she ran like a ballet dancer. Claire's mother worked at Leitner's Garden Center, and when the director of Saint Paul City Ballet came in inquiring about a donation to the ballet school, her mother took note of that and signed Claire up for ballet lessons.

Claire truly moved like a ballet dancer, and from her first ballet class as a seven-year-old to her last class as a senior in high school, Claire never stopped ballet. She later said, "I learned everything I needed to learn; everything else is now frosting . . . I remember that our studio felt like our home, my home studio." Claire took ballet at some other schools but always came back to Saint Paul City Ballet School. She said, "It felt like the right thing." She believed that she had a solid foundation—because of excellent teachers at Saint Paul City Ballet School.

Claire Westby, former dance artist with Saint Paul City Ballet, ca. 2019.
Courtesy of Erik Saulitis, photographer.

When her NYU teachers asked her where she trained, they were almost shocked to hear that it was a school in Saint Paul, Minnesota. They were equally amazed and felt it unique that she trained on wooden floors. In today's ballet world, marle © flooring is standard. Professionals quiver to dance on wooden floors because they are slippery. If the flooring is wooden, then rosin boxes are a necessity for the studio.

In New York City, Claire has been a member of the Liz Gerring Company ever since she graduated with a BFA degree from New York University. She dances modern, contemporary, and ballet in diverse performances and projects. Recently she set a work by Liz Gerring on the Alvin Ailey American Dance Theater. Claire feels that her first experience of a different dance style occurred with her first *caractère* class, even though the class is actually in the ballet pedagogy. The different steps amazed her, and she thought "*caractère* was so cool." Friday night *caractère* classes became a refreshing and fun end of the school week; plus, one of her dearest friends (whose name is also Claire) took the Friday night *caractère* class. Both were talented and versatile dancers, and the dancer Royal Anderson called them "Claire squared," an endearment that stayed.

Claire once told her former ballet director at Saint Paul City Ballet, "I definitely would not be where I am today without Saint Paul City Ballet." That statement is music for any director's ears.

Joan Westby: Former Saint Paul City Ballet board director and Manager of Leitner's Garden Center (Interview 10/24/21)

From floral and landscape design to painting and home renovations, Joan is an artist. Her generosity, positive spirit, and contagious laughter overflow into her pragmatic approach to life and her enthusiasm for ballet and opera. Joan once said, "Choose ballet to get started in dance, and then ballet gets you to wherever you want to go." She thinks of ballet "like the furnace of a home that heats the whole house."

At Saint Paul City Ballet School, Joan saw the teachers giving each student engaged attention and the needed encouragement as if they were on track to be a professional ballet dancer. From the creative movement child to the professional company dancer, everyone had a respected place in the whole organization; each person felt needed and affirmed. Joan believed that students at Saint Paul City Ballet School learned the importance of discipline, of a strong work ethic, and "working together to make something work for the best." Joan, along with her daughters Claire and Madeline, were significant contributors to Saint Paul City Ballet's growth.

Michael Leimbach: Wilson Learning, Vice President of Research and Learning; Dance Artist; and former Saint Paul City Ballet board director (Interview 2/24/20)

Michael was a gymnast who was proficient on the rings and the horizontal bars as a young adult. Then, as a college student, a friend introduced him to the Andaházy School of Classical Ballet in St. Louis Park. He was not in the gymnastic shape of his former days, so he decided to try a ballet class. The class technique fascinated Michael, and he continued taking classes.

Mr. A cast him into several ballets, and in the first one, *Schéhérazade*, at the Northrop in 1977, he performed two minor roles, but the opportunity to dance on stage in a full-length ballet made Michael a veritable balletomane. A fond memory of that time was meeting Karen Paulson Rivet, a beautiful young dancer. In later years, he would perform again, but this time for Karen as Saint Paul City Ballet's Artistic Director for *A Christmas Carol, the Ballet.*

After college, Michael began his doctoral studies in child psychology at the University of Minnesota and took a break from ballet. Once he achieved his doctorate, he went back to ballet. He moved to Saint Paul and decided to take ballet at Jo Savino's Classical Ballet Academy. He actually performed more ballets with Jo Savino than with the Andaházys.

After Jo Savino left for Mexico, Michael took another hiatus from dancing, but he came back to it when Saint Paul City Ballet leased the space at 1680 Grand Avenue. He began taking classes and performed in some of Saint Paul City Ballet's productions. Michael also gave his time and expertise as president of the board of directors during the significant growth and citywide awareness that Saint Paul City Ballet had garnered. The company and school received generous support from several Saint Paul-based organizations and people. Under Michael's helm, the board of directors expanded, and Kathrine Hill of the James J. Hill family legacy joined. An Advisory Board and a Friends of the Ballet volunteer organization were added and supported the ballet in various ways. To this day, Michael remains a balletomane— and a forever "friend of the ballet."

Connie Wagner: Adult student dancer and Benefactor
(Interview 6/17/21)

Connie never wanted to be on a stage and perform. She loved to dance, but she said that she did not need people to watch her. Connie performed at Saint Paul City Ballet because the director "pushed me in an encouraging and affirming manner; me, a middle-aged adult!" Connie found it was more challenging than she initially realized, but it ended up more exciting, too.

Connie fondly remembers how it felt to take ballet classes at Saint Paul City Ballet School. She said, "Everything at Saint Paul City Ballet—the large windows, the chandeliers, the piano music all came together and made you feel like you were in a palace . . . with happy people." She made friends with dancers of all ages and felt that the "intergenerational blend of ballet students was so good." Connie also said you could tell that the instructors were content, and so they did a good job. It all worked. Connie's remarks echo what many others would say—Saint Paul City Ballet had a welcoming ambiance that pervaded all aspects of the ballet school and company.

Everything changed in 2012 when the board of directors took over. It seemed to be all business. Connie quit after only two classes. She knows that if all had not changed, she would still be there taking ballet classes—and performing. Saint Paul City Ballet for Connie gave her poignant memories of grace, elegance, and peaceful feelings that cannot easily be replicated. She is glad that she risked taking ballet lessons as an older adult and that she did not "put off until tomorrow what she could do today."

Dancing in the Meadows. Elise Honerman, Miller Balley, and Emma Kosanke former dancers with Saint Paul City Ballet and Rivers Ballet (left to right), 2015. Courtesy of Erik Saulitis, photographer.

Dancing in the Meadows by woodcut artist and ballet dancer Emma Kosanke, 2021. After an original photograph by Erik Saulitis.

214

Pamela Neal: Parent Volunteer and Dr. Christine Neal, Emergency Medicine Residency in Roanoke, Virginia (2023), and former Saint Paul City Ballet dancer (Interview 10/20/21)

Pamela Neal was a generous volunteer who gave her time, expertise, and anything that was needed to produce a successful experience for the dancers at Saint Paul City Ballet. She sent the following statement expressing what she saw happening when her daughter danced at Saint Paul City Ballet.

"When my daughter and I arrived in the Twin Cities, there were several choices of ballet schools. We chose Saint Paul City Ballet School. After visiting the studio and meeting the director and some staff, we noticed its positive, uplifting, and professional environment. Exactly what I wanted for my daughter—all dancers were treated with respect and valued as a member of the school. For my daughter, Christine, the move to the Twin Cities from a small town in Wisconsin with a small ballet school to a larger city with a larger, more serious ballet program was a formidable change. Yet the non-competitive culture at Saint Paul City Ballet School abated her fears.

"The staff always remained supportive of each dancer's abilities and challenged the dancer to do his/her best . . . It was important to me that my daughter was able to become an independent, self-assured young woman who was able to take the responsibility of performance to the highest level possible." There are four determinants that Pamela feels make a strong, young person: confidence, organization, communication, and kindness. These attributes were encouraged at the school, and Christine embraced them. She has gone on to a career in medicine, taking these attributes with her.

Christine holds a prominent memory at Saint Paul City Ballet School of the kind and graceful presence of Gabriela Komleva, a master guest artist from Russia. Ms. Komleva was there teaching and coaching the upper-level dancers in the fairy variations from *The Sleeping Beauty*. Christine felt thrilled and a bit nervous about being personally coached by Ms. Komleva with the *Canari qui chante* variation—the "singing canary" fairy variation. Now, as a young woman, Dr. Neal realizes what a tremendous once-in-a-lifetime experience she had at Saint Paul City Ballet School.

Zoé Emilie Henrot, Artistic Director of Ballet Co.Laboratory. Saint Paul Cathedral steps, September 2021. Courtesy of the photographer, Alexis Lund.

Ballet Co.Laboratory

Zoé said that her story is "most amazing and most difficult," with valleys and peaks. Since 2020, the School of Ballet Co.Laboratory and its professional company have been a rising star in the Twin Cities star-studded dance sky.

Zoé Emilie Henrot: Founder and Artistic Director of Ballet Co.Laboratory (Interview 6/22/21)

Zoé grew up in Colorado and moved to Minnesota in July 2012 when her partner, Martha, entered a PhD program at the University of Minnesota. The number of small dance companies all over the Twin Cities both amazed and surprised her. Zoé also said, "As the historical tradition of ballet is so gendered, I did not feel comfortable enough to come out to the Twin Cities ballet community for a few years. I was concerned that parents might be uncomfortable with me working so closely with their students, knowing that I am queer. I came to find that within the Twin Cities dance community, I should feel free to be exactly who I am. I now feel very confident in bringing my full identity into the studio and my work."

Zoé learned that Saint Paul City Ballet had gone through some drastic changes in June 2012. Later that summer, Saint Paul City Ballet's Board of Directors decided to honor a commitment made to Joseph Morrissey earlier in 2012 to set one of his works on Saint Paul City Ballet's professional company in 2013. Zoé attended this 2013 mixed repertory performance in Minneapolis at The Cowles Center for Dance & the Performing Arts. The program included a *pas de deux* by Joseph Morrissey, *Bolero* by Greg Drotar, *Montana Memories* by Allison Doughty-Marquesen, and *Not An Étude*, original music by George Maurer with choreography by Ted Sothern, who later said, "That was the end of Saint Paul City Ballet as we knew it."

Zoé was pleasantly surprised to see a "forward-thinking" ballet. Her early understanding of the Twin Cities dance landscape was that classical ballets reigned within the ballet companies. Zoé believes in honoring the classics by "giving them a

American in Paris. Ballet Co.Laboratory,
June 2021. Zoé Emilie Henrot,
Da'Rius Malone, and Rosa Prigan.
Photography by Karin Lynn (left to right).

thank you and a bow." Ballet Co.Laboratory's teaching and company artists teach the classical ballet variations for core strength and know that ballet audiences enjoy seeing the classical works performed. Zoé believes that even if ballet students do not become professionals, they will hopefully become ballet and dance patrons. There's so much they will have learned from taking ballet: dedication, drive, working toward something, knowing that perfection doesn't exist, time management, and teamwork.

"I found out that Saint Paul City Ballet's professional dancers were all laid off after The Cowles Center performance in 2013. The dancers reached out to me while they were gathering independent dancers together as professionals for Saint Paul City Ballet. It worked, and all on a grassroots level." In the following seven months, the dance artists did

everything. They handled all their finances, administration needs, and artistic plans."

In 2013, Zoé and the dance artists for Saint Paul City Ballet became known as an artist-led company, separate from Saint Paul City Ballet School. The name changed in 2014 to St. Paul Ballet for both the school and the company. The Board of Directors wanted to merge the administrations of both, but Zoé stood her ground and said, "No, the dance artists wanted to continue working in the administration." St. Paul Ballet transitioned to a school-only model just weeks before the 2018–2019 season opened and the company was scheduled to perform in the Lakes Area Music Festival in Brainerd, Minnesota. Without a job and with grace and grit, Zoé founded Ballet Co.Laboratory in 2018.

The company artists and Zoé initially started the organization in a church space in downtown Minneapolis. Since 2019, Ballet Co.Laboratory's home has been firmly established in Saint Paul at 276 East Lafayette Frontage Road. Zoé's dedication to an artist-led company has never wavered. This model was recognized as a unique but successful business model in *Pointe Magazine* on March 22, 2021. The article described the company's dual-contract structure that provides its dancers with administrative employment in management, communications, development, or teaching—a design that became especially useful in keeping the dancers employed during the pandemic.

SCENE 6
Continental Ballet

With easy access to both Minneapolis and Saint Paul, the Bloomington Center for the Arts supports an art gallery, theater, ballet studio, dressing rooms, and Continental Ballet's administrative office. The center is an artistically pleasant approach to Continental Ballet's space and Genevieve Spooner, Continental Ballet's managing director and former Andaházy dancer. She greets visitors and dancers with a welcoming smile.

Riet Velthuisen: Founder and Artistic Director of Continental Ballet (Interview 8/2/21)

Riet Velthuisen was born in Ryswyk, Netherlands. Her strong Dutch accent, carries listeners away to Europe and beyond with her memories of ballet training and performing. In the Netherlands, Riet wanted to take ballet, even though her father did not want her to dance. He was afraid she would not get all the academic education she needed for future employment, but Riet wanted to dance. "I just had to do it." With youthful resolute, her father acquiesced to Riet's desire to dance, and in her late teens, she began ballet. Riet has never stopped.

She studied ballet and lived in France before she auditioned for a Netherlands ballet company. Riet performed with the Ballet Lagelander, which eventually merged with the Dutch National Ballet. She danced with the company in Amsterdam, The Hague, and toured throughout Europe. She met André Velthuisen while touring with the Dutch National Ballet. André was in the international hotel industry. He successfully managed some of Europe's most famous hotels, including those in the Netherlands, his native country. They eventually married and traveled with André's work to France, Japan, Aruba, and several states in America. Everywhere they lived, she continued taking ballet classes.

Once in Bloomington, Minnesota, André stopped traveling for his work; Riet seized this opportunity to establish her own school, Continental Ballet. Her brother suggested

219

Riet Velthuisen, Founder/Artistic Director of Continental Ballet with Yuki Tokuda of Continental Ballet, ca. 2018. Photography by Alexander Smirnov, a dance artist with Continental Ballet. Courtesy of Alexander Smirnov.

the name, which actually complements Riet's world-traveled experiences, and she began teaching ballet in her home in the early 1980s. Her number of students grew, and she moved into a space in a building on Nesbitt Avenue in Bloomington. In 1988, she merged her school and performing company together as a nonprofit. Continental Ballet is known for its commitment to performing ballets from the classical repertoire.

Genevieve Spooner came to Continental Ballet after she heard that they had a local Nutcracker. She took her children to Continental Ballet's Nutcracker and became totally impressed with the quality of the classical dancing. She enrolled herself and her daughters in ballet classes at Continental

Ballet. Eventually, Riet hired Genevieve to teach ballet at Continental, and she has been there ever since, wearing several hats.

Bloomington's city council decided to build a performing center that was annexed to the city's police department. The Continental Ballet Board of Directors actively helped Riet and Genevieve pursue a committed space in the building for ballet. They were actively engaged in the design of the studio, dressing rooms, and office space. The grand opening occurred in 2003. Continental Ballet had a dedicated home space at the Bloomington Center for the Arts. Success!

As with most nonprofit ballet/dance companies, Continental Ballet had its challenges, heightened during the 2020 pandemic.

Continental Ballet receives support from the City of Bloomington's Cultural Arts Fund as well as storage space in the Bloomington Center for the Arts. They have deep roots in Bloomington and are able to attract professional dancers who enjoy dancing a classical repertoire. With support from the community and quality dancers and teachers, Continental Ballet resiliently kept moving forward during the pandemic, and it continues to make its mark on the Minnesota ballet scene.

Swan Lake, Continental Ballet, 2022. Wesley Rocha-Santos as Prince Siegfried and Michaela Macauley as Odette. Photography by Genevieve Spooner. Courtesy of Continental Ballet and Genevieve Spooner.

Rick Vogt, 2018. Courtesy of Thomas McCartney, photographer.

Twin Cities Ballet of Minnesota and Ballet Royale

How does a couple that, between them, have trained and danced in Utah, Arizona, Nevada, New York, Washington, D.C., England, and West Germany, and had careers as an attorney and a pastry chef, decide to establish a ballet school and company in Lakeville, Minnesota? Here are their stories of a winding road to becoming professional ballet dancers, teachers, and directors of a ballet school and company.

Rick and Denise Vogt: Co-founders and Artistic Directors, Twin Cities Ballet of Minnesota; Co-founders and Directors of Ballet Royale Minnesota (Interview 6/17/21)

As a high school student, Rick Vogt watched an American Ballet Theatre's Nutcracker performance. Fascinated by the dancers' athleticism and strength, enamored by the whole presentation, and curious to find out more, some friends at school told him that Jo Savino's Classical Ballet Academy in Saint Paul was the best school. "I had no eventual goal to be a dancer; I just wanted a break from school."

Rick continued training, spending summers at San Francisco Ballet, in New York City at the Joffrey Ballet School and David Howard's School. Ballet drew him in, and Rick decided to put his academic studies on hold and pursue a professional ballet career. Rick danced with The Washington Ballet in D.C., Ballet West and Jazzin' Dance Company in Utah, Arizona Dance Theatre, and Nevada Dance Theatre. At that point, with eyes set on Europe, he was accepted as soloist and principal dancer at the Kiel Ballet in West Germany.

During this time, Denise received her serious training in England at the Harlow Ballet School, in particular with Leo Kersley (founding member of The Royal Ballet's predecessor, Sadler's Wells) and Thelma

Denise Vogt, 2018. Courtesy of Thomas McCartney, photographer.

Lister (formerly with Ballet Rambert). At sixteen years old, Denise trained for dance and drama at the London Studio Centre. "I loved it, and I trained for three years, every day from 9:30 a.m. to 5:00 p.m." At the London Studio Centre, she auditioned for the Kiel Ballet, and at nineteen years old, Denise headed to dance professionally with the Kiel Ballet.

From 1982 to 1986, she danced with the company and had an excellent experience with "every ballet form and *caractère* dance." She could speak a little German but had to learn it quickly. A respite from speaking German came when a new company dancer, Rick Vogt, joined the Kiel Ballet at the end of the 1984 season, and she could speak "American"

with him. Denise and Rick danced together for two more years. Denise then danced for the contemporary dance company Theater Osnabrück for one year. Rick stayed at Kiel. They married and danced for two years with the Kassel State Theater. They left Germany for Minnesota in late 1989, shortly before the Berlin Wall came down.

Back in Minnesota, they both took a hiatus from their professional dance careers. Rick returned to school and became an attorney but still taught ballet once or twice a week at various local schools. Denise worked as a pastry chef and caterer, then returned to full-time ballet, teaching ballet at several local schools, including Ballet Arts. Denise enjoyed teaching at Ballet Arts as well as the company class at MDT. For her, "It was fun to know and teach these beautiful people." In the mid-1990s, Denise worked at a dance school in Lakeville, establishing and directing its ballet program. As a choreographer, she set her Nutcracker on the school's ballet students. The Nutcracker increased in popularity over several years with enhanced improvements in production details.

After the 2002 Lakeville Nutcracker performances, Rick and Denise established a separate and independent nonprofit organization: Twin Cities Ballet of Minnesota (TCB), both as its artistic directors. As a nonprofit organization, Denise would have an artistic platform to further develop the professionalism of her Nutcracker and to create more choreography for more story ballets. Denise's creative energy has produced many new story ballets, including *Wizard of Oz–The Ballet, Cinderella 1944, Beauty & the Beast, Narnia: The Ballet*, and *Dracula*.

In 2009, with the success of TCB productions and growing support from the broad south metropolitan community, Rick and Denise decided to found and open their own ballet academy, Ballet Royale Minnesota. They soon needed to expand from their original leased space and decided to build, from the ground up, a properly designed classical ballet academy according to their specifications. Ballet Royale's state-of-the-art new facility took stage on the border of Burnsville and Lakeville—the first in Minnesota to be built with all new construction. As directors of Ballet Royale Minnesota, Rick and Denise oversee all aspects of the ballet and dance curriculum and administration. They are committed to the highest quality of training in an inclusive, healthy, and supportive environment. They share the gift and joy of ballet with all who buy a ticket to a TCB performance or walk across Ballet Royale's threshold.

Narnia: The Ballet. Twin Cities Ballet of Minnesota, premiere in May 2015. Andrew Lester as Aslan and Jennifer Christie as the White Witch. Courtesy of Erik Saulitis, photographer.

Dance Artist, Barry Leon. *Carmina Burana*. Choreography by Jean-Pierre Bonnefoux. Chautauqua Institution, 1991. Photography by Katharine P. Smith. Courtesy of Barry Leon.

Coda: Artist Story

Barry Leon: Dance Artist, Founder and former Artistic Director of the Buffalo Ballet Theater in New York, current Teaching/Coach Artist for the past ten years at Ballet Royale Minnesota (Interview 8/27/21)

Barry Leon's mother, in her youth, took ballet classes in Buffalo, New York, from a well-known Russian ballet teacher Alex Kaloff. She wanted to continue training, but during the Great Depression her family lost all their savings and she had to stop ballet. Later in life, she decided to go back and train with Mr. Kaloff, but he had a heart attack shortly after she began classes. As Alex recovered, he asked Barry's mother if she would take over the school and teach ballet until he could return; she gladly said, "Yes." She encouraged Barry and his sister to continue with ballet, and they often danced at Chautauqua's summer programs in upstate New York.

In 1969, when Barry was sixteen, he convinced his mother that he really needed to be in New York to study ballet. Barry explained, "There really was no reason to go to New York for ballet; my school had an incredible day program." Barry would go to academics in the morning for three hours, followed by classes at the ballet school, and then back to school for academics. At the end of his academic school day, he returned to ballet for more classes and rehearsals. An English

woman by the name of Katie Crofton, a former Ballets Russes dancer, directed the ballet program, along with Frank Bourman and a modern dance teacher, Graham Smith. "We had great training. There was no reason for me to leave. I think I just wanted to spread my own wings."

His mother took Barry to various New York City ballet schools to see who would offer him a scholarship. They went to the School of American Ballet, and they said Barry was too small. Then he went to the Joffrey Ballet School and also received no offers. Barry took a class one day at the Harkness House for Ballet Arts in New York City. "I was taking class in the gorgeous large studio with chandeliers when a woman, wrapped in a bathrobe, wandered into class and sat down. She wore pink ballet slippers, her hair all done up, and red lipstick smeared all over her lips." Barry knew there was something special about this woman. As she watched the class, he saw her approach the teacher, David Howard, and Barry heard her say, "I want him. Make sure he gets a scholarship." The woman was the ballet patron and philanthropist Rebekah Harkness. She told

Barry's mother, "He's small, and we're not sure, but I will take him anyway." Besides a scholarship, Rebekah Harkness offered every scholarship student a $45 stipend per week.

Barry attended the Harkness House for Ballet Arts for one year, one of twelve boys, all on scholarship. Rebekah Harkness was the third richest woman in the world at that time. She remarried several times, and each time she married into more money. Everything was provided for the dancers—great training, breakfast and lunch in the school's cafeteria, dance clothes, massages, and therapy if needed. Invited to join the Harkness Ballet's youth company after his first year, Barry was the youngest company member.

The Harkness Ballet was in Europe touring in 1970. At some point, Rebekah clashed with the artistic director and decided to disband the whole company. From Barry's understanding, she offered them no tickets to get back home from Europe. Some of the dancers stayed in Europe dancing; others came back to America, such as Bonnie Mathis, who joined American Ballet Theatre. The youth company became the Harkness Ballet to try to fulfill the European contracts that were already underway. Barry immediately went to Europe, and from late August 1970 through March 1971, the company performed in six European countries.

Barry said that Rebekah Harkness "was somewhat hard to deal with and wanted to direct the company with her choice of music, choreographers, and ballets because her funds completely supported the company." After Rebekah hired a new artistic director

who thought Barry was too small for the current repertoire, Barry ended up without work for almost a year and lived in New York City in a "cheap, tiny hotel room. It was horrible."

In New York City, he auditioned for American Ballet Theatre, and the director, Lucia Chase, told Barry, "I love you, but I just hired two dancers your size. I can't really hire you at this time." Barry then went to the Joffrey Ballet and tried to join the company by taking class. Several people told Joffrey, "He's a great dancer. You should take him." It was a six-week process, and finally, Joffrey ended up asking Barry to come to the theater during a rehearsal. Barry went to the theater and sat in the cold theater all day, watching with nothing to eat and with Joffrey taking slight notice of Barry, saying little to him. Finally, after a whole day of being basically ignored with no indication of an audition, Barry left saying to himself, "I've had enough. I'm done."

In 1972, he auditioned for Pennsylvania Ballet and joined the company for six years. Then in 1974, he met Greg Drotar, who previously had danced with Pennsylvania Ballet. Before joining Pennsylvania Ballet again, Greg had danced in the opening ceremonies of Disney World in Florida; in the movie *Mame* with Lucille Ball; performed in the Broadway show *Gigi*; and danced with Robert (Bob) Louis Fosse on Broadway.

One day Barry received a Western Union Telegram from Elliot Feld saying, "I saw you dance, and I'd love to have you in the company if you're interested." Barry did not have to audition. He just signed a contract. Barry was not even with the Feld company for a full year before he discovered that "I hated it . . . I found him extremely rude and abusive verbally." At twenty-four years old, Barry felt he could handle the toxic environment, but during one rehearsal, Elliot verbally kept "riding on some of the younger dancers." He said to himself that this man's choreography was great, but his personality was horrible. Barry went to his locker, took everything out, packed his bag, and left. He never went back.

In 1979, Greg and Barry left for Buffalo, New York. They stayed in Buffalo for the next ten years directing the school and establishing the Buffalo Ballet Theater. Barry reflectively added, "I don't know what led me to believe that I could direct a ballet school and company, being only twenty-six years old."

Barry spent summertime at Chautauqua in his youth, but he also taught ballet for Chautauqua's summer dance program from 1973-83. He danced in the company from 1988-98. In 1990, Barry met Ted Sothern, who had joined the company. Since that meeting in 1990 at Chautauqua, Ted and Barry have continued as dedicated partners and dance artists with fulfilling lives teaching, performing, directing, and living together in Minneapolis, Minnesota.

Svetlana Bak-Gavrilova, Gabriela Komleva, and Kirill Bak-Stepanoff (left to right).
Courtesy of Kirill Bak-Stepanoff and Svetlana Bak-Gavrilova.

SCENE 8

Minnesota Ballet Theatre and Minnesota Ballet School

Why does one leave his or her birth country, travel across seas, and begin a new life? Is it war, violence, poverty, a global sense of adventure, or a desire to go where friends or family have gone?

Kirill Bak-Stepanoff and Svetlana Bak-Gavrilova, Co-founders and Co-Artistic Directors (Interview 9/1/21)

Kirill and Svetlana arrived in the United States in 1998 from Saint Petersburg, Russia, with a work visa and a three-year contract for teaching ballet and performing at Classical Ballet Academy and Ballet Minnesota with Andrew and Cheryl Rist—performing as soloists and principal dancers. They chose Minnesota because they knew some Minnesota Russians, and "It was easier to go where you have friends," explained Kirill." Both Kirill and Svetlana left Russia, leaving behind successful ballet careers. They hoped to bring their ballet expertise and experience to America.

As a young boy in 1977, Kirill auditioned for and was accepted into the highly acclaimed Vaganova Academy of Russian Ballet in Saint Petersburg—renowned for its ballet, music, and academic training. On average, only one girl out of twenty and one-half of all boys are accepted after a rigorous three-part audition.

The first audition for aspiring young ballet dancers checks for good health and the proper height and size. If they pass, then the correct body structure is measured: the head not too big, the arms not too short, an arched foot, a deep plié, and good turnout. Third, the aspirants need to demonstrate musicality of movement and the ability to follow the barre and center exercises given by the teacher.

During his years at the Academy, Kirill left home at 7:35 a.m. and returned back home at eight or 8:30 p.m. Asked if he enjoyed his time at the Academy, he exclaimed, "Absolutely, yes!" Kirill graduated from the

Vaganova Academy in 1985. He went on to dance with the Boris Eifman Ballet for five years. After the Eifman Ballet, Kirill joined the Mikhailovsky State Opera Ballet Theatre, where he not only danced for seven years but where he also met Svetlana, also a graduate of the Vaganova Academy in 1992. They married and continued dancing together in the Mikhailovsky Theatre and touring around the globe.

At the end of the three-year contract with Andy and Cheryl Rist, they decided to stay in Minnesota and start their own ballet school. In 2001, Kirill and Svetlana were on their own. They applied for and received their green cards, then opened their first school in Eden Prairie, naming it the Academy of Russian Ballet. They restaged the classic ballets such as *Swan Lake*, *La Bayadère*, *Le Corsaire*, *Les Sylphides*, *Don Quixote*, and *The Nutcracker*.

They created an original ballet called *Great Pumpkin Rescues—Halloween Adventure*, and they choreographed their versions of *Peter and the Wolf* and *Carnival of the Animals*.

In 2018, the Academy of Russian Ballet's name changed to Minnesota Ballet School. They found that many in the general public thought the school was for Russians only. Since they teach all levels, and all are welcome to train with them, they decided that a Minnesota name would reach a broader population. Also in 2018, Svetlana and Kirill co-founded Minnesota Ballet Theatre, a non-profit organization, and they continue to stage performances with professional dancers.

Kirill and Svetlana said their journey from Russia to Minnesota has been good for twenty-three years, and they intend to sink their roots deeper into Minnesota soil.

Tutus created and designed by Ann Marie Ethen for Minnesota Ballet Theatre's productions, ca. 2018. Courtesy of Ann Marie Ethen.

Costume shop for New York City Ballet, 2010. Courtesy of the Saulitis family.

ACT THREE

L'Étoile du Nord

Lauren Shaul, company dancer with Minnesota Ballet, Duluth, 2022.
Courtesy of Erik Saulitis, photographer.

SCENE 1

Bold and Cold, Northern Minnesota
Minnesota Ballet in Duluth

Twenty bold Duluth Northlanders came together on a cold day in December 1965, establishing the Duluth Civic Ballet. They formed a board of directors with the mission to provide excellent ballet training for advanced ballet students and to have these students be part of an amateur performing company. The budget was set at one thousand dollars.

For the first year, Donna Harkins, a ballet teacher with a studio in Duluth Heights, "accepted no salary for leading the fledgling ballet in the first year. In her own studio, she tirelessly trained and rehearsed the young dancers chosen by audition."[152] A year later, in 1966, at Harkin's urging, the Civic Ballet hired Anna Adrianova Andaházy as their first artistic director, who flew weekly to Duluth to teach an evening class at the Civic Ballet's first studio—the former Dreamland ballroom. The weekly commute proved too time-consuming and expensive to continue, but a seed of excellence and professionalism in ballet training took root in the organization.

In constant pursuit of professionalism, the Civic Ballet's board hired Bernard "Bud" Johansen in the summer of 1967 to advise the ballet. As director and choreographer at the College of Saint Teresa in Winona, a former director of Rochester Ballet, and a former dancer with the Andaházys, he brought the professionalism needed. After teaching one class, assessing the organization, and visiting the Duluth Auditorium, Bud advised them to hire a full-time professional director.

The board of directors of the Duluth Civic Ballet found the means to hire a full-time director. This step moved the Civic Ballet forward in its professional growth, becoming an arts institution in Duluth that brings an appreciation of ballet and dance to northern Minnesota—a star in L'Étoile du Nord. The Duluth Civic Ballet became the Minnesota Ballet in 1994.

Minnesota Ballet dancers practice for the ballet's biggest production to date,
the three-act *Swan Lake*. The tutus were designed and created by Ann Marie Ethen.
Photography by Steve Kuchera. Courtesy of the *Duluth News Tribune*, March 22, 2018.

Karl von Rabenau: Artistic Director of Minnesota Ballet (Interview 7/8/21)

In August 2019, Karl became the new artistic director of Minnesota Ballet and his wife, Jennifer Miller, the ballet master. Karl claims Duluth as the city of his growing-up years. He attended the Duluth Ballet School during his middle school through early high school years. In 1983, he took the 7:00 a.m. bus on Saturday mornings, arriving in time for an 11:00 a.m. class at Minnesota Dance Theatre. The class included ballet, contemporary, and *pas de deux* classes. Affirmed and encouraged at MDT, he continued taking the Saturday morning classes for over two years. His mother and father were both artists—his mother a woodcut artist and lithographer, his father a potterer. They both encouraged his interest in ballet, and he continued training and dancing.

He brings to Minnesota Ballet deep and rich experiences in his ballet training and traveling. He trained at Boston Ballet in various capacities from 1985 to 1987, and then in 1986-87, he went to San Francisco Ballet for summer programs, followed by his first company contract with Omaha Ballet. At the invitation of Artistic Director Patricia Wilde, he joined Pittsburgh Ballet Theatre in 1988 and danced there for the next five years. Karl is immensely grateful for all his memorable experiences dancing full-length ballets and touring with the Pittsburgh Ballet Theatre (PBT). He became completely devoted to the art and continually strived to keep improving his technique. He also started thinking that after performing professionally, he would like to teach and pass on to students what he learned from some of his brilliant teachers and artistic directors.

In 1993, Milwaukee Ballet offered him a contract as a soloist. He was coming closer to the city of his youth. He danced for ten years with the Milwaukee Ballet, and then he took a "stage right" and retired. In 2003 he transitioned to the Milwaukee Ballet School & Academy, taking the next step in his balletic journey. For the next sixteen years, Karl taught at Milwaukee Ballet School & Academy, Point Park University in Pittsburgh, Pennsylvania, Central Pennsylvania Youth Ballet in Carlisle, PA, as well as throughout the country. In 2019 he received a phone call, seemingly out of the blue, inviting him to apply for the position of artistic director of Minnesota Ballet. His artist spirit said, "Yes," and he came back to his childhood home and to his ballet roots. With his wife, Jennifer, also a ballet dancer, they journeyed to Minnesota, continuing what Karl had always been called to do—ballet.

Classic tutu, created and designed by Ann Marie Ethen. Courtesy of Ann Marie Ethen.

Romanian Roots, Central Minnesota Stroia Ballet, Company and Studios

Carlos Cornel Stroia, born in Transylvania, Romania, attended the School of Choreography in Cluj-Napoca, Romania. He graduated with honors in 1974. He danced as a guest artist with companies in Italy, Germany, Cuba, and America (New York City at the Metropolitan Opera and Minnesota at Minnesota Dance Theatre).

Carlos is the founder of the Stroia Ballet Company and Studios in 1982, a regional company in Central Minnesota with studios in Baxter, Little Falls, and Sartell. Currently known as Stroia Dance Studios, under new owners, David and Alicia Le, who are building on the Stroia legacy that came before them.

Coda: Artist Story

Ann Marie Ethen: Design and Construction of Period Costumes, Tutus, and Stage Backdrops (Interview 8/26/21)

At ten years old, Ann Marie watched the full-length ballet of *Swan Lake* on television, completely enamored by its music and costumes. "I fell in love with ballet." She lived in St. Cloud, and the only dance school in the 1950s, St. Cloud School of Dance, did not teach classical ballet.

Ann Marie began ballet with Stroia Ballet in Little Falls, Minnesota, when she was thirty-one years old. "I was scared to death

because I had no background in music or ballet." As the studio grew in size and number, the company needed help finding backdrops for the Stroia ballet productions. Ann Marie mentioned, "I can draw a little bit." Quite an understatement—Ann Marie is a talented visual artist. If one goes and sees a classical ballet with Stroia Ballet, the backdrop is most likely a beautifully hand-painted one by Ann Marie. The first backdrop Ann Marie painted began her artistic journey into set and costume design. She researched what was appropriate for the time and culture of the ballet being performed, committed to being boldly accurate to the smallest detail. Her costumes were garments of excellent fabric and construction. Ann Marie consistently trained while making backdrops, garments, and tutus. Ann Marie also performed in the Stroia ballets and did promotional marketing for the company.

In the early 1990s, she performed in the Nutcracker with the Stroia Ballet Company in the stunning Hibbing High School Auditorium, with its marble floors, hand-molded ceilings, and cut-glass chandeliers. The school, built from the successes of the Iron Range, was a marvel of what a community could do when education and art were priorities.

For twenty-two years, Ann Marie trained, danced, painted backdrops, and made garments and tutus for Stroia Ballet. Without Ann Marie and her magnificent backdrops, stunning tutus and period garments, Stroia Ballet Company and Schools would never have had the broad awareness it has now. When Carlos Stroia came to Minnesota, he once told Ann Marie that "Ballet has to come from your heart," and for Ann Marie, all she does comes from her ballet heart, including her decision to leave Stroia Ballet and acquire a stronger technique. Similar to Anna Adrianova Andaházy, who took a leave of absence from the Ballets Russes to develop further her ballet artistry and technique with Mathilde Kschessinska in Paris, Ann Marie headed to the Twin Cities to learn from the masters who danced there. She left Stroia Ballet knowing that her years of dedicated generosity and artistry to ballet in Central Minnesota gave the Stroia Ballet the bedrock foundation from which to grow the organization.

Ann Marie continues to take ballet at Minnesota Ballet School in Eden Prairie. She also has made exquisite tutus, period garments, and beautiful backdrops for Minnesota Ballet Theatre. She has become well-known and much in demand for her exquisitely crafted tutus and period garments throughout Minnesota and beyond its borders to Rochester, New York; Dallas, Texas; Pittsburgh, Pennsylvania; and Ascoli Piceno in Italy. From her first ballet lesson as a young adult to the present time, she has not stopped taking ballet classes or designing and sewing ballet garments and tutus.

Ann Marie knows all the classical ballets, and she knows how dancers need to dance and move in period garments and tutus. She takes several measurements and designs and constructs breathtaking costumes for the dancer and his/her movements on stage. Ann Marie wants her garments and tutus to showcase the beauty and strength of a dancer's movement.

She said that if Carlos Stroia had never emigrated to Minnesota, her life trajectory would have been totally different. Reflecting on the past forty-two years, much of it immersed in the fortitude needed to "keep on dancing," she believes her life has been lived with more vitality and joy as a balletomane.

Rivers and Bluffs, Southern Minnesota

An interested group of students and their families who wanted to establish a quality ballet and dance program in their city became the source of Mankato Ballet Company's beginnings in 1983. The interest grew, and the small company decided to incorporate as a nonprofit in 1987 with its mission statement: "To nurture, encourage, and challenge students to achieve their potential for artistry and self-confidence through the classical dance experience."

Mankato Ballet Company

Riley Thomas Weber: Dance Artist, Ballet Master at Mankato Ballet Company (Interview 6/11/21)

Knowing Riley, with a gregarious and evanescent personality, one would never imagine that he was painfully shy and did not speak until he was nine. Music lessons with violin and cello helped him "speak out," at least at home initially. His music teacher noticed he had good feet and encouraged his parents to put him in dance.

Riley started with jazz at the local dance school in Fargo, North Dakota, then started ballet one year later. Riley began taking "straight-up-ballet" when he was twelve years old. He managed his rigorous ballet schedule four times a week in addition to his musical theater rehearsals. Riley spent his high school summers at a performing arts school where he was immersed in theater, ballet, and modern dance.

Riley enjoyed ballet but believed it would be over for him after high school. His real passion was music and playing his cello. He set his sights on the University of Minnesota for music and received an amazing cellist scholarship. But then Riley took an MDT adult open ballet class with Marcia Kegan. He had not danced in a year, but in the middle of the tendu exercise, Marcia came up to him and said, "You're beautiful!" That comment was characteristic of Marcia. Words of affirmation were given individually

Riley Weber. Courtesy of Galen Higgins, photographer.

to the dancers throughout class. After class, Marcia talked to him and said, "You're great, keep coming." An excellent teacher's words of encouragement at the right moment can positively change the course of a person's life. Riley chose a career in ballet instead of an orchestral career with cello.

Riley added a dance major to his studies at the U of M and danced with Ballet Minnesota. He also danced in a selection from the ballet *Raymonda* with Saint Paul City Ballet in 2011. During the performance, he felt something pop. He had four herniated discs needing three months of recovery. A life of ballet and performing changed in one day. Once healed, he started back at the U of M to finish his studies, but he only took one ballet class from Marcia. He was working at Grand Jeté, a dancewear store in Saint Paul, when he met the director of Mankato Ballet Company. She had sixty-five students and needed another teacher. Riley began teaching at Mankato Ballet Company at night. As of 2021, the number of students had increased to three hundred.

Riley started dancing again with Ballet Minnesota for one year. Riley said, "Ballet Minnesota will always be my home. Andy was a father to me, and he respected me." He took ballet classes to stay in shape. He had a 2016 contract to dance in Fargo-Moorhead's Nutcracker. "I loved it, but I came back to the Twin Cities," and back to teaching at Mankato Ballet Company. In 2017, Riley needed surgery on his four herniated discs that had ruptured again, plus a stress fracture in his spine. Two months after the surgery, Riley knew he could never dance again as he had. Teaching became his new passion, and in 2021, he celebrated his tenth year at Mankato Ballet Company. He is now ballet master for 350 students, and it keeps growing. He strives to have students feel supported and cared for and that their best is drawn out of them in ballet class. An excellent teacher following in Marcia Kegan's footsteps.

Rochester Ballet

Rochester Ballet appears in historical writings of other ballet schools and companies in Minnesota. Evidently, Rochester Ballet evoked an aura of professionalism and quality ballet instruction. No longer does a Rochester Ballet exist, but these following words will give life to its memory.

In the early 1950s, Bernard "Bud/Buddy" Johansen danced with the Andaházy Ballet Borealis company. At one point in his career with the Andaházys, he and Lóránt had a serious falling out. Bud Johansen left the Andaházys and headed south to Rochester and Winona, Minnesota. He directed the Rochester Ballet circa 1962 to 1966 and the ballet program at the College of Saint Teresa in Winona, circa 1966 to 1972. In 1963, when Loyce Houlton's The Contemporary Dance Playhouse was hosting auditions for a children's cast in the Bolshoi's production, Bud Johansen brought his students from Rochester, as did Lóránt Andaházy Jr. from Saint Paul. In the history of the Duluth Civic Ballet, Bud Johansen's name appears as Chairman of the Ballet Department at the College of Saint Teresa in Winona. He was invited to come and review the Civic Ballet and recommend their next artistic steps.

Program cover for Rochester Ballet School's final performance of *The Nutcracker*, 1998. Courtesy of Bobbie Herrell.

Coda: Artists' Stories

Balletomanes: Cynthia Betz (Interview 9/29/21), Bobbie Herrell (Interview 9/16/21), and Lisa Gray (Interview 9/28/21)

Cynthia Betz grew up in Rochester and took ballet lessons in high school at Rochester Ballet in the early 1960s from Bud Johansen. She remembers the studio with its "orange" door at the street level on Broadway Avenue. Mr. Johansen impressed Cynthia with his artistry and technique.

When Bobbie Herrell arrived in Rochester in 1968, Salvador Barillas directed Rochester Ballet. He was hired by the Rochester Ballet Guild after Bud Johansen left. In 1974, Salvador Barillas was hired at Kent State, and Bobbie bought the ballet school from him. She directed Rochester Ballet from 1974 to 1999, with ballet as its focus. The ballet methods she taught were Cecchetti and Royal Academy of Dance (RAD). Lisa Gray remembers Bobbie Herrell during her tenure as director of Rochester Ballet. The studio was still located downtown on Broadway Avenue. A creaky wooden staircase led up to the second floor with its large studio, no windows, and an old dressing room with two benches. That studio had seen many dancer days. Mrs. Herrell did not have a pianist. She played music on her record player in the corner. Lisa has a clear memory of Mrs. Herrell running back and forth to move the needle on the record.

Janet M. Johnson acquired Rochester Ballet from Bobbie Herrell in 1999 and merged it with her school Allegro. In 2021, Allegro celebrated thirty years and the retirement of Janet Johnson.

Paquita, Ballet Blake, 2019. Schuyler Kechely at Ballet Blake. Photography by Lance Thompson. Courtesy of Daniel and Julie Blake.

Ballet Blake

Daniel and Julie Blake met in 1997 at Houston Ballet Academy. They hoped to be together as dancers, acknowledging that a balletic couple would have its challenges. In 2001, Julie accepted a contract with Nevada Ballet Theatre until 2003. At that time, Daniel joined and danced for Minnesota Ballet in Duluth. He encouraged Julie to come to Minnesota. She did, and they danced together for the next five years, immensely enjoying their time with the company under the direction of Allen Fields and Robert Gardner. They danced leads in classical ballet roles and were married in Duluth in 2005, making it their home.

Daniel and Julie Blake: Co-directors and Co-owners of Ballet Blake (Interview 10/12/21)

In 2008, with Minnesota Ballet in Duluth touring more and the birth of their first child, Daniel decided to move on. David Marty, Director of the Reif Performing Arts Center in Grand Rapids, invited Daniel to join the staff and teach ballet. Julie had previously retired from dancing, saying "My cup runneth over now."

Daniel looked forward to enhancing the training and technique of the Reif Center ballet dancers. He taught at the Reif Center, envisioning it becoming similar to the intense training at the Houston Ballet Academy. After three full years, the Board of Directors did not agree with this vision. They kindly acknowledged Daniel's time and expertise he gave to the dancers at the Reif Center, and he and Julie began looking for another city in Minnesota that needed a ballet teacher. They considered Rochester because there was no classical ballet school there, only a performing ensemble of students from various dance schools with varied ballet programs. Competition schools dominated the dance scene. From 2012 to 2020, Ted Sothern traveled to Rochester every week and worked with this performing ensemble. A ballet teacher for years in the Twin Cities, Ted taught excellent ballet classes for this performing ensemble and set appropriate choreography for the students based on their ages and abilities.

Daniel and Julie moved down to Rochester in 2014 and launched their school with a "soft" opening. Within seven years, Ballet Blake, with emphasis on the classical ballet tradition, had found its niche in the Rochester dance scene.

Minnesota Conservatory for the Arts
An affiliate program of Saint Mary's University of Minnesota

A river city gem, the Minnesota Conservatory for the Arts (MCA) in Winona is located on the Teresan campus of Saint Mary's University of Minnesota. Its beginnings go back to 1973 when the power plant at the College of St. Teresa had enough space for a one-room dance studio, named The Ballet School, under the direction of Mme. Stefannié Valéncia-Kierlin. Mme.Valéncia-Kierlin created a full ballet curriculum, and MCA grew as her vision grew to include several other dance disciplines, performing arts, and visual arts. With Mme. Valéncia-Kierlin's untimely passing in 1999, MCA hired new artistic and managerial staff.

Tammy Schmidt: Director of Dance (Interview 9/28/21)

The Minnesota Conservatory for the Arts became an affiliate program of St. Mary's University, School of the Arts in 2003. It is the only Minnesota higher education institution where pointe work is offered. The Conservatory has no recitals, and all rehearsals for performances occur outside the ballet and dance classes. Dancers interested in performing in the Nutcracker, which is produced every other year, need to audition. College students may also perform. Teachers at MCA must have a BFA in dance or sufficient professional experience. As Director of Dance, Tammy Schmidt continues to enhance and expand the dance programs while honoring the artistic vision of the founder, Mme.Valéncia-Kierlin.

Variation:
University of Minnesota

Carl Flink: Director of the Department of Theatre Arts & Dance, College of Liberal Arts; and Artistic Director, Black Label Movement (Interview 9/16/21)

Carl, raised in a home on the isthmus area between Lake of the Isles and Cedar Lake, is a Minneapolitan at heart. He played soccer as a youth and always wanted to dance, but I was a "sports guy and a good student." He never imagined that he would become a dance artist. In high school, he mentioned to a friend that he was interested in dance. Later that day, a group of athletes surrounded him at his locker, expressing their concern that he was interested in dance.

Carl continued playing sports and never followed through with dance while in high school. He began post-high school at Carleton College, but that college was not "my cup of tea." He came back home after his freshman year, took some time off, and then decided to go to the U of M. He visited the campus, picked up a catalog, and saw the dance offerings. He signed up for a class and loved it. "It's kind of funny to think about a course catalog being life-changing."

At nineteen years old, he went from that one class, and within a month, he was dancing between thirty-eight to forty hours a week. Bonnie Mathis and Susan DeLange were his ballet teachers. He performed in a number of Delange & Dancers' studio performances.

Bonnie Mathis would bring him to Ballet Arts to do partnering. In fact, what he enjoys most about dance is its physicality, especially the art of partnering. "I graduated with a degree

Carl Flink and Emilie Plauché Flink in Flink's *Duet for Wreck* in 2012. The Cowles Center, Goodale Theater. Courtesy of the photographer, Bill Cameron, and Black Label Movement.

in political science and women's studies and three classes short of a major in dance." Carl laughed, calling himself "the barbarian out of the north who decided to be a dancer."

What amazed Carl was that Bonnie Mathis "delighted in me." He believes that Bonnie was, in some way, a pioneer in the ballet world and opened up new thinking of ballet in the twenty-first century—a step away from the ballet hierarchal and aristocratic lineage. She looked at ballet as a physical form, and she helped Carl "find dance within my body." She would tell Carl, "I want you to be right where your turnout is. We'll expand from there."

Carl's primary dance career began not in Minnesota but in New York City with the José Limón Company. One of the greatest gifts from the eight years of dancing in Limón's company was that Carl became "a dance artist who toured all over the world, all over the country." This experience with Limón was transformational. "There's just something magical about the fact that other artists and communities want to bring you into their culture and their community, not in a few days, but the moment you're there."

During his career with the José Limón Company, Carl and Emilie, another dancer in the company, were married. In 1998, he decided to pause his dance career and go to law school. He was accepted at Stanford Law School in Palo Alto, California. Emily continued dancing in the Limón Company. For his last two years in law school, Emily decided to join him in Palo Alto, and after law school finished, they both came back

Carl Flink and Penny Freeh in the 2016 VocalEssence Production of Virgil Thomson's *Four Saints in Three Acts* at The Cowles Center, Goodale Theater. Freeh and Flink co-choreographed the production with Flink as director. Courtesy of the photographer, Bill Cameron, and Black Label Movement.

to Minneapolis. Carl found a job at a law firm, but his mind was "just always in this world of movement." He heard of the dance professorship position available at the U of M and decided to apply. He was accepted and offered a position as an associate professor. "I was hired in part, not just to be a professor, but also to replace the director."

Shortly before this interview, Carl traveled to West Africa and Côte d'Ivoire. He traveled not for sightseeing but to connect with professional dance artists during an international dance festival. Asked how he

252

was selected to go, he said, "Quite frankly, I don't know how it actually happened. My name bubbled up with a group of artists I've stayed connected to throughout the years." The festival was a successful event, and he believed that he had connected with people at an extraordinary cultural level. The goal of the organization is to have an international dance festival every two years, and Carl has already been asked back. If this happens, his goal is to go with several performers. Carl says that because of his career with the Limón Company and multiple New York City artists, he has a fairly significant national and international network. "I've been lucky, lucky enough in my time as a dance artist."

Since 2009, Carl spoke highly of a collaboration with David Odde, a biomedical engineer at the University of Minnesota. They call this project "the moving cell project." Together, they developed a technique called *bodystorming*, where they use space bodies and photographic strategies to rapidly model scientific research. Carl explained that an interesting aspect of *bodystorming* is that it is also a way to challenge and encourage scientists to speak in plain English

In another scientific realm, Carl met John Bohannon, a former correspondent for *Science Magazine* who founded a competition called "Dance your PhD." In 2011, John collaborated with Carl and his dance company, Black Label, to create a TED talk, *Dance versus PowerPoint, a Modest Proposal.* In the TED talk, the Black Label dancers carried John Bohannon on stage, and as John spoke, the dancers, "like his little minions," moved to what he said. This highly successful TED talk has over five hundred thousand views on the TED circuit.

At the height of the Covid-19 pandemic in September 2020, Carl created a film with the theme "touch when touch is gone" for a Minneapolis TED talk. They worked with Jon Hallberg, a doctor at the University of Minnesota who created a process that allowed the dancers to take off their masks. The dancers went through extensive testing with this process so that they could reasonably feel like everyone was free of Covid. "And it worked!" After the initial TED talk, and the recent 2020 one, Carl has had three TED talks in between.

Since 2005, Carl has been at the University of Minnesota for sixteen years, and within his first year as a university dance professor, Carl founded his company Black Label Movement. In Carl's position as Director of the University's Dance Program, he oversees its expansive dance curriculum. He explained that ballet is one of the many techniques offered to dancers and dance majors. The program's mission is Contemporary Dance in Global Contexts. The program offers ballet training in conjunction with contemporary/modern, American jazz, African Diasporic Movement and hip-hop styles. Dance majors are not required to take ballet, but many still use it as a fundamental basis for their training.

Variation:
Carleton College, Northfield, Minnesota

Mary Moore Easter: Founder of the Carleton College Department of Dance (Interview 8/11/21)

Mary Moore Easter describes herself as a moving artist and now a writing artist, but she does not often write about dancing because "the medium of writing is both what's seen and heard, and the medium of dance is the body. If it isn't the body, there is no dance . . ." Her story takes one on an eclectic dance journey of nearly fifty years.

Mary taught at Carleton College for forty-one years, retiring in 2008. She exclaimed, "Oh my goodness. Wow. It took that length of time to develop the theater and dance department that we ended up with." She was hired to teach modern, and her colleague taught ballet classes. Carleton College had a history of visits and residences by Nancy Hauser, a Twin Cities modern dancer.

Mary spoke about her dance training as in "bits and pieces." She thought she was going to be a music theory teacher in college, like her mother, but "dance seized me." She had taken many ballet classes, but it was clear to her that she would not be a ballerina. Plus, she wanted to be a Graham dancer. In the summer of 1969, Mary began training at a Nancy Hauser six-week workshop taught by Margret Dietz, a former dancer with the Mary Wigman company in Germany. An old knitting mill warehouse became the dance

Portrait of Mary Moore Easter by Lyn Swigart taken for her solo dance tour, *Mary Easter Dances* in 1979, from Carlton College to the east coast and back to Minneapolis, ending at the Walker Art Center. Courtesy of Mary Moore Easter.

training ground for the workshop. Located in Dinkytown on the West Bank of the University of Minnesota, the old factory had a performance space on the first floor and open and spacious studios with large factory windows on the second floor. "That was where I was absolutely hooked."

Margret Dietz taught dancing at the University of Minnesota and was the artistic adviser for the Nancy Hauser Dance Company. Going to that first class taught by Margret Dietz was "a stunning experience for me, and I was in class with members of the Nancy Hauser company." Nancy trained with the modern dancer Hanya Holm, who, like Margret Dietz, also drew from the Wigman style of modern dance. So, Mary put aside her aspirations to be a Graham dancer and embraced the Wigman-Dietz-Holm German Expressionist style instead. After her workshop training, Mary joined a dance group in Minneapolis called Choreogram, directed by Margret Dietz.

Mary brought her modern training to the Carleton College campus and began building awareness that dance is an art and a dance program needs its own department—not part of the Physical Education department. "I was seeking to build a program that had artistic weight to it." Mary's colleague at Carleton, Toni Sostek, taught the ballet classes, and they intended the classes to be complementary to each other for the dance students. Serious dance students would take a combination of four dance classes each week, two ballet and two modern classes. Mary would often hold choreography rehearsals on the weekends. Her dancers presented at least one concert each year. Mary also invited guest teachers and choreographers to teach and rehearse the student dancers because, as Mary said, "dance is much wider than me and what I'm doing." For example, in May 1970, Margret Dietz came to Carleton College and presented her choreography in her *Choreogram Dance Concert*. Fast-forward

to 2006, Mathew Janczewski set one of his works, *Quartet*, on four Carleton dance students, two men and two women. They took *Quartet* to the Kennedy Center in Washington, D.C. "A Minnesota thing at the Kennedy Center."

During the last four years that Mary taught at Carleton College, dance received recognition for its value and had full department status. Up until that time, dance was called a program. Mary reminisced, "I actually thought I was leaving it [dance], but I wasn't. And then I like to say that modern choreographers discovered something they called the 'mature presence.'" In 2009, Mary performed a solo concert three months after her retirement, using her husband's sculpture pieces and her choreography. At sixty-eight years old, Mary danced within her "mature presence" ability. This work became her swan song for choreography, but some other opportunities for performing came her way when choreographers needed a mature presence. She performed and toured with Shapiro & Smith's *Tableau Vivant* at The Cowles Center for Dance & the Performing Arts and on tour to Marshall, Minnesota. *Tableau Vivant* presented an older cast, mixed in with younger dancers, on stage together.

In 2021, Mary Moore Easter, at eighty years old, is forever a dance artist.

Variation:
St. Olaf College, Northfield, Minnesota

Anthony Roberts: Artist in Residence in Dance and Janice Roberts: Professor of Dance (Interview 9/8/21)

Together Anthony and Janice Roberts brought stellar ballet and dance experience and expertise to St. Olaf College. To date, they have about fifty years of teaching, choreographing, performing, improving, and enhancing the St. Olaf College Dance Department. The department is a charter and accredited member of the National Association of Schools of Dance (NASD), one of only two member schools in Minnesota, along with the University of Minnesota. The NASD establishes national standards for undergraduate and graduate degrees and other credentials for dance and dance-related disciplines.

Since the 1990s, Anthony and Janice have, as artistic athletes, immersed themselves in

Jock-ularity. Dance students at St. Olaf College, Northfield, 2007.
Choreography by Anthony Roberts, premiered at the Walker Art Center, 1995.
Courtesy of Erik Saulitis, photographer.

the hyper-physical demands of the art form that they have dearly loved for decades. Being immersed so completely, the amount of growth and enhancements of the dance program and curriculum has been extensive. It is almost impossible to list all that they have done and accomplished during their St. Olaf tenure. Here are examples of some of their works and successes.

One of their first improvements gave students in the performing company the option to take technique class at or near their individual level. When they first began at St. Olaf, all company students took the same class, no matter how strong or advanced some may have been. Additionally, for seniors in the dance major, a Senior Dance Seminar Class culminates their dance training. Each dance major has to select, create, and present a Senior Dance Capstone Project.

They initiated student participation in an annual regional dance conference—the American College Dance Association. At this annual conference, students and faculty engage in three days of performances, workshops, panels, and master classes. Their dance works could also be adjudicated with open and constructive feedback.

From the 2000s on, Janice led the dance department in working to secure a new building that would house art and dance. Prior to the new building, the dance department held classes in five different buildings and had no central office space. The new building gave a visual identity to the dance department. Anthony and Janice also saw the need to have a dance technology course named Movement, the Camera, & the Creative Process. In this course, students gain experience as directors, performers, videographers, editors, and critics.

From 2004 to 2006, Anthony created an evening-length work called *Swing a Club: Facing Cancer* which received high

Aqueous. Dance students at St. Olaf College, Northfield, 2006. Courtesy of Erik Saulitis, photographer.

accolades. This work toured nationally to Arizona, Colorado, Iowa, and Oregon, in addition to Minnesota performances in Northfield, Bloomington, and Minneapolis. In May 2007, Janice and dance department colleague, Heather Klopchin, received a National Endowment for the Arts grant for a historical modern dance project, *Dreams*, choreographed by Anna Sokolow in 1961. They brought in Lorry May, director of the Sokolow Dance Foundation, to reconstruct the Sokolow choreography for Anthony and the student dancers.

From the 2010s to the present, they continued to boldly enhance the dance department's programs by developing new courses and course requirements for the dance majors. Also, non-dance majors are welcome and encouraged to take these new courses. They developed Dance Anatomy & Kinesiology and Conditioning: Practice and Principles and received another NEA grant to support Janice's one-of-a-kind collaborative interdisciplinary project that engaged the Northfield communities. They have continued to invite guest artists to teach classes.

In the 2020s, Janice initiated and oversaw a collaboration with Penumbra Theatre to provide diversity, equity, and inclusion training to the dance faculty, staff and students. They also wrote a proposal, approved by the administration, to establish a tenure position offering movement and theory classes that focus on African diaspora dance.

On August 31, 2022, Anthony and Janice will take their final bows at St. Olaf College. In their retirement notice sent to the provost and dean of the college, they wrote, "Our St. Olaf colleagues and students have excited, challenged, supported, and propelled us along meaningful and rich careers . . . We will strive to encourage the Dance Department to look beyond the mere replication of our skills as it continues to evolve into the most equitable, inclusive program it can be."

Apotheosis: Sacred Dance

The word *apotheosis* comes from the ancient Greek verb *apotheoun*, meaning "to deify," and *theos* is the Greek word for "god." Among the ancient Greeks, it was sometimes fitting to grant someone "god status," and at the beginnings of ballet in Europe, the French nobility deified Louis XIV, christening him *Louis-Dieudonné* (Gift of God). At only fifteen years old, he took center stage and danced the role of Apollo, the Roman sun god. In Marius Petipa's original score of *The Sleeping Beauty*, the ballet ends with an apotheosis—a dancer performs as Louis XIV. In the twenty-first century, there is no apotheosizing of people, and the word, *apotheosis*, can be used in reference to a perfect example or ultimate form.

Throughout human history, with its cultural diversity of race, color, and ethnicities, dance continued to express the ultimate inexpressible form—a visible presence of an invisible Higher Power. Hafez, a fourteenth-century Persian lyric poet, wrote:

> *I sometimes forget that I was created for Joy.*
> *My mind is too heavy for me to remember*
> *that I have been called to dance, the*
> *Sacred dance of life.*
> *I was created to smile, to love, to be lifted up,*
> *and to lift others up.*
> *O Sacred One, untangle my feet from all the*
> *ensnares.*

> *Free my soul that we might dance,*
> *And that our dancing might be contagious.*[153]

In Judaism, the world's oldest monotheistic religion, Hebrew Scriptures Psalm 150 says, "Praise God with timbrel and dancing," and in 2 Samuel 6:14, "David danced before the Lord." In early Christian times, dance and its costumes represented heavenly bliss, as danced by angels. An early Christian theologian, Clement of Alexandria (150–216), wrote, "Then shalt thou dance in a ring together with the angels, round Him who is without beginning nor end."[154] Throughout the Middle Ages and the early Renaissance, sacred dance received moral reprobation. In 1667 the Parliament of Paris "issued a decree proscribing all religious dances . . ."[155] Yet, humans move, and dance is movement, and sacred dance continued to move through the centuries, garnering moral reprobation at times.

In Minnesota's ballet history, the most significant sacred dance that integrated dance into a Christian liturgical setting was Anna Adrianova Andaházy's *Los Seises*. Her inspiration was a sacred dance performed in Seville, Spain. The seises, choristers of Seville Cathedral, perform each of the six days following the feast of Corpus Christi in June. Their costumes today are those dating from the beginning of the seventeenth century, but the dance and its tradition date back to the fourteenth century.[156] From February to April 1973, the Andaházy Ballet Company's *Los Seises* performed eleven times in Washington, D.C., between the National Cathedral and the National Presbyterian Church. At this time, the Andaházys had two ensembles performing *Los Seises*, and the second ensemble stayed back in Minnesota, rehearsed by the ballet mistress Kay (Page) Greaser. Rehearsals took place in the St. Louis Park studio. Kay also taught Adult Beginning Ballet classes in the 1680 Grand Avenue studio.

Minnesota currently has several church groups that have Praise Dancers, people of all ages dancing during church services and events, believing "For in Him we live and move and have our being."[157]

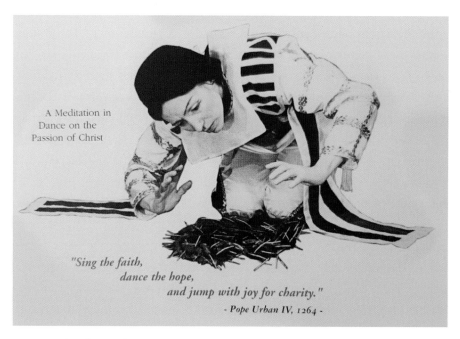

Los Seises, Andaházy Ballet Company. Jane (Harrington) Keyes, who performed the 'Crown of Thorns' solo in the 1965 KTCA-TV premiere. Choreography by Anna Adrianova Andaházy. "Andaházy Souvenir Pamphlet, 2000." Courtesy of Marius Andaházy.

Los Seises. Andaházy Ballet Company. Basilica of St. Mary, Minneapolis. Choreography by Anna Adrianova Andaházy. Dancers: Laurel Charles, Barbara Christian, Heidi Fisk, Lori (Kartheiser) Gleason, Elizabeth Heffernan, Jennifer Johnston, Kathleen O'Brien, Sharon Weiher Peterson, Linda Purdy, Karen Paulson Rivet, ca. 1973. "Andaházy Souvenir Pamphlet, 2000." Courtesy of Marius Andaházy.

CrossCurrent Dance Theatre. Brenda Jerich and Sonja Hinderlie. Choreographer Sharon Hinck,
ca.1994. Music from *The Mission*, a 1986 British period drama film by composer Ennio Morricone.
Photographer unknown. Courtesy of the Saulitis Family.

Coda: Artists' Stories

Sonja Hinderlie: Dance Artist, Sacred Dance and Ballet (Interview 10/20/21)

Sonja trained in ballet both in Illinois and California beginning at age five. She is also a cellist and singer, and at times her music and her ballet vied for Sonja's time and attention. She had been interested in sacred dance or dance for worship since 1973 after meeting Sarah Linner Quie at Holden Village, a Lutheran Christian center in the Cascade Mountains of the U.S. state of Washington. Sarah had trained with Loyce Houlton during her high school years and then graduated with a sacred dance major from St. Olaf College.

Impassioned by this vision of dance as a sacred art, Sonja's interest in sacred dance to communicate scripture and the glory of God in worship was piqued. Sonja and her husband, Johan Hinderlie, left Holden Village, and they serendipitously met Sarah again at a Carla DeSola sacred dance workshop in Minneapolis in 1982. Sonja said, "We danced together at this event, and a special bond developed between us with a sacred dance vision." Sonja and Johan were living at this time in Cambridge, Wisconsin, where arts were thriving. Sonja opened a ballet studio and gymnastics program in this small town.

In 1984, the Hinderlies moved to Minneapolis, and Sonja reached out to Sarah who had been training a small group of dancers for a liturgical dance group at St. Anthony Park Lutheran Church. In 1982, Sarah incorporated St. Anthony Park School of Dance, also using the church space. The dance school grew and needed a larger dance space. Sarah moved to a magnificent and architecturally beautiful open space, Aasgaard Hall of Luther Seminary on Como Avenue in Saint Paul. The dance school continued growing by leaps and bounds, and Sarah hired Sonja to teach in 1986, and Monica Wolney was the manager.

The liturgical dance program at St. Anthony Park Lutheran Church continued under Sarah's instruction. When she and her husband, Joel, planned to move to Pennsylvania, Sarah asked Sonja to take over the liturgical dance group at the church; Sonja agreed and directed the group for three years. Sonja also became manager for St. Anthony Park School of Dance in 1987; she and Monica Wolney were the two main teachers. Sonja hired Anna Goodrich in 1991, who had been teaching jazz and ballet for Sarah. She also hired ballet teacher Dana Bliss. Together Anna and Dana raised the level of ballet technique at the school. Cross Current Dance Theater, a concert sacred dance company directed by Sharon Hinck, did their rehearsals at Aasgaard Hall, and she became another teacher for the school in the fall of 1990.

In 1991, St. Anthony Park School of Dance moved to a commercial space on Energy Park Drive in Saint Paul. The sacred dance partnership with Cross Current Dance Theater continued, and Sonja joined the Cross Current Dance Theater company. Sacred dance classes for children became part of the dance school's class offerings. At the school's Christmas and spring performances, other partners in sacred dance from the Twin Cities performed as guest artists. Anointed Soles, directed by Brad and Cindy Garner, performed works with classical and contemporary music to sacred dance choreography. Cross Current Dance Theater also performed on stage with larger pieces that entertained both young and old.

The 1990s were golden years of sacred dance with expansion to other churches and an increased appreciation for its liturgical relevance. Several clinics and workshops were held at Mount Carmel, a retreat site in Alexandria, Minnesota. Individuals and groups came from churches to receive training on how to begin a sacred dance program at their churches. Sonja, as program director at Mount Carmel, frequently incorporated sacred dancing into worship services. In 1993, Sonja purchased St. Anthony Park School of Dance from Sarah. At that time, the Quies had moved to South Bend, Indiana. Sonja hired Wilor Bluege, a former Andaházy ballet teacher, in early spring of 1996 to teach more advanced ballet classes at the school. With excellent teachers and managers,

including Kate Barloon, the school continued to grow and develop, needing even more space.

One of her teachers who trained with Marius Andaházy, arranged for Sonja to meet Marius. Sonja, her teacher, and Marius met for dinner in June 1996 at a small restaurant in Saint Paul. Sonja and Marius discussed a shared vision for sacred dance and ballet. His parents had produced *Los Seises*, a ballet depicting the Passion of Christ, for several years. After hours of conversation, Marius took them to his 1680 Grand Avenue studio, recently closed. With complete trust in Sonja's integrity, he handed the keys to the Grand Avenue studio space to Sonja. St. Anthony Park School of Dance moved from Energy Park Drive to Grand Avenue in July 1996.

At the same time, Sarah, who had since started an active dance school in South Bend, Indiana, moved back to the Twin Cities. Cross Current Dance Theater's ending became an opportunity for Sarah and Sonja to establish a new ensemble, St. Anthony Sacred Dance Company. Many Cross Current Theater dancers joined this ensemble. From 1997 through 1999, the company had bookings two or three times a month at various churches and venues. After 2000 and through 2008, the company had six to eight bookings a year. Some of these were large events at Central Lutheran, Calvary Lutheran of Golden Valley, St. Catherine University, St. Olaf Catholic Church, Mt. Olivet Lutheran, Westminster Presbyterian, the Basilica, and the Saint Paul Cathedral. It was a flourishing time for St. Anthony Sacred Dance Company, and several of the dancers also joined the Andaházy Ballet Company for its performances of *Los Seises* from 1998 through 2002 at St. Olaf Catholic Church. Sonja was privileged to be part of *Los Seises*.

St. Anthony Sacred Dance has not officially closed any invitation to perform sacred dance, but the recent focus has been on inviting young people to become involved in sacred dance. One of its last projects occurred in 2013 at Trinity Lutheran Church in Stillwater, where St. Anthony Sacred Dance Company and guest dancers collaborated with the Valley Chamber Chorale dancing to a Mass by Zoltán Kodály. Twenty dancers of all ages performed, augmented by multimedia and banners. It was a grand finale of all the years that Sarah and Sonja had partnered with others to bring God glory through dance.

Paula Christensen: Dance Artist for Sacred Dance and Ballet (Interview 10/26/21)

I believe that sacred dance enhances ballet (or any form of dance) in that, ultimately, all movement comes from the Creator of movement. The Apostle Paul said, "In Him, we live and move and have our being." Dance brings Paula a deeper joy, appreciation, and awareness that dance is movement, and all movement emanates from the Creator; it is a gift from Him, and dancing is a gift back to him.

For Paula, ballet enhances sacred dance because it gives dance a graceful and beautiful framework from which to do its "speaking." Ballet helps sacred dancers to stretch and extend their lines in a movement prayer to God. Sacred dancers are able to have a common base from which to share and perform and from which to expand into other movement with grounding, strength, and grace.

Paula described *Los Seises* "as a spiritual journey in dance." The music, props—Marius Andaházy called them "instruments" of Christ's death—costumes with white-plumed hats, red velvet and white satin garments, and Anna Adrianova Andaházy's choreography intensely portrayed the agony and death of Christ. Paula said, "*Los Seises* was a giving of myself and my living, moving, and being, so the audience could share the experience of an intimate prayer dance."

Terpsichorean. Self-portrait of the artist, Charles Gilbert Kapsner, 2009.
Oil on canvas, 20 x 24 inches. Courtesy of the Private Collection of
Charles Gilbert Kapsner.

Coda Générale:
Ballet Collaborators

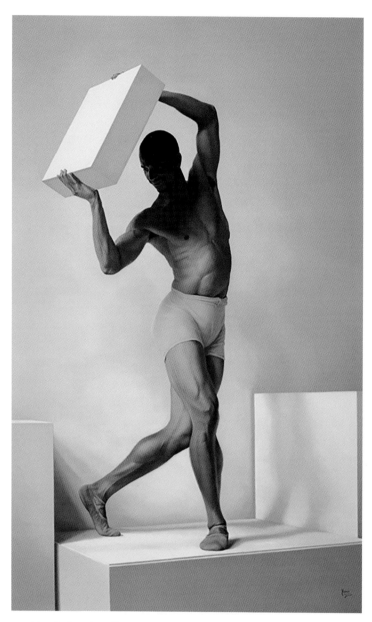

North Carolina Dance Theatre (currently Charlotte Ballet).
Jhe Russell, 2009. Artist, Charles Gilbert Kapsner.
Oil on panel, 30 x 48 inches. Courtesy of the
Private Collection of Charles Gilbert Kapsner.

Charles Gilbert Kapsner: Visual Artist, Ballet Supporter
(Below is his curriculum vitae, written by his wife, Catherine Stoch, a writer and supporter of the arts.)

"Remember nature is your teacher, I am your guide," was a prevailing theme in the Florence, Italy, studio of Nerina Simi, where Charles Gilbert Kapsner's greatest learning as a painter occurred. His artistic roots are planted in the fifteenth century, yet he remains a contemporary painter whose compositions fuse old and new. He works to ensure that both *art and artist* are accessible and that the images serve as educational tools. "This is my life," he said. "There's no difference between work and life for me."

In 2018 Charles was designated as an ARC Associate Living Master by the Art Renewal Center. He is also a member of the Oil Painters of America, Portrait Society of America, Coast Guard Art Program, and the Salmagundi Club. In addition, he received a Career Achievement Award from the Florence Biennale, Master Artist from the Five Wings Arts Council (serving five counties in central Minnesota), Public Service Commendation from the United States Coast Guard, and Superior Volunteer Service Award from the Adjutant General of the Minnesota National Guard. Primarily a studio painter, he prefers the "Vanitas" style of still life painting in which the various objects depicted symbolize the brevity and vanity of human existence.

Interwoven through decades and in between his studio time are community-based art projects, including two frescoes in the elementary school in his hometown of Little Falls and a commission for the Committal Hall at the Minnesota State Veterans Cemetery completed in 2019. The commission that is perhaps the most

Duet, Saint Paul City Ballet School. Eleni Ayo Caros (pink tutu) and Megan Thrasher (blue tutu), ca. 2006. Artist, Charles Gilbert Kapsner. Oil on panel, 16 x 20 inches. Courtesy of the Private Collection of Charles Gilbert Kapsner.

impactful of Charles's career is a series of five 8' x 10' oil paintings that depict the faces and stories of the men and women of each of the five U.S. military branches.

Dance collaborations include sketches and paintings of dancers from the Stroia Ballet Company & Studios, Minnesota Ballet in Duluth, Saint Paul City Ballet, and Charlotte Ballet (previously North Carolina Dance Theatre). As shared by Jean-Pierre Bonnefoux, artistic director at the Charlotte Ballet:

Charles Kapsner captures the graceful athleticism of a dancer's body. This collaboration has given the North Carolina Dance Theatre artists an opportunity to experience firsthand how art inspires art.

His works can be found in public and private collections in the United States and Europe. Charles calls Central Minnesota home (near Little Falls, on the Mississippi River), where he lives with his wife, Catherine, and the many forest creatures that surround him on a daily basis.

Coda: Artists' Stories

Judith Brin Ingber: Dancer, Choreographer, and Writer
(Interview 9/14/2021 and several other conversations)

Judith Brin Ingber has an air of gravitas that commands deep respect. Her knowledge of Minnesota's dance history and her own dance and choreographic story have a profound depth. The following artist's story will be like the tip of the iceberg of her amazing life as a dancer, choreographer, dance artist, writer, and historian.

Judith grew up in Minneapolis and trained with Lóránt and Anna Andaházy. With their company, Ballet Borealis, she performed at the Northrop in *Schéhérazade* under the baton of Antol Doráti of the Minneapolis Orchestra. In later years, she continued her ballet training at Ballet Arts with Bonnie Mathis and Lirena Branitski and ballet class with the James Sewell Ballet company. Judith graduated from Sarah Lawrence College under Bessie Schönberg, taking ballet class from Henry Danton.

After graduation, she worked as an editorial assistant for *Dance Magazine* and performed in Meredith Monk's breakthrough *Juice: A Theatre Cantata in Three Installments* on the spiraling ramps of the Guggenheim Museum in New York City. She returned to Minneapolis in 1970, working with Suzanne Weil at the Walker Art Center. Judith proposed that she search for young Minnesota dance choreographers. A proposal that resulted in the Young Choreographers Evening directed by Judith. Wildly successful, this program has continued for fifty years, now called the Choreographers Evening. In the mid-70s, Judith lived in Israel, working for Inbal Dance Theatre and teaching for the Batsheva Bat Dor Dance Society. She also choreographed a work for young audiences for the Batsheva Dance Company. With her writing interest and expertise, she also co-founded *Israel Dance Annual*, Israel's first dance magazine.

After returning to Minneapolis, and after the sudden death of Nadine Jette, then director of the University of Minnesota's Physical Education dance program, Judith became the first director of the dance program for the newly combined Department of Theatre Arts & Dance. She continued to teach in the dance program for twenty years. Her dance and dance history acumen included invitations to teach at international dance programs from England to Poland to Israel. In 1986 she co-founded Voices of Sepharad as choreographer and dancer, touring extensively in the U.S. and abroad until 2006. The Voices of Sepharad explores a rich Jewish cultural tradition with performances in song, music, and dance.

Judith was honored in 2006 with a special citation from the Minnesota Sage Awards for Dance. She continues writing and creating, including her latest duet for Stephanie (Grey) Fellner and performing in *LVD* by Helen Hatch and Berit Ahlgren.

Ruthena Fink: Dance Artist, Owner of the Grand Jeté, 1983 to 2021 (Interview 6/1/21)

Ruthena (Sternberg) Fink began dancing by "happenstance," as she explained. As a young child, about ten years old, Ruthena accompanied her friend, Carolyn, to the Mary Bellefour School of Dance in the High-

Schéhérazade, Andaházy Ballet Borealis. Ruthena (Sternberg) Fink (left on knee), Michele Della Rocca (right on knee), Rennie Palmer (standing on left), and Mary Arsenault (standing on right). Andaházy Ballet Borealis Souvenir Pamphlet, 1961-62 Season. Courtesy of Marius Andaházy.

land neighborhood of Saint Paul. She just walked in without registering and remembers the class being a mixture of tumbling, ballet, and "this and that." At her church, a woman and her dancer daughter knew of the Andaházys because of the Hungarian community in Saint Paul. The daughter danced there and suggested that Ruthena try taking ballet classes at the Andaházy school. The studio was close enough to her home, so she started attending classes with the Andaházys as an eighth grader, about thirteen years old, and continued training with them from 1959 to 1964.

Ruthena's first performance was at the Northrop, which was so exciting for her. It was *Aurora's Wedding* taken from Act III of *The Sleeping Beauty* and one of the popular Ballets Russes works performed by the Andaházys. She was a Page in the ballet and did little more than walk onto the stage with a tree, put it in place, blow a horn, and then exit. She also performed in *Schéhérazade* for two years at the Northrop with the Andaházys. "The costumes and scenery were amazing. One doesn't see many productions like that today." She particularly enjoyed watching Mr. and Mrs. A perform the lead roles of Zobéide and the Golden Slave. Mr. A made an incredible jump to Zobéide as the Golden Slave, landing on a pile of pillows. Ruthena also performed in several other of their ballets.

Ruthena remembers that Mrs. A was the epitome of a ballerina, "very delicate and often wore a pink or white flowing chiffon skirt for teaching. Mr. A was quite the opposite . . . very masculine, leather jacket, and he loved to ride his motorcycle. In class, I remember he often had a stick he used for timing and rhythm—not for making corrections on dancers." He also entertained students with stories of the Ballets Russes days or his family's home back in Hungary before World War II. Ruthena said that she only cried once in class, but she cannot remember why.

After high school, Ruthena attended Grinnell College from 1964 to 1968 and took whatever dance classes they offered, but mostly contemporary. Once home, she began taking classes at Minnesota Dance Theatre from 1969 to 1971 at The Contemporary Dance Playhouse. Class with Loyce was more balletic from waist down and contemporary from waist up. Her ballet classes were not strictly Vaganova or Cecchetti—her own amalgamation of different ballet styles. She enjoyed performing for two years in Loyce's Nutcracker. As a dancer, Loyce expected you to give 100 percent; it was all business when you were around her. After the Nutcracker performance, at the celebration party at the Playhouse, the

other side of Loyce came out—kind, generous, and presenting gifts to all the dancers. "One could see that Loyce truly loved the dancers and was so kind to them."

From 1972 to the late 1970s, Ruthena took classes at Jo Savino's school called the Classical Ballet Academy, and his company was the Saint Paul City Ballet. Since she was married and living in Saint Paul, his studio was a better location for Ruthena than MDT in Minneapolis. With Jo Savino, she had the opportunity to perform in full-length ballets: *Giselle*, *Coppelia*, and *Firebird*. A performance of *Giselle* in Rochester, Minnesota, remains a fond memory for her. Not only did she walk on stage as Bathilde in the first act with two dogs, but she also "entered the convent;" that is, the Rochester community of the Sisters of Saint Francis provided lodging for them. She remembers staying in a small, austere, sparsely decorated room and the sweet smell of cinnamon rolls waking her up in the early morning.

When Jo Savino needed to vacate his first studio in Saint Paul, he moved to a building in the Frogtown neighborhood of Saint Paul. Ruthena, like many others, followed him there. When Savino said his goodbyes to Minnesota, she followed his best teacher and dance artist, Janet Smith, to Dance Spectrum. She heard that St. Anthony Park School of Dance had moved to the former Andaházy space at 1680 Grand Avenue. Ruthena decided to continue taking ballet classes there from Wilor Bluege and other staff, many of whom were Andaházy trained. She continued training at 1680 Grand Avenue, supporting its name change to Saint Paul City Ballet in 2002. Ruthena also performed with Ballet Minnesota in *Swan Lake* (2007), *Cinderella* (2008), and *Coppélia* (2013–14).

In 1983, Ruthena was thirty-seven years old, and after working at Macalester College as director of student financial aid, she decided to take a career path change and opened her store, the Grand Jeté on Grand Avenue in Saint Paul. For thirty-eight years, she embraced the opportunity to see the evolution and expansion of ballet in the Twin Cities. From the roots of Lóránt and Anna Andaházy on one side of the Mississippi River to Loyce Houlton and Minnesota Dance Theatre on the other side, ballet established firm and deep roots, but with differing creativity and focus. Her store became the go-to store for all kinds of dancers. From pointe shoes to ballroom dance shoes to leotards, tights, and dance belts, Grand Jeté had whatever was needed. She often received an SOS call within hours of a performance to help a dancer or company with an emergency shoe or costume need.

Ruthena made it a point to learn about the various schools and companies in the area—and even beyond into the states sur-rounding Minnesota. Grand Jeté's business encircles a large demographic area. She attends many of the Twin Cities ballet and dance performances. It is almost a rarity not to see her there.

Another rewarding aspect of her business was seeing some dancers come to the store as young children and then watching them progress in their dancing skills and technique until it became time to say goodbye as they entered college or began a professional dance career. It was also a joy to see them come back to the store or see them performing on a Twin Cities stage.

On December 31, 2021, Ruthena took her swan song bow after thirty-eight years of serving a broad dance community and being an invaluable supporter of dancers of all ages and dance disciplines. She graciously retired and sold her business to Solveig Mebust, a former dancer at Saint Paul City Ballet. Solveig has a music education degree with a PhD forthcoming from the University of Minnesota. Solveig said that she "came back to dance as an adult, first at St. Paul Ballet and now at Ballet Co.Laboratory, and now at Grand Jeté where dance remains 'an integral part of my life.'"[158]

Emily Kleinschmidt: Dance Artist and former Grand Jeté employee (Interview 7/15/21)

Emily Kleinschmidt is a tall, lithe, smart, and savvy young woman. She remembers beginning her dance training as a young child at Dance Spectrum. She enjoyed the variety of dance styles, such as ballet, tap, and jazz, but preferred ballet. In high school, she trained at MDT and also attended the Saint Paul Conservatory for Performing Artists. Emily performed in MDT's Nutcracker, and she absolutely enjoyed when Lise Houlton's friend, Martine Van Hamel, held the Kaatsbaan audition at MDT. To further enhance her ballet and dance training, Emily also traveled to Upstate New York to attend Kaatsbaan. She has received a mixed variety of training that opened her to concert dance and the value that modern, postmodern, and pedestrian movement bring to the dance world: an underlying belief that dance is movement.

In her last year in high school, she changed ballet schools and danced at Classical Ballet Academy. During that year, she decided to continue ballet training and to choose a dance major at the collegiate level. Emily applied and was accepted to the University of Utah, which has an excellent ballet program. She graduated with honors and received her BFA degree in ballet as well as a writing degree. Emily came to the university versed in other dance disciplines and could easily adapt to other styles. She could see the value of a solid ballet foundation that allows a dancer to perform modern and contemporary dance at a higher caliber, even if the purpose of the choreography is not to use codified steps.

When Emily graduated from Utah and returned home, she became an apprentice at Twin Cities Ballet of Minnesota for one year; then, the Covid-19 pandemic hit, and most companies were not hiring apprentices, but Ballet Co.Lab (BCL) was hiring and paying apprentices. For the pandemic year, BCL came up with creative solutions for maintaining the health and safety of dancers while continuing to train and perform. Besides being an apprentice, Emily also helped on the administrative side of the company. With her writing degree and excellent writing skills, she drafted grants for the company, and the BCL manager edited them. Likewise, other apprentices did various jobs helping run the "ballet business." The idea behind both dancing and learning other work skills was to give dancers practical work experience to be used after they stopped dancing. Emily believes there are other skills one needs to legitimately learn in order to make it work for them in the dance industry. Working at Grand Jeté gave Emily employment, new work skills, and allowed her to share her ballet knowledge and experience with the customers she helped.

As far as dancing and performing, the "back line of the corps de ballet" is the bulk of

Emily Kleinschmidt. A versatile and resilient dance artist on a new work journey, bringing her dance experiences, training, and skills to the new job. Photography by Lauren Baker. Courtesy of Emily Kleinschmidt.

the people who make up the ballet industry. Emily said, "No one cares about the person in the back, but history does, and I do!" In 2021, she made a decision to move on and out of the ballet and dance world. She believed there is much one has to commit to if a ballet career is chosen. She decided it was not for her.

All her years in ballet were not for naught. It showed her that embracing excellent standards in ballet carries through to other work areas as well. Arts administration appeals to her because one makes something happen; one works with a purpose, not just for the dollars. Emily is currently working as the Annual Giving Manager at the International Institute of Minnesota. Her discipline, work ethic, writing, and administrative skills as a dance artist have carried Emily into her new career. As a dance artist, Emily learned new steps for new dances. It's a new dance for her now, and she already knows some of the steps.

Maryann Smith Johnson: Dance Artist and Physical Therapist (Interview 2/20/21)

Aurora's Wedding, Janet (Hansen) Smith in the "Bluebird Pas de Deux" performing with the Andaházy Ballet Borealis, ca. 1960. Courtesy of Maryann Johnson.

Maryann Johnson grew up watching her mother, Janet Smith, dance, teach, and perform with the Andaházys. At seven years old, a free spirit, who wanted to dance and always danced around their home, Maryann began ballet lessons with the Andaházys. At ten years old, she remembers Mr. A telling everyone to bring in a record with music they like for dancing. She preferred pop music, so she brought in a Simon and Garfunkel record, while most other dancers brought in a classical piece of music. Whatever music the dancers chose did not matter; the Andaházys encouraged creativity and a love of dance— they drew that out of the students they taught and affirmed their efforts at learning ballet, whether they had a ballet aesthetic or not.

She vividly remembers watching the dancers rehearse *Los Seises* and how the soloist with the crown of thorns completely gave over to the piece. Another time, while watching Janet perform the Hammers and Nails Dance role in *Los Seises*, she saw the hammer hit her mother's thumb, opening an artery. Blood spurted onto the floor of the church's sacristy, and when she doffed her hat, blood was on her hat and more on the floor. People thought it was a miracle, and some started crying. It was quite an audience response. A technically strong and talented ballerina, her mother also danced for Jo Savino and partnered beautifully with him. Maryann said

277

Maryann Smith Johnson performing with the Ballet of the Dolls. Courtesy of Maryann Johnson. Photography by Thomas F. Florey.

that Savino "was a force in the Twin Cities dance community."

Maryann became a strong dancer with the Andaházy training, and continued training at Jo Savino's ballet school. She traveled to New York City in 1980 with other dancers from Savino's school for summer intensives. Rick Vogt, Susan Hovey, and Maryann trained at the David Howard and Joffrey ballet schools; Laural Nelson trained at the School of American Ballet. James Sewell was already living and dancing in New York City, and the dancers stayed in Laura Sewell's apartment—James's sister. Dance and ballet became a focus of Maryann's life, and for her senior academic year in high school, she attended Pennsylvania Ballet in Philadelphia.

Maryann spoke extensively about all the dancers she knew and worked with in the Twin Cities. She took classes with MDT teachers Bonnie Mathis, Lirena Branitski, Frank Bourman, and Marjorie Thompson. She learned that these two forces on both sides of the Mississippi, the Andaházys in Saint Paul and Loyce Houlton in Minneapolis, taught ballet quite differently. "The Andaházys were very classical; Loyce created a hybrid of ballet and Graham to create the Houlton technique."

Maryann's historical memory of the Twin Cities ballet and dance from the 1970s through the 1990s is extraordinary. She can name most of the movers and shakers who made a lasting mark and legacy in Minnesota. From Frank Bourman of theatre dance place to Andy and Cheryl Rist of Ballet Minnesota to Bonnie Mathis and Marcia Chapman of Ballet Arts to Myron Johnson with Children's Theatre and the Ballet of the Dolls, and current dance artists like Berit Ahlgren. The list is broad, extensive, and deep.

Maryann spoke about one significant personal memory when Myron Johnson said to her, "If you stay in town, I'm starting a company, and I want you to join." Both Maryann and her mother, Janet Smith, joined Myron's company, Ballet of the Dolls, and danced and performed for several years with Myron's hybrid blend of theater, dance, and ballet. She said, "I loved dancing with the Dolls."

Her recollection of the Twin Cities dance scene is incredibly fascinating, with stories replete with colorful personalities. She acknowledged an artistic divide that existed between the two cities—Saint Paul, more classical and traditional; Minneapolis, more progressive and contemporary. The Minneapolis side fit her personality better. She also said that the "winds of change" are moving through the Cities, and the great divide is lessening its historical hold on the dancers. She believes that ballet's history can be kept alive when people honor its tradition while at the same time moving forward with new ideas.

As a dance physical therapist, Maryann is known throughout the Twin Cities as the go-to physical therapist for dancers. Her background in performing and teaching makes her an invaluable asset to the dance community. Plus, she has a pleasant, kind, and uplifting personality. Maryann is a vibrant force and a true gift to Minnesota's ballet and dance history.

Joseph Bingham: Co-Director, Operations & Productions for The Cowles Center for Dance & the Performing Arts (Interview 10/21/21)

In 2002 Joseph Bingham began ballet training at MDT, then went to Continental Ballet and danced with them for eight years. He has spent another twelve years as their lighting designer and stage manager and found he enjoyed this "behind the scenes" ballet work. Since 2012, he has been a freelance dance stage manager and lighting designer throughout the Twin Cities. In 2015, Joseph began working full-time at The Cowles Center, bringing his dance background and backstage knowledge and experience to the Goodale Theater. The Cowles Center opened in 2010, designed and renovated by combining two Minneapolis historic buildings: the Hennepin Center for the Arts and the Shubert Theater, the current Goodale Theater.

In 2019 he became co-director of The Cowles Center, managing it well, especially overseeing its artistic business during the 2020 pandemic. Along with Jessi Fett, the co-director of programming and education, he hopes to continue to build a broader reach for The Cowles Center, extending its availability and influence beyond the companies that have frequented the center since its opening in 2010.

The mission statement for The Cowles Center states: *The Cowles Center is a dance and performing arts hub that promotes movement and growth for artists through supportive programs and spaces; engages audiences through dynamic performances; and educates learners of all ages through robust and inclusive education initiatives.* The Cowles Center's website includes moving text, graphics and photos revealing Minnesota's stunning dance versatility.

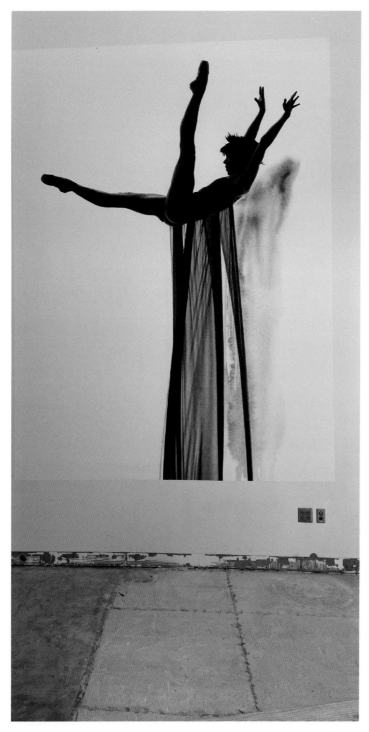

The Cowles Center for Dance & the Performing Arts. The renovation work in 2021 of the front lobby shows an image of Penny Freeh. Blue coloring was added to the black-and-white image, and instead of a horizontal orientation, the image is rotated to look like Penny was propelled upward.
Courtesy of Erik Saulitis, photographer.

Summer Splash. Emily Tyra with James Sewell Ballet. ca. 2008.
Courtesy of Erik Saulitis, photographer

Eve Schulte with James Sewell Ballet, 2010.
Courtesy of Erik Saulitis, photographer.

Encore: Modern and Contemporary Dance

By the early twentieth century, dance and movement for movement's sake pushed aside ballet's sovereignty as the premier concert dance form; even so, balletic training still remains a hallmark of a versatile and well-trained dancer. These dance artists' stories, accompanied by historical and contemporary images, highlight movement for movement's sake, demonstrating Minnesota's cultural vibrancy and dance versatility.

In the late nineteenth and early twentieth century, the first generation of modern dancers embraced a new approach to gesture and movement called "expressive" dancing. The catalyst for this new movement was Frenchman François Delsarte (1811–1871), who developed a system of gesture and expression. From France to America, Delsarte's system moved westward, gaining interest. In 1893 at St. Benedict's Academy in the small town of St. Joseph, Minnesota, the Niobe Group performed a choreographic piece called *Tableaux*, where "Like ballet, Delsarte placed the body in an imaginary circle, and designated horizontal motions within it—forward, oblique, lateral—which intersected with certain vertical body 'zones'—upper, middle, lower."[159]

Niobe Group, students of St. Benedict's Academy in a Delsarte *Tableaux* dance pose created in 1893. St. Joseph, Minnesota. Courtesy of Saint Benedict's Monastery/SBM.04f.

A Movement Choir, Mary Wigman, ca. 1928. Dance Collection of the New York Public Library at Lincoln Center. Astor, Lenox and Tilden Foundations.

Coda: Artists' Stories

Gertrude Lippincott (1913–1996): Dance Artist, Choreographer, Teacher, and Costumer

Gertrude Lippincott was born in Saint Paul and was undoubtedly one of the great early modern dance pioneers in Minnesota. She began her career in dance when she was asked to join the University of Minnesota's Dance Group in the early 1930s. Gertrude was originally asked to join the dance group because she owned a car, but her propensity and passion for dance quickly became obvious. Before graduating from the University of Minnesota in 1935 with a degree in psychology, she married professor Benjamin Lippincott who encouraged her modern dance studies, and she studied with some of the best modern dancers the world had at that time.

Traveling with her husband exposed Lippincott to the Mary Wigman technique in Boston and London and to leading modern American dancers such as Martha Graham, Hanya Holm, and Louis Horst. She established a Modern Dance Center in Minneapolis in 1937. When World War II broke out, her husband's tour of duty sent him to the Far East as an Air Force historian. Gertrude decided to head to the "nearer East"—New York City. She earned a Master of Fine Arts degree in education with an emphasis in dance from New York University in 1943.

She became a nationally known dancer, choreographer, and teacher. "According to Gertrude, she eventually performed 107 concerts in twenty-one states, seventy-two master classes in twenty-two states, and residencies and performances in 250 colleges and universities."[160]

In June 1991, during the conference, "Celebrating 60 Years of Dance Education in Minnesota," Judith Brin Ingber, dance artist, art and dance historian, and former dance critic for *Dance Magazine*, described how Gertrude believed in the importance of cultural representation and diversity of social classes and educational entities in dance. "It's safe to say that she had the first integrated modern dance company in America."[161] Tony Charmoli, a former dancer in Gertrude's Modern Dance Group and later renowned as a television and Broadway choreographer and director, wrote that Gertrude's company included all races and ethnicities that "were not segregated, but acted as one, loaning their talents to the Group as a whole."[162]

Gertrude also strongly believed that modern dance costuming "was a personal relationship between a dancer and her outfit that went beyond visual beauty, a relationship achieved by being involved in the costume's

285

design and creation."[163] The Minnesota Historical Society maintains a collection of her artistically stunning costumes worn during her dancing career.

Modern dance has flourished in Minnesota, and Gertrude's generosity to dancers and to dance has been modern dance's seed and fodder. "Right it is that we remember her work and praise her, though she would likely only nod slightly and wish to conclude with her characteristic conclusive remark, 'Righto.'"[164]

Robert (Bob) D. Moulton (1922–1979): Dance and Theater Artist, Choreographer, and Teacher

"What we do today is built in large part on the foundation, 'The spade work,' Robert Moulton calls it, that Mrs. Lippincott did for us."[165]

Bob realized he loved to dance after learning to tap as a young boy in Fargo, North Dakota. He went on tapping for Geraldine Butler's floor shows during his high school years in Duluth. Then, World War II erupted, and he fought in the European theater, survived the Battle of the Bulge, and other critical battles against the Nazis. In Soissons, France, he met his future wife, Marion Skowlund (Maggie Moulton), a member of the American Red Cross dispatched to Europe during the war. Bob believed his dancing career would be over because of the war, but similar to Anna Adrianova's Foxhole Ballet performances for army soldiers, he finished his European theater experience dancing in black full-dress tails for American army officers and then joined a performing unit after the war.

Returning to civilian life, Bob enrolled at the University of Minnesota to study theater and achieve his doctorate in theatrics. He loved to dance, so he joined Orchesis, the University of Minnesota's dance performance organization. A red-letter day occurred when one of the teachers, Margaret Pataky, introduced him to Gertrude Lippincott. This meeting ignited a fifteen-year dance collaboration between Gertrude and Bob. From 1949 to 1964, their partnership toured America with professionally produced dance performances, live music, and gorgeous costumes. In the Twin Cities, they held performances at Macalester College, Hamline University, the University of Minnesota, and the Women's Club.

Gertrude introduced Bob to the professional New York City avant-garde modern dancers, such as Louis Horst. Later he credits Horst for teaching him this valuable insight: That whatever material one begins with, "whether it's a play, music, or a dance idea—the material will show you a form, and from the form will come the techniques you need."[166] Martha Graham wanted Bob to dance in her company, but he did not want to leave what he and Maggie had in Minnesota. He said, "No, thanks." Not many dancers would have said "no" to Martha Graham.

At home in Minnesota, he was the first choreographer for the Guthrie Theater when it opened in 1963, and he choreographed several plays for them. As an artistic director and professor for forty-two years at the University of Minnesota's Department of Theatre Arts & Dance, students experienced how he loved to move, teach, and direct.[167] As a preeminent dancer and choreographer, Bob

brought his performing talents, education, and dance in its many forms beyond the borders of Minnesota to the Royal Winnipeg Ballet, the Canadian Contemporary Dancers, and the Calgary Ballet.

Judith Brin Ingber knew Bob well, and when he was dying of stomach cancer, Judith and Bob decided it was best not to tell Gertrude. Bob died before both Gertrude and his wife, Maggie. After his death, the Robert Moulton Theatre Arts Scholarship Fund, University of Minnesota Foundation, was established.

Barbara Barker Warner (1939–2002): Former Director of the Department of Theatre Arts & Dance, University of Minnesota

Barbara Barker first met Gertrude Lippincott in 1986, at her interview to head the University of Minnesota's dance program. "Reed-narrow, resilient, and dignified, she appeared among the assembled dance community both as 'the Oracle,' and as she who remembers—the keeper of history."[168]

One day when Barbara and Gertrude were walking into Norris Hall at the University of Minnesota, Gertrude gestured to the building next to Norris Hall and said, "that's where I went to high school." Barbara sud-

denly realized the seventy years of bonding that Gertrude had for the University of Minnesota that included her "father, a husband on the faculty, her undergraduate degree, her partnership with Bob Moulton, and . . . years as a teacher in the University of Minnesota dance program."[169]

In Barbara's memorial notes, she also said that Gertrude had no personal agenda other than strengthening both the Minnesota dance community and the University of Minnesota's dance program.

Nancy McKnight Hauser (1909–1990):
Dance Artist, Choreographer

Nancy Hauser danced for an amazing seven decades, bringing to Minnesota the emergence of modern dance in the twentieth century. As a young girl, Nancy grew up on Long Island and later in Manhattan, New York. Hauser found the ocean peaceful, and in her later years, as she battled lung cancer, her children took her to Minnesota's "ocean," Lake Superior, for respite.

Nancy studied "natural dance" in her youth, and as a young adult, she danced on Broadway for two years in Norman Bel Geddes's production of *Lysistrata*, choreographed by the modern dancer Doris Humphrey. Another modern dancer, José Limón, also danced in *Lysistrata*. The turning point in Nancy's life occurred when the German expressionist dance company, under the direction of Mary Wigman, performed in New York City in 1930. The impresario Sol Hurok brought the Wigman Company to New York and announced at the performance that Wigman would be opening a school in New York City, directed by her assistant, Hanya Holm. In her later years, Nancy said, "There's no question that Hanya Holm determined my way of thinking."[170] Holm came to the United States in 1931, and Nancy was one of the twenty students standing outside the door at the opening of the Wigman school.

Holm's influence spread across numerous universities and colleges where she taught her technique. Her choreography for *Kiss me Kate* was the first choreographic composition accepted for copyright by the Library of Congress. In 1958, Holm won an award from the Federation of Jewish Philanthropies for her outstanding contribution to the modern dance movement in America.[171] Nancy brought Holm's expressionist dance to Wisconsin, where she was hired as a teacher in the Department of Recreation in 1938. She then crossed the St. Croix River, came to Carleton College in Minnesota, and taught dance from 1944–46 and again from 1949–56. Nancy also taught at Macalester College for three years. While dancing barefooted, with cutting-edge movements, seeds of modern dance continued to form deep tap roots in Minnesota.

In 1956, Nancy founded the Dance Guild Theater. During this time, she choreographed for the Contemporary Dance Group, whose dancers included Loyce Houlton and Sage Cowles. Nancy's modern dance influence grew and by the late 1960s, the Nancy Hauser Dance Company thrived, and with her children, she co-founded the Guild of Performing Arts in the warehouse district of Minneapolis. A former knitting mill's large open spaces became like manna for the Guild as it transformed from knitting spaces to dance and music studios, offices, an in-house theater, and a gallery space for artists and photographers. The Nancy Hauser Dance Company received support from the National

288

Endowment for the Arts for touring to small colleges across America, and also for the Artist in the Schools program that sent the company as far away as Hawaii, Tennessee, and Nevada.

In the 1970s, many dancers who trained under Nancy became teachers in the Urban Arts Program which sent high school students to the Guild. She also taught at the University of Minnesota and, in the late 70s and early 80s, taught at Hanya Holm's Summer Dance program at Colorado College in Colorado Springs, often bringing some of her dance company to study and perform there. Nancy once said, "People seem to have lost track of why art exists. . . . The arts are a really deep emotional need in people, and it allows something which lifts the soul. . . . Being involved in the arts is not an intellectual thing. It's a connection with all that's essential."[172]

John Munger (1946–2013): "Dance everything"

In "Remembering John Munger," Lightsey Darst, dance critic and poet, wrote that John was a "dance everything" in the Twin Cities arts community: dancer and choreographer, student and teacher, writer and administrator, activist and curator . . . from a globe-trotting childhood to his days studying with modern dance pioneer Hanya Holm, to his work on the Minnesota Dance Alliance . . . The man was a linchpin.[173]

In June 1972, John recalled arriving at Hanya Holm's annual summer session in Colorado. Hanya was choreographing the first summer opera, and she needed a short male, and invited John to audition that night. John said, "Dumbfounded at my luck, I said hell yes." At rehearsal/audition that evening,

"Hanya was a tiny black-clad sparrow of a woman who looked at me keenly and said, 'Well, we see what we can do.'" At one of the following evening rehearsals, it rained ferociously, and Hanya was late. When she finally arrived, she had taken a direct fall to her face, marked by a purple-hued bruise above one eyebrow. To her waiting dancers, Hanya said, "I have a sore noggin and you have sore legs. Let's go to work."

She was seventy-nine at the time. John attended seven of Hanya's summer sessions, and he never once saw her waste rehearsal time. Never. She simply believed, "The most important thing about time is that it does not stop."[174]

Margret Dietz (1913–1972): Dance Artist, Choreographer

Margret Dietz, a German-born expressionist dancer, choreographer, and teacher, began her dance career with Mary Wigman in 1932. She just missed dancing with Hanya Holm, who had left in 1931 to start the Mary Wigman School in New York City. When the Nazis took complete control of Germany in 1933, Margret continued to dance to keep her spirit lifted as the dark shadows of Hitler's control deepened. In the early 1940s, she danced and was an assistant to Mary Wigman at the Wigman School in Dresden.

In 1942, as Nazi control became tighter and Wigman's refusal to fly the Nazi flag above her school became more dangerous for them, Wigman and her school in Dresden moved to Leipzig. Wigman's life in Leipzig came under scrutiny by the Nazis, and the Gestapo frequently interrogated her. She would not let her students down and did all she could to keep her school open. When Wigman moved her school to Leipzig, Margret received government orders to join a group of twelve other dancers, all of them anti-Nazis, who were to entertain the Nazi army officers at the Russian front. A cruel punishment. Margret later referred to this as being forced to dance at gunpoint. The dancers were sent by train wherever conditions were harsh, dangerous, and deadly—truly experiencing *danse macabre*. Of the twelve, Margret was the only one to return alive to Leipzig, where she found Wigman and her

Margret Dietz, ca. 1930s. Charlotte Randolph, Photographer. © 2023 Artists Rights Society (ARS), New York / VG Bild-Kunst, Bonn.

school. She had carried with her a cherished photo album of Mary Wigman's solo dances, taken by the famous photographer Charlotte Rudolphe.[175]

After the war, Margret taught dance to the children of Berlin, "They learned how to dance, and they learned how to live through faith in an art which," she taught them, "no bomb can destroy." She made them stand firmly on a floor full of holes and made them feel warm in winter in a room that had windows but no windowpanes.[176]

Margret eventually came to America in 1953. A master teacher and guest lecturer, she brought her modern expressionism to major universities. In 1966, she moved to Minnesota after the University of Minnesota offered her an associate professor position. In 1968, Margret and Nancy Hauser began collaborative efforts. "Hauser relied on Margret's theatrical and pedagogical experience. Margret admired Hauser's choreographic abilities, especially her dramatic flair."[177] During the summer, they taught a workshop together at the Guild, and in the fall, Margret moved her company and school to a larger space in Hauser's Guild of Performing Arts. Margret's titles were guest artist and artistic adviser.

In 1968 Nancy asked Margret to choreograph a dance for her company. In contrast to Nancy's choreography, with its themes often reflecting current events, Margret decided to create a joyful piece that reflected her Germanic roots: *Emperor Waltz* by Johann Strauss II in the tradition of the Grand Viennese Waltz. In this work, Margret achieved "what Wigman called 'the perfect marriage of content and form.' She balanced control and abandon, precision of form and ecstatic release . . . "[178]

In the early 1970s, the College of Saint Benedict in St. Joseph, Minnesota, invited Margret to be the master teacher and choreographer for their summer workshops. A popular teacher, the college assisted Margret in founding her company Choreogram. While at St. Benedict's in 1972, Margret died suddenly of a heart attack and was buried in the cemetery of the Sisters of the Order of Saint Benedict on the college campus.

In her Convocation Talk at Benedicta Arts Center of the College of Saint Benedict in March 1971, Margret said, "Experience or no experience, every one of you has a relationship to Dance, because you breathe. And breath is movement, and movement is nothing less than expression of life . . . Your movements are produced by the same miraculous instrument the Dancer uses: the human body."[179]

Mathew Janczewski: Founder and Artistic Director of ARENA DANCES (Interview 2/17/21)

When Mathew was first approached and asked to be interviewed for *Grace & Grit*, he responded, "You know I do not teach ballet." The interview did happen, and his story needed to be told. His broad and stellar dance influence over the past twenty-plus years has made a salient mark on the Minnesota dance scene. Mathew's passion for dance and for passing on dance to adults and the younger generation is palpable. His email signature line includes the following quote from Bill T. Jones, which speaks to his passion: "I want my dancers to be in a place of engagement with themselves and their dancing . . . You

ARENA DANCES, Mathew Janczewski, Artistic Director, in rehearsal
with his company 2009. Courtesy of Erik Saulitis, photographer.

must approach it like any serious spiritual pursuit with a form we call practice. Respect your body, which is your instrument. Understand it. Understand its boundaries, its history, how it fits into the world."

After Mathew earned a BFA in dance from the University of Minnesota, he performed with Jazzdance! by Danny Buraczeski from 1992–97; he founded his own nonprofit company, ARENA DANCES, in 1995, and performed with them three times; he danced twice internationally with Shapiro & Smith Dance during his 2007–14 tenure there; and as Mathew was making his own work, he also danced with several independent contemporary choreographers—Robin Steihm, Shawn

McConneloug, Morgan Thorson, Cathy Young, and Beth Corning.

He created over thirty-five works with his contemporary style of dance, and his creative energies continue to make new work. Believing in the transformative power of dance, Mathew reaches beyond his dancers to serve other companies, the young, aging, and underserved people in the Twin Cities. In 2005, he received both the Sage Award for Outstanding Performance and the McKnight Artist Choreographer Fellowship. *Dance Magazine* named him as one of their "25 to Watch" in 2008.

His positive impact on the Minnesota dance community goes beyond his studio and outreach. His podcast, *Studio Stories: Reminiscing on Twin Cities Dance History*, happens every Thursday at noon. Mathew interviews dance artists who have made a valuable impact on the dance and cultural landscape in the Twin Cities. For Mathew, "Stories are our most potent tools. We need to unearth old stories that live in a place and begin to create new ones." These stories are easily accessed by contacting ARENA DANCES or in the announcements on the weekly Twin Cities e-newsletter *DanceMN*.

Mathew openly acknowledges with gratitude the immense support of his contemporary dance endeavors from his company, friends, and the Twin Cities dance community. In essence, the community gratefully acknowledges his broad impact on Minnesota dance and dance history.

Mathew Janczewski. Photography by Aaron Warkov. Courtesy of Mathew Janczewski.

Colleen Callahan: Dance Educator, President of Dance Educators' Coalition in Minnesota (Interview 8/31/2021)

Colleen trained in jazz and tap; modern dance came later when she majored in dance and minored in history at Brigham Young University in Utah. She said, "I realized as a dance major, I had become a dance history connoisseur. I was on a dance mission, making life and art connect." The university's faculty were phenomenal teachers who represented the major modern dance companies across the country. She student taught at East High School in Salt Lake City with Connie Jo Hepworth, experiencing an award-winning high school dance program in action as dance history, composition, and technique wove into the curriculum.

After graduation, Colleen came home to Minneapolis and, for fifteen years at North High School, taught her African-American students how to create work that contained their interests and issues. She continued teaching for twenty years at Southwest High School in Minneapolis.

Colleen is a compilation of stories about the visionaries of modern and contemporary dance, such as Lippincott, Holm, Dietz, and also the pioneer dance educators. Colleen Callahan leaves a legacy as a modern dancer and a beloved dance educator.

Karen Long Charles: Artistic Director and Executive Director of Threads Dance Project (Interview 9/23/21)

Karen Charles's passion is dance. She began dancing at a local dance school in Atlanta, Georgia, learning ballet, tap, and jazz at five years old. She continued dance training and received a major in dance at Texas Christian University. At college, Karen experienced modern dance for the first time, and she continues to believe that ballet and modern do not have to be separate. In 1989, Charles auditioned for the Alvin Ailey Company and danced as a fellow recipient until an injury made her stop. She eventually headed back to Atlanta and back to school, achieving an MA in education administration. Karen kept dancing and also opened a dance school. After eighteen years in Atlanta, Karen and her husband moved to Minneapolis.

In 2010, her father passed away, and she inherited ten thousand dollars. With this inheritance money, and to honor her father, she said that she was going to dance, doing what she loved, even if she failed. What Karen loved and dreamed of doing became reality: She founded Threads Dance Project. In 2011, Threads Dance Project was incorporated, and the company had its first performance at the Lab Theater in Minneapolis. Karen said that she prayed people would come. They did come, and engaged audiences continued to grow. In January 2021, they opened the year with an exciting move to their own space in the Seward Neighborhood of Minneapolis. Karen schedules both ballet and modern dance classes; they complement each other and make the strongest dancers.

Karen has brought in guest teachers from Alvin Ailey and hopes to expand these experiences for the community. She feels that her life experiences enable her to honor and acknowledge difference, and she makes her dance studio a place where diversity is celebrated. As an educator in dance, Karen feels that she handles differences well.

Karen has led her Threads Dance Project for the past thirteen years, and even though she truly missed performing on stage, once she started her company, that desire and need went away. "I don't need to dance. I really do enjoy the creative process now."

Jim Lieberthal: Dance Artist, Choreographer, Actor, and Writer (Interviews 10/28/21 and 10/30/21)

One could almost count on seeing Jim Lieberthal in the audience of any dance concert or program in the Twin Cities—no matter what discipline. He brings an appreciation of ballet, dance, and theater from his varied training with the Wigman and Horton modern dance methods, jazz, ballet, and the Kabuki and Noh theater techniques. Jim's sincere openness to all dance forms, and his positive accolades given generously to dancers, make him a welcome presence at various events. Jim could sit down with any Twin Cities dancer or company member and discuss the history of dance in the Twin Cities with its historical divisions, mergers, and changes in leadership.

He was honored with a McKnight Fellowship for Choreography, creating *Mer-Peace* in 1988, and received a 2013 Sage Award for Performance in *Listen* by choreographer Rosy Simas. Jim's DynamicShapeConstruction has produced commissioned work for both Threads Dance Project and Kanopy Dance Company in Madison, Wisconsin. Quite the masterful collaborator, Jim often works with multiple artists in creating artistic work in various medians. In 2022, along with the brilliant dance videographer Hector Cortes of Snack Media, Jim created FLIGHTwatch solo and duo sections for the opera Split-Second/

Kats. This image of Kats D, currently known as Gadu Doushin, expresses Jim's exuberant appreciation of dance. Courtesy of Erik Saulitis, photographer.

LIFE. The other co-creators on the project were Ashley Jian Thomson and Javan Mngrezzo, with music by John Adams. Jim has also been an originator and contributor to 16 FEET Collaborative for four seasons.

Jim Lieberthal is an apex of dance gratitude, expressed so well by his affirmation of many Minnesotan talents who work together creatively "between the poles of ballet and modern dance."

Myron Johnson: Theater Dance Artist (Interview 9/22/21)

Myron Johnson said he fell into theater by accident. He was only seven years old when he remembers walking to Cedar Riverside and seeing auditions for The Moppet Players' new production. He auditioned, got into the play, and never left the theater. He worked at the Children's Theatre Company (CTC) in Minneapolis for twenty-five years.

Theater had Myron's heart, but so did dance. When he was eight years old, John Linnerson's sister owned The Moppet Theatre and encouraged him to take classes with Loyce Houlton at The Contemporary Dance Playhouse, and he did. At that time, John Clark Donohue, one of the founders of the Children's Theatre Company, was the artistic director, and speaking about Donohue and Loyce, Myron said, "They were both as creative as any human could possibly be." What happened next? Myron said he was torn between Loyce, who wanted him to continue taking dance classes and performing, and John, who wanted him to be more engaged with acting at Children's Theatre Company. Myron felt he could do both, but when he was about fifteen years old, theater drew him in. Also, the Children's Theatre Company now offered dance classes which made it possible for him to still dance and do theater.

When Myron turned seventeen, he began training in Paris at the Marcel Marceau school for two years. Upon his return to America, he began directing plays at the Children's Theatre Company. Myron said the theater experienced "wildly popular sold-out audiences, but everything crashed with John's arrest for sexual abuse in 1984." In 1987 Myron founded Ballet of the Dolls—the name chosen as a nod to the 1967 film *Valley of the Dolls*. Myron began his dance company with rehearsals at Ruby's Cabaret in southeast Minneapolis. His home in the old Harmony Glass warehouse served as the theater space for the Ballet of the Dolls's performances. From his warehouse home theater space to another space in the warehouse district, the company kept performing. In 1989 they performed 280 times. "Crazy!" Myron exclaimed.

From the warehouse district to the Loring Playhouse to a huge leap to buy the Ritz Theater in Northeast Minneapolis, the Ballet of the Dolls finally had its own space. The company's performances became more theatrical than dance. Myron's choreography "deconstructed" the classic ballets such as

Myron Johnson. Courtesy of Myron Johnson.

Giselle, *Swan Lake*, and Myron's Nutcracker became *Nutcracker Not So Suite*.

As often happens when artists move to economically deprived city neighborhoods, gentrification begins and the artists need to move out. In Northeast Minneapolis, Ballet of the Dolls claimed the Ritz Theater as their home until 2013, but increased costs eventually caused them to close their theater doors. For Myron, he was "burnt out from his nonstop career." He realizes how awesome Minneapolis is for dance and theater. He hopes to see more spaces become available and affordable for artists. "Without an outlet for their art, it becomes small and less inspiring." Myron continued talking but eventually said, "I could go on forever, but that is the gist of it."

Helen Hatch: Dancer and Choreographer (Interview 9/7/21)

Helen Hatch has been dancing since she was five years old, first at a community center in South Minneapolis, then at Ballet Arts. She recognizes the excellent ballet training she received in Minneapolis at Ballet Arts from her teachers Bonnie Mathis, Kathie Goodale, Julia Sutter, and Lirena Branitski. She also experienced contemporary and modern choreography from local dance artists Wynn Fricke, James Sewell, and Penny Freeh.

After graduating from high school in 2007, she attended Fordham University and earned a BFA. At Fordham, she expanded her modern and contemporary training while continuing ballet. In 2011, Helen returned home to Minneapolis, took classes at Minnesota Dance Theatre, and Lise Houlton offered her a full contract in 2012. Helen performed with MDT until 2017. She had decided that "I wanted to do more choreography and connect more with the dance community in the Twin Cities."

Helen founded Hatch Dance, a project-based company with one to two shows a year. She also teaches ballet and says, "I love teaching ballet, one of my passions, but my choreography is more contemporary." Helen sees and teaches ballet through a different lens now. "All the different voices and people I have worked with, plus my own personal ballet technique, help my students see possibilities . . . Their dance is their ownership to develop for themselves, not for me as their teacher."

Hannah Benditt: Dance Performance Artist, Creator, and Founder of Community Collective Movement (Interview 9/29/21)

Hannah Benditt says she had a rich background growing up with parents who were "very much art supporters." Her mother signed her up at Continental Ballet when she was young because "I had a lot of energy." And now her mother says, "I created a monster because Hannah has never stopped dancing." Hannah continued her ballet training at Ballet Arts in the Edina Community Center with Joanne Gordon. She continued training with Ballet Arts as she got older. Speaking of her years at Ballet Arts, Hannah said, "It was such a special place—a rich, full, and well-rounded experience. I remember being hooked on Ballet Arts and *The City Children's Nutcracker*."

The phenomenal ballet and modern dance teachers—Lirena Branitski, Marcia Chapman, Julia Sutter, and Kathie Goodale—kept Hannah dancing and performing with Ballet Arts. From her teachers, she learned that "movement is the best way to portray music." When Hannah's age and technique were strong enough for pointe shoes, she experienced a pivotal life decision: "I decided I wanted to dedicate my life to dance." Her teacher, Karen Paulson Rivet, was the most inspiring of them all. "The way she taught, and how passionate she was for ballet, made me really love ballet. I credit continuing my dance career to her; I was so entranced by Karen. She really cared for us as humans."

From Hannah's experiences at Ballet Arts, she continued to train after high school. She attended University of Missouri-Kansas City Conservatory where she had the opportunity to perform with Kansas City Ballet as a guest artist. Her dance BFA has an emphasis in modern, ballet, and choreography. Hannah moved back to the Twin Cities in 2015 and joined St. Paul Ballet for two seasons. She realized that it was more classical than what she wanted, so Hannah jumped into the world of freelance dance, which was nerve-racking for her because of no consistency. Plus, she began to feel lonely because freelance work is such solo work, even though she took open ballet classes with Minnesota Dance Theatre, Ballet Co.Lab, and James Sewell Ballet.

During the 2020 pandemic, Hannah founded the Community Collective Movement—a space that would be a "hub" where independent dance professionals could take classes together in a neutral space, not on someone else's turf. Hannah said that she is so honored that one of the teaching artists, Maryann Johnson, agreed to teach at Community Collective Movement. "She is literally the only reason that I am still dancing." Maryann teaches a ballet class that comes from her physical therapy perspective.

The Community Collective Movement gives teaching artists the space and time to share their knowledge, experience, and expertise. Social media marketing brought awareness and success to the Community Collective Movement. Independent dance artists need a platform where they can move together at their level of expertise, share knowledge of choreographic trends, seek pedagogical help and advice, and build relationships with each other. With grace and grit, the Community Collective Movement is this platform satisfying these needs—an innovative endeavor destined to stay.

Jumping. Erik Saulitis, self-portrait, ca. 1993. He believes that his dance images further bring the passion and beauty of dancers to life. Courtesy of Erik Saulitis, photographer.

Acknowledgments

How do I succinctly express my gratitude for a myriad of people who encouraged me to dig in, research, and write; to those who applauded my efforts and shared their historical resources with me? Thoughts and words tumultuously spilled out into long drafts that made no written sense. Finally, acknowledgments took shape in these words below.

For my husband, Erik Saulitis, I owe my utmost gratitude for his unceasing support and help. His photographs decorate *Grace & Grit*'s written word with stunning visualizations of ballet and dance. Thank you is also due to the many copyright holders who kindly gave permission for the use of their images. Every effort was made to obtain permission from the copyright holder for all the images, but that was not always possible.

Tremendous thanks go to Afton Press's publisher, Ian Graham Leask, and the staff for their time, expertise, and advice. Without them, Minnesota's ballet history, with its cultural and artistic legacy, would not be documented.

I thank Marius Andaházy, who generously shared with me boxes filled with photos, newspaper clippings, and historical documents about his parents' lives as dancers, choreographers, and ballet school directors. I thank both Lise Houlton and John Linnerson for lending me Loyce Houlton's memoirs, *Twilight Tales, Volumes One and Two*. With these two memoir tomes, I was privileged to write about Minnesota Dance Theatre's history as told through Loyce's articulate and colorful stories.

I owe a tremendous debt of gratitude for all the dance artists I interviewed, to the critical readers Marius Andaházy and Sonja Hinderlie, and to Catherine Stoch for editing my Author's Note. A special thank you is also due to Colleen Callahan, Judith Brin Ingber, Jane Keyes, Diane Masterman, Paula Christensen, and Ruthena Fink for their invaluable help lending me first source ballet, dance, and dance educator documents.

Grace & Grit is a ballet history, but Minnesotans also enjoy the cultural landscape of various dance disciplines and dance educators. These dance artists and educators, some of whom I had the privilege to interview, continue to create, inspire, and pass along the breadth and depth of dance "beyond the ballet barre." Many fascinating modern and contemporary dance stories in the "Encore" chapter of my book give these dance movers my written bravos.

I am beyond grateful for the support, encouragement, and affirmation I received from my family and many friends. All of you, named and unnamed, were collaborators with me since 2019 as *Grace & Grit: A History of Ballet in Minnesota* became a reality.

Bibliography

Adams, Doug and Diane Apostolos-Cappadona. *Dance as Religious Studies.* New York: The Crossroads Publishing Company, 1990.

"Advertisement for the Duluth Civic Ballet/ Hy Somers." *Statesman*, May 6, 1971.

Amy Woods. "Modern Dance Pioneer Gertrude Lippincott Dies at 82." *Star Tribune*, June 7, 1996.

Andaházy, Lóránt and Anna Adrianova. "Andaházy Ballet Borealis Souvenir Pamphlet, 1952."

Andaházy, Lóránt and Anna Adrianova. "Andaházy Ballet Borealis Souvenir Pamphlet, 1961–62." Minneapolis: Published to announce the 1961–62 season, with performances by the Andaházy Ballet Borealis, at the Northrop Memorial Auditorium at the University of Minnesota, Minneapolis, December 6, 1961.

Andaházy, Marius J. "Andaházy Souvenir Pamphlet, 2000."

"Avalon Theatre." Placeography.org, Minnesota Historical Society. Accessed October 19, 2021.

Anderson, Jack. *The One and Only: The Ballet Russe de Monte Carlo.* London: Dance Books Ltd., 1981.

Anderson, Jack. *Ballet & Modern Dance, A Concise History.* Trenton: Princeton Book Company, 2018.

Anderson, Zoë. *The Ballet Lover's Companion.* New Haven and London: Yale University Press, 2015.

Annas, Julia. *Plato.* New York: Sterling Publishing Co., Inc. Published by arrangement with Oxford University Press, Inc., 2009.

Bahn, Paul G. *The Cambridge Illustrated History of Prehistoric Art.* New York: Cambridge University Press, 1998.

Bales, Melanie and Karen Eliot, eds. *Dance on Its Own Terms.* New York: Oxford University Press, 2013.

Barnes, Jonathan, ed. *The Cambridge Companion to Aristotle.* New York: Cambridge University Press, 1995.

Beatty, Jack. *The Lost History of 1914: Reconsidering the Year the Great War Began.* New York: Walker Publishing Company, Inc., a division of Bloomsbury Publishing, 2012.

Blackwolf and Gina Jones. *Earth Dance Drum: A Celebration of Life.* Salt Lake City: Commune-A-Key Publishing, 1996.

Blasis, Carlo. *An Elementary Treatise Upon the Theory and Practice of the Art of Dancing.* Translated by Mary Stewart Evans. New York: Dover Publications, Inc., 1968. Originally published as *Traité Élémentaire, Théorique et Pratique de l'Art de la Danse.* New York: Kamin Dance Publishers, 1944.

Brandner, Eric, ed. "The Words, Emotions and Hard Realities of the Greatest Entertainment Mobilization the World has Ever Seen." *On Patrol*, Fall 2015. www.uso.org.

Brin Ingber, Judith. "Nancy Hauser." *Minnesota Dance, A Publication of Minnesota Dance Alliance*. September/October 1989.

Brin Ingber, Judith. "Gertrude Lippincott 'Righto'." *Minnesota Dance, A Publication of Minnesota Dance Alliance*. January/February 1990.

Brin Ingber, Judith. "Entertainment or Art?" *Minnesota Dance, A Publication of Minnesota Dance Alliance*. January/February 1993.

Brooks, Lynn Matluck. "'Los Seises' in the Golden Age of Seville." *Dance Chronicle*. Taylor & Francis, Ltd., 1982.

Brower, J. V., A. J. Hill, and Minnesota Historical Society. *The Mississippi River and its source: A narrative and critical history of the discovery of the river and its headwaters, accompanied by the results of detailed hydrographic and topographic surveys*. Minneapolis, MN: Harrison & Smith, State Printers, 1893. https://bit.ly/46yuyhB/.

Callahan, Colleen and Mary Kay Conway. Editors of the recorded speeches, August 1992. Dance Educators Coalition. *Celebrating 60 Years of Dance Education in Minnesota. (Honoring the Contributions of Gertrude Lippincott, Mary Rae Josephson-Adamson, Florence Cobb, Molly Lynn.)* Hennepin Center for the Arts, Minneapolis, MN 1991.

Carmen, Imel, ed. *National Dance Association of the American Alliance for Health, Physical Education, and Recreation*. "Focus on Dance: VII, Dance Heritage." Washington, D.C.: AAHPER Publications, 1977.

Carson, Julia M. H. *Home Away from Home, The Story of the U.S.O.* New York: Harpers & Brothers Publishers, 1946.

Cathcart, Rebecca M. "A Sheaf of Remembrances." *Collections of the Minnesota Historical Society*, 1915.

Chujoy, Anatole and P. W. Manchester. *The Dance Encyclopedia*. New York: Simon and Schuster, 1967.

Clarke, Mary and Clement Crisp. *The History of Dance*. New York: Crown Publishers, Inc., 1981.

Close, Cynthia and Anne Hevener, eds., "Dancing Through Time." *Artists Magazine*. November/December 2021.

Coe, Robert. *Dance in America*. New York: E. P. Dutton, 1985.

Commemoration Service of Gertrude Lippincott. "In Memorium, Gertrude Lippincott, June 29, 1913, to June 2, 1996." Frederick R. Weisman Museum, University of Minnesota, June 29, 1996.

Conyn, Cornelius. *Three Centuries of Ballet*. Houston-New York: Elsevier Press, Inc., 1953.

Crisp, Clement and Edward Thorpe. *The Colorful World of Ballet*. New York: Octopus Books, 1978.

Crowle, Pigeon. *Enter the Ballerina*. New York: Pitman Publishing Corporation, 1955.

Darst, Lightsey. "Remembering John Munger." *MnArtists, Arts Writing from Mn, Beyond Mn*, May 2013. https://bit.ly/49VsC5A.

David, Bruno. *Cave Art*. London: Thames & Hudson Ltd., 2017.

Deocariza, April. "Inaugural Five Moons Dance Festival Honors Oklahoma's Native American Ballerinas." *Pointe Magazine*, April 18, 2021. https://pointemagazine.com/five-moons-dance-festival.com.

Demidov, Alexander. *The Russian Ballet Past and Present*. Translated by Guy Daniels. Garden City, New York: Doubleday & Company Inc., 1977. Originally published in Russian, Moscow: Novosti Press Agency Publishing House.

DeSola, Carla. *The Spirit Moves: Handbook of Dance and Prayer*. Washington, D.C.: The Liturgical Conference, Inc., 1977.

Diehl, Judith and Kathryn Karipides. "Dance." *Encyclopedia of Cleveland History, Fine Arts and Literature*. Cleveland: Case Western Reserve University, 2022. https://case.edu/ech/articles/d/dance.

Dmitriyev, Anatoly, ed., *Complete Collected Works*. Moscow: Muzgiz, 1952. https://imslp.org/wiki/ The Sleeping Beauty, Op.66 (Tchaikovsky, Pyotr Ilyich) (Act 3).

Doak, Robin S. *Assassination at Sarajevo: The Spark That Started World War I*. Minneapolis: Compass Point Books, 2009.

Drummond, Sir John. *Speaking of Diaghilev*. London: Faber and Faber Limited, 1997.

Evans, Greg. "Tony Charmoli Dies: Three-Time Emmy-Winning Choreographer For TV & Broadway Was 99." *Deadline*, August 11, 2020. https://bit.ly/3T8HK9I.

Exley, Helen, ed. *Dance Quotations*. New York: Exley Giftbooks, 1993.

Findlay, J. N. *Plato: The Written and Unwritten Doctrines*. London: Routledge & Kegan Paul Ltd., 1974.

Fokine, Vitale, trans., Anatole Chujoy, ed. *Fokine, Memoirs of a Ballet Master*. Boston: Little, Brown and Company, 1961.

Folwell, William W. *A History of Minnesota*. Saint Paul: Minnesota Hist. Soc., 1956.

Fonteyn, Margot. *The Magic of Dance*. New York: Alfred A. Knopf, 1979.

Franks, A. H. *Twentieth Century Ballet*. New York: Pitman Publishing Corporation, 1954.

Freeman, Elizabeth Carlin, Marie Winckler Nickell, Linda Lee Soderstrom. *Margret Dietz, A Dancer's Legacy*. St. Cloud: Sentinel Printing, 2010.

Garafola, Lynn. *Diaghilev's Ballets Russes*. New York: Oxford University Press, 1989.

García-Márquez, Vincente. *The Ballets Russes, Colonel de Basil's Ballets Russes de Monte Carlo 1932-1952*. New York: Alfred A. Knopf, 1990.

Goode, Gerald, ed. *The Book of Ballets, Classic and Modern*. New York: Crown Publishers, 1939.

Gregory, John. *Understanding Ballet*. London: Octopus Books Limited, 1972.

Guest, Ivor. *The Ballet of the Second Empire*. London: Sir Isaac Pitman and Sons Ltd., 1974.

Guest, Ivor. *The Dancer's Heritage, A Short History of Ballet*. London: The Dancing Times, 1967.

Guest, Ivor. *The Empire Ballet*. London: The Society for Theatre Research, 1962.

Gust, Kelly. "Ballerina and a dream—the Result, Marriage." *Contra Costa Times*, August 1975.

Hafiz, "Created for Joy," poem, https://creating miracles.wordpress. com/2021/04/25/created-for-joy.

Hastings, Baird. *Choreographer and Composer*. Boston: Twayne Publishers, A Division of G.K. Hall & Company, 1983.

Hazan, Fernand, ed. *Dictionnaire du Ballet Moderne*. Paris. Translated by John Montague and Peggie Cochrane as *Dictionary of Modern Ballet*, American ed. Cohen, Selma Jeanne. New York: Tudor Publishing Company, 1959.

Heyworth-Dunne, Victoria, Jane Ewart and Megan Douglass, eds. *Ballet: The Definitive Illustrated Story*. New York: DK Publishing, 2018.

Homans, Jennifer. *Apollo's Angels*. New York: Random Press, 2010.

"In rivers, the water that you touch is the last of what has passed and the first of that which comes; so with present time." https://www.leonardodavinci.net/quotes.jsp.

Jacobs, Laura. *Celestial Bodies, How to Look at Ballet*. New York: Basic Books, 2018.

Jean Worrall. "Art on the Rocks Flourish in Grand Marais Colony." *Minneapolis Sunday Tribune*, August 12, 1956

Karkar, Jack and Waltraud. *And They Danced On*. Wausau: Aardvark Enterprises, 1989.

Kemp, Martin. *Leonardo*. New York: Oxford University Press, Inc., 2004.

Kemp, Martin. *Leonardo da Vinci, Experience, Experiment and Design*. Princeton: Princeton University Press, 2006.

Kendall, Elizabeth. *Where She Danced: The Birth of American Art-Dance*. New York: Alfred A. Knopf, Inc., 1979.

Keyes, Alicia & Jane, v3. *Mom, tell me about my dad*. Keyes personal photo memoir, 2020.

Keyes, Jane & Alicia, v2. *Patricia Garland, Dancer*. A photo memoir, 2021. Submitted by Judith Brin Ingber to the New York Public Library Performing Arts, Dance Division at Lincoln Center, and accepted in 2018.

Kirk Honeycutt, "Black Swan: A Review." *The Hollywood Reporter*, October 2010.

Kirstein, Lincoln. *Movement & Metaphor: Four Centuries of Ballet*. New York: Praeger Publishers, Inc., 1970.

Kirstein, Lincoln. *Four Centuries of Ballet, Fifty Masterworks*. New York: Dover Publications, Inc., 1984.

Klas, Alexandra (Sandy). "I Remember My Aunt Frances Boardman—Music Critic, Who Covered an Archbishop's Funeral." *Ramsey County History*, Summer 2005.

Kochno, Boris and Adrienne Foulke, trans. *Diaghilev and the Ballet Russe*. New York & Evanston: Harper & Row Publishers, 1970. Originally published as *Diaghilev et Les Ballets Russes*. New York: Harper & Row Publishers, 1970.

Kyra, Laubacher, "Ballet Co. Laboratory's Unique Business Model Has Kept Its Dancers Securely Employed Throughout the Pandemic." *Pointe Magazine*, March 2021. https://dancemedia.com/.

Ladinsky, Daniel. *I heard God Laughing*. New York: Penguin Books, 2006.

Lawson, Joan. *A History of Ballet and Its Makers*. London: Dance Books Ltd., 1976.

Lee, Carol. *Ballet in Western Culture. A History of its Origins and Evolution*. Boston: Allyn and Bacon, 1999.

Lee, Jennette. "NorthWest Ballet: The End of an Era." *Minnesota Dance, A Publication of Minnesota Dance Alliance*, May/June/July 1989.

Leonardo da Vinci quotes. BrainyMedia Inc., 2022. https://bit.ly/3wSxHdB.

Lieven, Prince Peter, L. Zarine, trans. *The Birth of Ballets-Russes*. Boston and New York: Houghton Mifflin Company, 1936.

Luhmann, Gretchen. "Donaldson's." Minnesota Historical Society. https://bit.ly/3PSeOz4.

"Lyceum Theatre." Cinema Treasures. https://bit.ly/3wSy8of.

Lydon, Kate. "Straight From the Heart. Gelsey Kirkland looks back . . . and ahead." *Dance Magazine*, September 2005.

Mackrell, Judith. *Bloomsbury Ballerina*. London: Weidenfeld & Nicolson, 2008.

Manor, Giora. *The Gospel According to Dance: Choreography and the Bible from Ballet to Modern*. New York: Danad Publishing Company, Inc., 1980.

Mark Yost. "On pointe." *St. Paul Pioneer Press*, December 4, 2004.

Marra, Ben and Linda. *Faces from the Land: Twenty Years of Powwow Tradition*. New York: Harry N. Abrams, Inc., 2009.

McDonagh, Don. *The Rise and Fall and Rise of Modern Dance*. Chicago: A Capella Books, 1990.

McDonald, John K. *House of Eternity: The Tomb of Nefertari*. Los Angeles: The J. Paul Getty Trust, 1996.

Mikhail Fokine. Mariinsky Theatre Souvenir Booklet. Saint Petersburg: The Museum of the Mariinsky Theatre, 2008.

"Minneapolis Auditorium." Minnesota Historical Society. https://bit.ly/3NxC1V8.

Minnesota Ballet in Duluth. https://minnesotaballet.org/about/history/.

MN Dance Pioneers Oral History Project, Part One: Marius J. Andaházy and Jane Keyes, Narrators; Judith Brin Ingber, Interviewer; Nancy Mason Hauser, Cameraperson. Conducted at Nancy Mason Hauser's home, Saint Paul, MN, November, 2018.

Munger, John. "High Places Must Be Deserved: Memories of Hanya Holm." *Minnesota Dance, A Publication of Minnesota Dance Alliance*. January/February, 1993.

Nelson, Paul. "Dayton's: More than a century of Minnesota retail." *Minnpost*, September 29, 2015. https://bit.ly/3LVAxmn.

Nichols, Dawn, ed. "Vision." *Visitation School Magazine*. Winter–Spring, 2016.

Nijinsky, Romola, ed. *The Diary of Vaslav Nijinsky*. Berkeley and Los Angeles: University of California Press, 1936.

Obituary of George H. Bonnarens. *Star Tribune*, March 3, 2004.

Obituary of Karen Paulson Rivet. *Star Tribune*, October 12, 2016.

Obituary of Lirena Grisha Branitski, *Star Tribune*, February 2, 2022.

Obituary of Tony Charmoli. *Deadline*, August 11, 2020.

Old Minneapolis, Facebook. "Victor Stengel School of Ballet," February 26, 2012. https://www.facebook.com/oldmpls/photos/a.119636488056535/355030234517158/.

Percival, John. *The World of Diaghilev*. London: The Herbert Press Limited, 1979.

Pritchard, Jane, ed. *Diaghilev and the Golden Age of the Ballets Russes 1909–1929*. London: V&A Publishing, 2010.

Ramsey Professional Building, Saint Paul: https://www.emporis.com/buildings/260253/ramsey-professional-building-st-paul-mn-usa.

Rilke, Rainer Maria. *Rilke's Book of Hours*. Trans. by Anita Barros and Joanna Macy. New York: Penguin Group, 1996.

Robert, Grace. *The Borzoi Book of Ballets*. New York: Alfred A. Knopf, 1947.

Roberts, Debbie. *Rejoice: A Biblical Study of the Dance*. Shippensburg: Revival Press of Destiny Image Publishers, 1982.

Sahakian, William S. and Mabel Lewis. *Plato*. Boston: Twayne Publishers, a Division of G. K. Hall & Co., 1977.

Sasha, Anawalt. *The Joffrey Ballet: Robert Joffrey and the Making of An American Dance Company*. New York: Scribner, 1996.

"Ultimate Guide to Sleeping Beauty." San Francisco Ballet 2019 Season. https://www.sfballet.org/your-ultimate-guide-to-sleeping-beauty/.

Savino, Joseph. *A Dream, Love and Dedication, Dancing on Four Continents*. A Pictorial Autobiography. Bloomington: AuthorHouse, 2011.

Séailles, Gabriel. *Leonardo da Vinci*. New York: Parkstone Press International, 2010.

Shawn, Ted. *Every Little Movement, A Book About François Delsarte*. Brooklyn: Dance Horizons, 1968 (publication date uncertain).

Sheila Regan. "Three decades of dance." *Star Tribune*, February 19, 2020.

Stokesbury, James L. *A Short History of World War I*. New York: William Morrow and Company, Inc., 1981.

Stravinsky, Igor. "The Diaghilev I knew." *Atlantic Monthly*, November 1952.

Studio Stories, "Reminiscing on Twin Cities Dance with Jim Lieberthal," Episode 71, Season 5, October 2021, https://www.arena-dances.org/.

Sturgeon, Alison, ed. *A Short History of World War II*. New York: DK Publishing, 2020.

Svetloff, V. *Anna Pavlova*. Trans. by A. Grey. New York: Dover Publications, Inc., 1974.

T.B. Walker Art Gallery, 807 Hennepin Avenue, Minneapolis, 1890. Minnesota Historical Society, https://bit.ly/3NDbZji

University of Rochester. Special Collections 2000.3, University of Rochester. https://bit.ly/3Rzx55S

University of Texas. Special Collections

& Archives, University of Houston Libraries. https://legacy.lib.utexas.edu/taro/uhsc/00023/hsc-00023.html.

Volynsky, Akim, and Stanley J. Rabinowitz, trans. *Ballet's Magic Kingdom: Selected Writings on Dance in Russia, 1911–1925.* New Haven: Yale University Press, 2008.

Walker, Kathrine Sorley. *De Basil's Ballets Russes.* New York: Atheneum, 1983.

Weinberg, Sandra Snell. "Growing Up in St. Paul: My Years at the Andaházy School of Classical Ballet." *Ramsey County History,* Winter 2006.

Windreich, Leland, ed. *Dancing for de Basil: Letters to her parents from Rosemary Deveson, 1938–1940.* Toronto: Arts Inter-Media Canada/Dance Collection Danse Press/es, 1996.

Zide-Booth, Rochelle. "Have Tutu, Will Travel." Memoirs of dancing in Sergei Denham's Ballet Russe de Monte Carlo.

Notes

1. Lynn Garafola, *Diaghilev's Ballets Russes* (New York: Oxford University Press, 1989), 23.

2. Maria Rainer Rilke, *Rilke's Book of Hours,* trans. Anita Barrows and Joanna Macy (New York: Penguin Group, 1996), 64–65.

3. Kathrine Sorley Walker, *De Basil's Ballets Russes* (New York: Atheneum, 1983), 239.

4. Lincoln Kirstein, *Movement & Metaphor: Four Centuries of Ballet* (New York: Praeger Publishers, Inc., 1970), 5.

5. Vitale Fokine, trans. *Fokine, Memoirs of a Ballet Master*, ed. Anatole Chujoy (Boston: Little, Brown and Company, 1961), v.

6. Clement Crisp and Edward Thorpe, *The Colorful World of Ballet* (New York: Octopus Books, 1978), 5.

7. Cornelius Conyn, *Three Centuries of Ballet* (Houston-New York: Elsevier Press, Inc., 1953), 117.

8. Blackwolf Jones and Gina Jones, *Earth Dance Drum: A Celebration of Life* (Salt Lake City: Commune-A-Key Publishing, 1996), xx.

9. William W. Folwell, *A History of Minnesota* (Minnesota Historical Society, 1956), 220.

10. Folwell, 222.

11. Laura Jacobs, *Celestial Bodies, How to Look at Ballet* (New York: Basic Books, 2018), xiii.

12. Victoria Heyworth-Dunne, Jane Ewart, and Megan Douglass, eds., *Ballet: The Definitive Illustrated Story* (New York: DK Publishing, 2018), 146.

13. Anatole Chujoy and P. W. Manchester, *The Dance Encyclopedia* (New York: Simon and Schuster, 1967), 672.

14. Conyn, 137.

15. Jennifer Homans, *Apollo's Angels* (New York: Random Press, 2010), 4.

16. Homans, 7.

17. Homans, 13.

18. Baird Hastings, *Choreographer and Composer* (Boston: Twayne Publishers, A Division of G.K. Hall & Company, 1983), 35.

19. Carlo Blasis, *An Elementary Treatise Upon the Theory and Practice of the Art of Dancing,* trans. Mary Stewart Evans (New York: Dover Publications, Inc., 1968). Originally published as *Traité Élémentaire, Théorique et Pratique de l'Art de la Danse* (New York: Kamin Dance Publishers, 1944), 4.

20. Homans, 3.

21. Mary Clarke and Clement Crisp, *The History of Dance* (New York: Crown Publishers, Inc., 1981), 140.

22. Heyworth-Dunne, Ewart, and Douglass, 30.

23. Homans, 75–76.

24. Homans, 95.

25. Heyworth-Dunne, Ewart, and Douglass, 235.

26. Homans, 114.

27. Homans, 111.

28. Heyworth-Dunne, Ewart, and Douglass, 38.

29. Blasis, 36.

30. Heyworth-Dunne, Ewart, and Douglass, 57.

31. Chujoy and Manchester, 775.

32. Hastings, 74.

33. Heyworth-Dunne, Ewart, and Douglass, 46.

34. Carol Lee, *Ballet in Western Culture. A History of its Origins and Evolution* (Boston: Allyn and Bacon, 1999), 148.

35. Clarke and Crisp, 146.

36. Chujoy and Manchester, 328.

37. Conyn, 140.

38. Heyworth-Dunne, Ewart, and Douglass, 46.

39. Ivor Guest, *The Ballet of the Second Empire* (London: Sir Isaac Pitman and Sons Ltd., 1974), 158–159.

40. Guest, 123.

41. Chujoy and Manchester, 329.

42. Heyworth-Dunne, Ewart, and Douglass, 67.

43. Lee, 153.

44. Lee, 159–160.

45. Lee, 158.

46. Lee, 166.

47. Guest, 14–15.

48. Homans, 174–175.

49. Jack Anderson, *Ballet & Modern Dance, A Concise History* (Trenton: Princeton Book Company, 2018), 121.

50. Conyn, 164.

51. Heyworth-Dunne, Ewart, and Douglass, 81.

52. Heyworth-Dunne, Ewart, and Douglass, 114.

53. Heyworth-Dunne, Ewart, and Douglass, 88.

54. Conyn, 30; Heyworth-Dunne, Ewart, and Douglass, 88.

55. Jane Pritchard, ed., *Diaghilev and the Golden Age of the Ballets Russes 1909–1929* (London: V&A Publishing, 2010), 7.

56. John Percival, *The World of Diaghilev* (London: The Herbert Press Limited, 1979), 13.

57. Boris Kochno, *Diaghilev and the Ballet Russe*, trans. Adrienne Foulke (New York & Evanston: Harper & Row Publishers, 1970). Originally published as *Diaghilev et Les Ballets Russes* (New York: Harper & Row Publishers, 1970), 2.

58. Pritchard, 15.

59. Kochno, 4.

60. Kochno, 2.

61. Pritchard, 26.

62. Heyworth-Dunne, Ewart, and Douglass, 145.

63. Conyn, 59.

64. Anderson, 134.

65. Anderson, 135.

66. Kochno, 16.

67. Kochno, 42.

68. Pritchard, 56.

69. Jacobs, 185.

70. Jacobs, 187.

71. Romola Nijinsky, ed., *The Diary of Vaslav Nijinsky* (Berkeley and Los Angeles: University of California Press, 1936), 137.

72. Chujoy and Manchester, 673.

73. Pritchard, 7.

74. Pritchard, 224.

75. Garafola, 76.

76. Kochno, 278.

77. Kochno, 279.

78. Percival, 132.

79. Vincente García-Márquez, *The Ballets Russes, Colonel de Basil's Ballets Russes de Monte Carlo* (New York: Alfred A. Knopf, 1990), 320.

80. García-Márquez, 87.

81. García-Márquez, 98.

82. Sandra Snell Weinberg, "Growing Up in St. Paul: My Years at the Andaházy School of Classical Ballet," *Ramsey County History* 40, no. 4 (Winter 2006): 21.

83. García-Márquez, 136.

84. V. Svetloff, *Anna Pavlova*, trans. A. Grey (New York: Dover Publications, Inc., 1974), 128.

85. Jane Keyes, Private Collection of Andaházy memoirs and research. Accessed 2021.

86. Advertisement in *Statesman* 41, no. 25, May 6, 1971. Duluth, MN.

87. Elizabeth Kendall, interview, June 4, 2021.

88. Weinberg, 19.

89. Private Collection of Marius Andaházy. Performance Program: Andaházy Ballet Borealis, 1961–1962 Season.

90. James L. Stokesbury, *A Short History of World War I* (New York: William Morrow and Company, Inc., 1981), 316.

91. Andaházy, Performance Program.

92. Stanley S. Hubbard, interview, July 19, 2021.

93. Weinberg, 21.

94. Andaházy, Performance Program.

95. García-Márquez, 98.

96. Grace Robert, *The Borzoi Book of Ballets* (New York: Alfred A. Knopf, 1947), 72.

97. Andaházy Souvenir Pamphlet, Copyright Marius J. Andaházy, 2000, 2.

98. Leland Windreich, compiled and edited, *Dancing for de Basil: Letters to her parents from Rosemary Deveson, 1938–1940*. (Toronto: Arts Inter-Media Canada/Dance Collection Danse Press, 1996), 5–6.

99. Marius Andaházy interviews: June 14, 2021; August 28, 2021; September 13, 2021.

100. Andaházy Souvenir Pamphlet, 4.

101. García-Márquez, 137.

102. Walker, 88.

103. Private Collection of Marius Andaházy, Anna Adrianova memoir letter, Paris, 1961.

104. Andaházy Souvenir Pamphlet, 2.

105. Marius Andaházy, additional interview notes, December 21, 2021.

106. Andaházy Souvenir Pamphlet, 2–3.

107. Marius Andaházy interviews: June 14, 2021; August 28, 2021; September 13, 2021.

108. Julia M. H. Carson, *Home Away from Home, the Story of the USO* (New York: Harpers & Brothers Publishers, 1946), 134–135.

109. Alexandra (Sandy) Klas, "I Remember My Aunt Frances Boardman—Music Critic, Who Covered an Archbishop's Funeral," *Ramsey County History*, 40-2 (Summer 2005): 27.

110. Stanley S. Hubbard, interview, July 19, 2021.

111. Jane Keyes, Private Collection of Andaházy memoirs and research. Accessed 2021.

112. Ibid.

113. Jane Keyes Souvenir Book, *Patricia Garland, Dancer*, and Quotations Recorded by Sandra Snell Weinberg, 2020.

114. Jane Keyes, Private Collection of Andaházy memoirs and research. Quotations from Anderson, Weinberg, and Keyes, 2020.

115. Walker, 240.

116. MN Dance Pioneers Oral History Project, 11/14/2018. Part One.

117. Loyce Houlton, "Twilight Tales," The Contemporary Dance Playhouse, vol. 1, 1.

118. Houlton, vol. 1, 8.

119. Chujoy and Manchester, 933.

120. The Performance Program for The Contemporary Dance Playhouse, 1966, 3–4.

121. Clarke and Crisp, 224.

122. Houlton, "Twilight Tales," Legacy of Graham, vol. 1, 22.

123. Interview with John Linnerson, 2/18/21.

124. Interview with Zide-Booth, 9/1/21.

125. Zide-Booth Memoirs, *Have Tutu, Will Travel*, 22.

126. Jacobs, 66–67.

127. Houlton, "Twilight Tales," Spectre, vol. 1, 18.

128. Houlton, "Twilight Tales," Spectre, vol. 1, 26.

129. Houlton, "Twilight Tales," Resident Theater, vol. 1, 11–12.

130. Houlton, "Twilight Tales," Resident Theater, vol. 1, 22.

131. Houlton, "Twilight Tales," Resident Theater, vol. 1, 35.

132. Houlton, "Twilight Tales," The Miracle of Lichine, vol. 1, 15.

133. Houlton, "Twilight Tales," Early Alliances with the Stars of ABT, vol. 1, 17.

134. Houlton, "Twilight Tales," Jacob's Pillow, Tomorrow Spoleto! Vol. 1, 15.

135. Houlton, "Twilight Tales," Nutcracker Fantasies, vol. 2, 2.

136. Houlton, "Twilight Tales," Nutcracker Fantasies, vol. 2, 8–9.

137. Houlton, "Twilight Tales," Nutcracker Fantasies, vol. 2, 10–11.

138. Houlton, "Twilight Tales," Interims, vol. 2, 18.

139. Houlton, "Twilight Tales," Unforgettable Women, vol. 2, 10.

140. Houlton, "Twilight Tales," Unforgettable Women, vol. 2, 14.

141. Houlton, "Twilight Tales," Escapades in HCA and Germany, vol. 2, 4.

142. Interview with John Linnerson, 2/18/21.

143. Houlton, "Twilight Tales," Extraordinary People, vol. 2, 1.

144. Houlton, "Twilight Tales," Extraordinary People, vol. 2, 4.

145. Houlton, "Twilight Tales," Fini! vol. 2, 8.

146. Sheila Regan, "Three decades of dance," *Star Tribune* (Minneapolis, MN), February 19, 2020, E1.

147. Obituary of Karen Paulson Rivet, *Star Tribune* (Minneapolis, MN), October 12, 2016.

148. Zide-Booth, 3.

149. Jack Anderson, *The One and Only: The Ballet Russe de Monte Carlo* (London: Dance Books Ltd., 1981), 166.

150. Anawalt Sasha, *The Joffrey Ballet* (New York: Scribner, 1996), 116.

151. Sasha, 125.

152. Minnesota Ballet in Duluth. https://minnesotaballet.org/about/history/.

153. Hafiz, "Created for Joy," https://creatingmiracles.wordpress.com/2021/04/25/created-for-joy/.

154. Clarke and Crisp, 37.

155. Clarke and Crisp, 38–39.

156. Clarke and Crisp, 40.

157. New Testament, Acts 17:28.

158. Mebust interview, 1/15/2022.

159. Elizabeth Kendall, *Where She Danced: The Birth of American Art-Dance* (New York: Alfred A. Knopf, Inc., 1979), 25.

160. Colleen Callahan and Mary Kay Conway, eds., *Celebrating 60 Years of Dance Education in Minnesota*, A Commemorative Tribute, honoring the contributions of Gertrude Lippincott, Mary Rae Josephson-Adamson, Florence Cobb, Molly Lynn (Minneapolis: Hennepin Center for the Arts, 1991), 2.

161. Callahan and Conway, 5.

162. Imel E. Carmen, ed., *Focus on Dance: VII, Dance Heritage* (Washington, DC: AAHPER Publications, 1977), 44.

163. *Minnesota History* (Spring 2016): 27.

164. Judith Brin Ingber, "Gertrude Lippincott 'Righto'," *Minnesota Dance, A Publication of Minnesota Dance Alliance* 11, no. 3 (January/February 1990): 7.

165. Ibid., 1.

166. Judith Brin Ingber, "Entertainment or Art?" *Minnesota Dance, A Publication of Minnesota Dance Alliance* 14, no. 3 (January/February 1993): 7.

167. Ibid., 1 and 7.

168. *In Memorium, Gertrude Lippincott, June 29, 1913, to June 2, 1996.* Written for the Commemoration Service of Gertrude Lippincott, June 29, 1996. Frederick R. Weisman Museum, University of Minnesota, (Barbara Barker Warner, speech, p. 1).

169. *In Memorium* (Barbara Barker Warner, speech, p. 2).

170. Judith Brin Ingber, "Nancy Hauser," *Minnesota Dance, A Publication of Minnesota Dance Alliance* 11, no. 1 (September/October 1989): 1.

171. Anatole Chujoy and P. W. Manchester, *The Dance Encyclopedia* (New York: Simon and Schuster, 1967), 472.

172. Ingber, 1.

173. Lightsey Darst, "Remembering John Munger," MnArtists, Arts Writing from Mn, Beyond Mn, May 10, 2013, https://bit.ly/3wnDc3x.

174. John Munger, "High Places Must Be Deserved: Memories of Hanya Holm," *Minnesota Dance, A Publication of Minnesota Dance Alliance* 14, no.3 (January/February 1993): 10–11.

175. Elizabeth Carlin Freeman, Marie Winckler Nickell and Linda Lee Soderstrom, *Margret Dietz: A Dancer's Legacy* (St. Cloud: Sentinal Printing, 2010), 26–27.

176. Freeman, Nickell, and Soderstrom, 30.

177. Freeman, Nickell, and Soderstrom, 64.

178. Freeman, Nickell, and Soderstrom, 65.

179. Freeman, Nickell, and Soderstrom, 93.

Index

Note: Page numbers in bold refer to images.

317